Bill Adams'
Yester Days
Volume III

Bill Adams *(signature)*

This book contains 101 columns that originally appeared in the *Peoria Journal Star* from Monday, February 3, 1992 until Monday, March 21, 1994. They contain more than 160 photos, most of which appeared with the original columns, but many more have been added.

The three volumes of *Yester Days* books are a complete collection of the 302 columns that first appeared in the *Peoria Journal Star* beginning on Monday, May 9, 1988.

This book is dedicated to my father and mother...

Virg and Ann Adams

They instilled in me a pride of my home town that has stayed with me since childhood and many of the memories I have of Mom and Dad have been relived, in various ways, in this newspaper column.

Preface

The first volume of *Yester Days* was published in the fall of 1992. It contained the first 101 of my *Yester Days* columns that began in the *Peoria Journal Star* on Monday, May 9, 1988, and ran through Monday, April 30, 1990. (The only column not to appear on a Monday, was the one on Tuesday, December 26, 1989, because of the *Journal Star's* policy not to publish on Christmas Day).

The second book, *Yester Days - Volume II*, picked up where the first one ended, and was published in the fall of 1993. It began with the column of Monday, May 7, 1990 and continued in chronological order through Monday, January 20, 1992, except for its last 12 columns.

Those last 12 columns originally ran once a month in the *Journal Star*, from October 28, 1991 through September 28, 1992, during the Peoria Area's TriCentennial Year. They were all included in Volume II so that the entire series, which was dedicated to Peoria's 300-year history, could be contained in one book.

This book, *Yester Days - Volume III*, continues on with the final 101 columns of the 302 that ran in the *Peoria Journal Star* for nearly six years. These final columns ran in the newspaper from Monday, February 3, 1992 until the final *Yester Days* column appeared on Monday, March 21, 1994.

I hope these last 101 columns will be as enjoyable as the first 201. So, let's take one last nostalgic trip back into Peoria's past.

Once again you may find that some of the stories will

...seem like only yesterday!

Bill Adams

Special thanks again

to CILCO and the *Peoria Journal Star* for their continued participation in publishing all three volumes of *Yester Days* books. Again, without their continued commitment, it would have been impossible to have done so.

© Copyright 1994 by the *Peoria Journal Star*, Inc.

No portion of this book may be used or reproduced without written permission from the publisher, except in brief quotations used in reviews.

ISBN 0-9634793-2-6

Published by the *Peoria Journal Star*, Inc.
1 News Plaza
Peoria, Illinois 61643

Cover design, book design and production by Logan Images, Inc., Peoria, Illinois
Printed by Logan Printing Company, Peoria, Illinois

Cover photo of the Civil War Statue in Peoria County Court House Plaza, photographed by Al Harkrader.

A portion of the proceeds from the sale of this book will be donated to the Peoria Area Community Foundation for the funding of literacy programs.

Acknowledgements

As in the past, many people participated in the collecting of these 101 stories and more than 160 photos, other than those mentioned along the way.

Once again, my special thanks to Mrs. Jean Shrier and all her Reference Desk Staff at the Peoria Public Library's downtown branch...especially Mrs. Betty Roberson.

To Chuck Frey and his Special Collections Staff at the Bradley University Library, especially Karen Deller and Sherri Schneider, and also to the Peoria Historical Society.

To Paul Stringham for all his streetcar material and photos and other historical data.

To Edna Roten and Dick Deller for their special permission to reuse photos from Lee Roten's Historic Peoria Photo Files.

To the *Journal Star*, WEEK, WMBD, NBC, CBS, ABC, Dumont, International News, Big Band Jazz, The War the West and the Wilderness, Underwood & Underwood, Madison Theater, Leonard Maltin, CB&Q Railroad, Montague L. Powell Collection, Gary DeNeal and Helen Stoutemyer, for allowing us to reprint their photos.

To Dick & Marlene Caldwell, Marv Hult, George Brignall, Nena Gullette, Al Larson, Marian Coffeen, Verna Eichorn, Phillip O'Connell, Charles Anderson, Jay Janssen, Bill Becker, Geraldine (Rapp) Carius, Curtis White, Nanette Meals, Roger Seghetti, Keith Barr, Lila Crotty Smith and Charles Ginoli for also providing photos.

And, once again, special thanks to my daughter, Lesa Adams Collier, for her continued dedication in researching for column material these past six years.

Table of Contents

Area employers group celebrating its 75th year

This story on the Central Illinois Employers' Association's 75th anniversary is the first of two parts.

On February 19th, the Central Illinois Employers' Association will celebrate 75 years of service at its annual luncheon meeting in the ballroom of the Hotel Pere Marquette. Four hundred people will meet, representing more than 360 member companies.

Its president, John J. Gibson, is only the sixth the organization has had over the past 75 years. While Donald L. Richardson of Illinois Bell was the 1991 chairman of the board, Rita S. Kress of the Kress Corporation has taken over for 1992, and its treasurer, Glen D. Blake, retired at the end of 1991. Its total board represents 18 Central Illinois businesses.

The organization has changed its name three times since it began in 1917 as the Peoria Manufacturers' and Merchants' Association, and its mission also has changed over those 75 years. Its one mission today is to serve all employers - private and public, manufacturing and service, big and small - in all areas of human resource management.

Assisting Gibson in this regard is a most able staff: Sharon Durst-Fender, manager; Cindy Hamilton, administrative assistant; and secretaries Lucille Hunt and Colleen Hubert.

First industries

As most people who read this column know by now, the Peoria area has had a rich and varied history over its 300-year existence (which also is being celebrated this year), but none of its history is more varied than that of its industry.

Fur trading was Peoria's first major industry, but every log cabin was, by necessity, also a home factory. Green timber was sawed or split to make bunks, tables, and other furniture, and corn was beaten on a wooden block to make bread. Deerskins were dressed and fashioned into jackets and moccasins, while native wool and flax were spun and woven for outer garments.

The blacksmithing and gunsmithing trade came early on, and in 1822 a horse mill was grinding grain in Peoria. It didn't take long until flour milling became Peoria's major industry, and by 1860, ten mills were operating here.

Breweries and distilleries

In April 1837, a German named Andrew Eitle operated Peoria's first brewery, and this industry not only continued to flourish until Prohibition came along, but also revived after its repeal.

About 1843, a Peoria merchant, Almiran S. Cole, built Peoria's first distillery, and by 1878, 14 distilleries were in operation.

Before the turn of the century, Peoria not only had the world's largest distillery (Great Western), but it was also the home of the "Whisky Trust," which virtually controlled the industry in the entire United States.

The cooperage business (barrel making) also flourished here as a result of the distilling and brewing industries - all of which also revived after Prohibition was repealed in the early '30s.

Agriculture implements

In 1837, the same year that Eitle opened Peoria's first brewery, William M. Nurse & Son began manufacturing the first fanning mills here, and out of this evolved another major Peoria industry, the manufacture of agriculture implements, with the development of the combined grain thresher, separator and cleaner.

In 1843, Toby and Anderson manufactured Peoria's first steel plows. This soon was followed by Avery, Acme Harvester, Hart Grain-Weigher, Kingman Plow, Rhea-Theilins, Union Corn Planter, Selby and Starr.

Other early industries

In 1893, Rouse, Hazard & Co. (who hired Charles Duryea) began manufacturing bicycles here, and in 1895, they built a large factory in Peoria Heights. Other bicycle manufacturers followed, including Ide Manufacturing, Luthy & Co., Peoria

PEORIA CORDAGE CO. - Artist's rendering of the firm headed by E. C. Heidrich, Jr., who became the first chairman of the board of the Peoria Manufacturers' and Merchants' Association in 1917.

A. LUCAS & SONS - Located at 1328 SW Washington St., the firm was founded by Adam Lucas in 1857 on Liberty Street.
(Photo courtesy Peoria Public Library)

Rubber & Manufacturing, American and Patee. Out of this, Peoria became a major national bicycle manufacturing center.

Other early Peoria industries produced such products and services as architectural iron, art glass, artificial ice and cold storage, awnings and tents, binder-twine, boats, bookbinding and printing, bricks, brooms, cereal foods, pharmaceuticals, cigars, crackers and confections, cellulose, electric meters, engraving, fish, foundries, furniture, gloves, glucose, harness & saddlery, monuments, overalls, parlor game boards, pottery, paper boxes, peanut roasters, planing mills, meat packing, stoves and ranges, sickles, soap, starch, steam boilers, stone, straw board, vinegar, watches, wagons, carriages, automobiles, trucks, airplanes, women's dresses, white lead, wire products and, of course, tractors and earth-moving equipment.

Because of WWI

By the time World War I came along, Peoria's local businesses were becoming more complicated in many ways. And because of the war (believe it or not today), finding and hiring good people became a serious problem, and local businesses needed a way to coordinate employment.

So, at noon on Monday, October 29, 1917, a group representing the area's major manufacturers met in the Grill Room at Block and Kuhl's Department Store, for the purpose of forming an association. E. C. Heidrich, Jr. of Peoria Cordage Co. presided and 15 firms out of 27 listed, were represented: Acme Harvesting Machines, Avery, Harry Bates Co., Bemis Bag, Brass Foundry, Carr & Johnson, J. W. Franks & Son, Herschel Manufacturing, Keystone Steel & Wire, Kinsey & Mahler, Peoria Cordage, Peoria Drill & Seeder, Wahlfeld Manufacturing, Peoria Malleable Castings, and National Cooperage.

It's interesting to note that of the many varied businesses in operation in 1917, seven are still a part of this year's 75th Anniversary of the organization: Bemis Bag, Brass Foundry, Keystone, A. Lucas & Sons, Wahlfeld Manufacturing, Caterpillar (originally Holt Caterpillar) and CILCO.

NEXT WEEK, we'll take a closer look at this 75-year-old organization and some of its member companies, then and now.

Group's name changed along with its purpose

This is the second of two parts on the Central Illinois Employers' Association's 75th anniversary

The Central Illinois Employers' Association will begin celebrating 75 years of service at its annual luncheon February 19 in the Pere Marquette ballroom. This assembly of 400 people, representing more than 360 member companies, will break bread before listening to its guest speaker, Donald O. Fites, chairman of the board and CEO of Caterpillar. Fites also represents a founding member company of the association.

Fledgling organization

Gordon L. Hostetter was hired Sept. 1, 1917, as secretary of the fledgling organization. He and a part-time secretary (who provided her own typewriter) was its total staff.

The first meeting took place at noon Oct. 29, 1917, at Block & Kuhl's, and E. C. Heidrich, Jr. of Peoria Cordage Co. presided. This original group of 15, representing only manufacturers, decided to enlarge its scope to also include retail and wholesale merchants. E. B. Hazen of the Brass Foundry suggested that a nominating committee be selected to pick 15 names to be elected as its first governing board.

The committee met at the Creve Coeur Club on Oct. 30, and acted as charged, and on the evening of Nov. 6 at the (Peoria) Country Club, 21 members again met, and the association's first board was elected. Its officers were: Heidrich, president; L. E. Roby (Peoria Drill & Seeder), 1st vice president; Warren Kinsey (Kinsey & Mahler Foundry), second vice president; and Hazen, third vice president.

These officers agreed that the "manufacturers and merchants form an association to supply necessary labor and make labor conditions attractive..." A lease with Charles J. Off was approved for office space in the Hippodrome theater building.

Successions

Hostetter served as its first secretary until May 15, 1918. Then, L.E. Roark took over for the next 26 years, until Jan. 1, 1945. Edward D. Stoetzel then served, with his title later changing to executive secretary, until Aug. 30, 1968. On Sept. 1, 1968, Newton A. Brokaw came from Cincinnati, Ohio, to serve for about 2 1/2 years.

After 34 years with Keystone Steel and Wire Co., Louis W. Hesse retired as their vice president for industrial relations to succeed Brokaw on June 1, 1971, as executive vice president, and then president, until Sept. 30, 1982.

On Oct. 1, 1982, the current president, John J. Gibson, took over when Hesse retired. Gibson had also worked at Keystone for 22 years, and left as vice president of personal services for Keystone Consolidated Industries, when they moved their corporate headquarters to Dallas, Texas.

Name changes

During these past 75 years, the group's name has changed from Peoria Manufacturers' and Merchants' Association to Central Illinois Industrial Association to Central Illinois Employers' Association. The last name change occurred Jan. 1, 1986, to better reflect its current service to more than 360 member companies, ranging in size from one employee to more than 30,000.

Seven firms have weathered the many changes that have occurred during the organization's 75 years, and here's a quick look at how they began:

■ BEMIS BAG COMPANY - In 1858, with $2,000 of his own savings, Judson Moss Bemis and his cousin, Simeon Farwell, went to St. Louis and opened a bag factory under the name of J. M. Bemis & Co. With six sewing machines, two small printing presses and some wooden type, they began making cotton bags. In 1912, the firm chose Peoria for its first paper mill, at the foot of Sloan Street, where the company is still located. It began operations here January 10, 1914.

■ BRASS FOUNDRY - The company was founded in 1887 (the same year Peoria's Christmas parade began) by A. T. Antcliff, Edward Couch and William Heyl (who later formed the hardware company) and W. D. Dickson.

It was originally the Brass Foundry and Heating Co., located at 1028 South Adams, and started with one machine lathe and a small pit furnace for melting brass. In 1893, the company was incorporated and in 1895,

The original location of the Brass Foundry & Heating Co. at 1028 South Adams Street.
(Photo courtesy Peoria Public Library)

E. B. Hazen bought a small interest and became its bookkeeper. In 1898, the firm moved to the corner of First and Franklin Streets, and in 1906 to its present location at 713 SW Adams.

Brass Foundry, by the way, made the blocks for Charles Duryea's first Peoria trap automobile engines.

■ CILCO - Between 1911 & 1913, a series of mergers involving seven companies took place to form Central Illinois Light Co., which would provide Peoria and 26 surrounding communities with gas, electric, and steam service.

■ KEYSTONE STEEL & WIRE CO. - Back in the 1880's, Peter Sommer, a Tazewell County farmer, got an idea to simplify the making of wire fence. In March 1889, he and his sons, P. W. and John, built a hand-operated, fence-making machine and made fence for use on their own farm. They then made fence for a neighbor, Gottlieb Kurth. Others saw it and ordered some for themselves.

In November, the Sommers' built a power machine. The father and sons formed a partnership, which later became Keystone Steel & Wire Co.

■ A. LUCAS & SONS - The business was established in 1857 by Mr. Adam Lucas in a small shop on Liberty Street, making vault doors and locks.

In 1859, Lucas moved to the 200 block of South Washington, and in 1863 to 207 Fulton. The firm changed to A. Lucas & Sons in 1889 when Adam took his sons, Emil and Hugo, into partnership.

The company enlarged and incorporated in 1897, the same year it moved to South Washington at Cedar Street.

■ WAHLFELD MANUFACTURING CO. - The firm was founded in the 1100 block of South Washington in 1889 by August Wahlfeld, a newly arrived young man from Havana, Illinois, and before that from Hanover, Germany.

Wahlfeld came to the United States as a boy, and worked nine years at Peoria's J. T. Rogers Lumber Co. before going into lumber milling for himself.

■ CATERPILLAR - The Holt Caterpillar Co. began producing tractors in East Peoria with about 40 employees in 1910. Holt moved here from Stockton, California, after Murray M. Baker contacted them about an idle Colean Co. plant and its equipment that was available here at an attractive price.

In 1925, Holt merged with its biggest competitor, C. L. Best Tractor Co. of San Leandro, California, and formed Caterpillar Tractor Co.

Well, Peoria and central Illinois have certainly had a varied and colorful history, and none more interesting than its past 75 years with, what we know today as, the Central Illinois Employers' Association.

When it was "Roaring Peoria"

My, how times change! Here we are, with our town celebrating its 300th anniversary with year long festivities, a town that's often used as the standard by which other American towns are compared (Will it play in Peoria?). For the second time in recent years, Peoria has been chosen an All-America City, and this past fall, the Par-A-Dice riverboat, one of the largest attractions for bringing visitors to our town, began plying our Illinois River with its floating casino.

But gambling and ah... er... other means of entertaining visitors, isn't anything new to our town. It's just that gambling has been legitimatized and is now looked upon as an industry rather than a vice.

Well, that isn't the way it was back in the 1920s, '30s and well into the '40s, when Peoria was infamously known as "Roaring Peoria," and gambling was the king-pin of it all.

In 1956, the Journal Star ran a series on that "Old Peoria," referring to it with the headline, "As Wide Open as the Gateway To Hell."

The Peoria charisma

Now, I was a product of the 1920s and I recall much of that period as a child and young adult. Call it being naive if you must, but as I look back on it, I was unaware of the hoodlum element under the surface of it all. But I agree with the newspaper's description of it as a "bawdy town, but always with a twinkle in its eye," and, good or bad, Peoria has always had a certain charisma.

Those Depression days after 1929 were difficult times, when more people were out of work than working. Gambling and prostitution were easy ways to make a buck for some, with men controlling the former, and women the latter.

At one time a madam who ran a "home" at Fayette and Washington streets, conducted "Miss Fern's Midnight Cotillion" each Saturday night in her grand ballroom. It was said to be as well-known from coast-to-coast as New Orleans' famous Quadroon Ball.

Prairie Alley, one of Peoria's three "red light" districts, was also well-known nationally, while practically every house near North Washington and Eaton became a brothel.

A gambler's paradise

But, most of all, Peoria became a town where gambling joints were more common downtown than banks, restaurants and churches. The best known, and probably most lucrative, was the Empire at 139 S. Jefferson. It offered various types of gambling, but was best known as the home of the baseball pool. It was said to take in as much as $75,000 a month, and frequently paid off jackpots of $5,000 or more. And I'm here to tell you that $5,000 back then was some hunk of change!

Its proprietor, Bill Urban, was a kidnap victim in 1930, and the manager of his Alcazar, Frank Dougherty, also was kidnapped a few weeks later. It's believed that Urban paid $80,000 before he was released.

In the same block as the Empire was the Saratoga. It was a cigar store with bowling alleys upstairs, but it also had a short gambling career before Peoria's reform mayor, Carl O. Triebel, was elected in the mid-'40s and put a lid on it. The Saratoga's gambling operation lasted less than a year.

Urban's Alcazar was around the corner from the Empire on Fulton Street, across from City Hall. It also sold baseball pool tickets, and featured slot machines. In that same 400 block of Fulton was the old Sportsmen's Club, which later became the Clover Club and operated by Jack Adams.

Also in the 400 block of Fulton was the Mint but its gambling was done on a smaller scale. It's said its operators refused to deal with the mob.

Unlucky to be too lucky

Across Madison Avenue from City Hall was the Palace Club, which became the headquarters for the Shelton gang. It was sometimes unlucky to be too lucky at the Palace Club. Winners often wound up with a busted head and their pockets picked after they left the premises with too big of a winning roll.

In the 100 block of South Madison was the Palace Arcade, not to be confused with the Palace Club. It also featured gambling,

THE ALCAZAR "Cigar Store" (with the street light in front of it) at 414 Fulton Street in the mid-1930s. The white faced building across the alley on the left is the Sportsmen's Club.
(Photo from the Grassel files/Peoria Public Library)

THE CLOVER CLUB at 416 Fulton Street. It had formerly operated as the Sportsmen's Club.
(Photo from the Grassel files/Peoria Public Library)

with a horse betting operation on the second floor.

Further down Fulton Street, in the 300 block, were the Lyceum and the Windsor. The Lyceum was originally established by Pete Weast before the turn of the century, but was now strictly a gang operation. It also featured horse betting but was held in somewhat low esteem by the city's other gamblers.

The Windsor offered roulette and faro, in addition to other games of chance. As featured in this column recently, its proprietor, Clyde Garrison, was wounded and his wife, Cora, killed in a kidnap attempt in 1930, shortly after those of Urban and Dougherty.

A tough river town

Yes, our town certainly had a bold tradition as a tough river town back in those "Roaring Peoria" days. The vice and rackets flourished, and it's said a well-placed bribe could be more effective than a well-aimed bullet.

That's no doubt why so many of those kidnappings and murders were never solved. Of all the stories I've read about those days, the only one I'm aware of that was solved was the kidnapping of Dr. James W. Parker in 1932. And that was probably only because the job was done by amateurs who weren't aware (nor had the money) to pay off the local officials who always seemed to have their hand out.

"Roaring Peoria" gained such a reputation that newspapers from other midwest cities sent their ace reporters here to cover the story.

Yep, our town had charisma all right, but not the positive kind it has today.

... and it seems like only yesterday!

Telling the story of the house on Perry

This is the first of three parts

Some time ago, Marv Hult gave me a copy of an unpublished book titled "The House That David Built." It was written by Julia Proctor White, the daughter of the original owners of the house that still stands at 245 NE Perry Street. Mrs. White gave the book to Marv as a "thank you" for saving the building after he bought and refurbished it in 1959 for his Hult Advertising Agency, and it's still the home of Hult, Fritz, Matuszak and Associates today.

Julia's story is a fascinating one, not only of the house, but of her family and their lives there, until they sold it in 1907.

Getting started

The home was originally built by a contractor named Flynn for David Choate Proctor and his family in 1877. Proctor was a half-brother to I. Francis, Ezekiel A. and John C. Proctor, who had all settled in Peoria in the 1840s. He joined them here in 1856 and went into the wholesale grocery business with Joseph W. Parrish.

Then, in 1867, he and Richard Culter established the Culter & Proctor Stove Co. They manufactured heating and cooking stoves and ranges, and their firm once occupied a solid city block, surrounded by Fayette, Commercial, Hamilton and Water streets.

In the spring of 1869, David Proctor journeyed east, where he married Sarah Storrs on May 5. She was the only child of Mr. and Mrs. Charles Storrs of Brooklyn, N. Y. He brought his bride back to Peoria, and their first home was in one side of a small double house at 613 N. Jefferson. Peoria seemed very remote to the eastern big-city girl where, just across the Mississippi River, it was still the "Wild West," with its buffalos and Indians.

Walking on Peoria's brick and wooden pavements of those days wasn't too difficult for Sarah, but the single planks laid over the crossings of the dirt streets were a great hazard and she would often return home muddy and discouraged.

Growing family

A son, Charles, was born to the Proctors in the hot summer of 1873. Then, two years later when a daughter, Julia, came along, David knew he must look to the future and build a house of their own. He searched for a site not too far from his business, but well removed from the noise and dust of the center of town.

He found the ideal location at the corner of Perry and Fayette streets. It was a good-sized vacant lot, except for a small wooden building at the rear, which held a carpenter's shop with a living room over it and a small addition for a stable.

What he wanted

David wanted a substantial, unpretentious, moderate-sized house (although it would have six fireplaces) with four rooms downstairs and four up and wide halls down the center. It must have a high attic to keep the summer heat from the upper story and a good heavy roof, with two rooms for servant's quarters over a large kitchen at the rear.

Knowing so much about what he wanted, David hired a contactor named Flynn, whom he knew would select only the best materials and would know how to put it together without the added cost of an architect.

But David would allow one more luxury. No more wash stands with bowls and pitchers for Sarah. Each of the four big bedrooms would have a stationary basin with hot and cold running water. These and the bathroom's basin and man-sized tub would have their plumbing concealed by fine black walnut wooden cabinets.

211 Perry St.

In the autumn of 1877, when David was 45 and Sarah 32, the new brick house with central heating was completed. It had a wooden porch across the entire front and a stout wooden fence surrounding the yard. (This fence was later replaced by a low, stylish iron fence.) A strong fence was necessary because in those days, horses, pigs and cows still wandered freely down Fayette Street. Its address was, then, 211 Perry Street.

Little Charlie's great joy became the milkman, the ever smiling Billy Roszell, whose Mount Holly Dairy horses and wagon would stop on Fayette Street, without a command from the driver, every day, while Roszell poured milk into the pans of Susan, the cook.

Left — The house at the corner of NE Perry and Fayette streets as it appeared in 1877. It originally had a porch extending across its entire front, and a short, wooden fence around the yard. Note the hitching post at the curb.   (Photo courtesy of Marvin Hult)

Right — David C. and Sarah (Storrs) Proctor as they appeared when the house was built in 1877.
(Photo courtesy of Marvin Hult)

Failing health

The summer of 1880 was a hot one. Sarah had never gotten used to Peoria's summer heat, so David insisted that she take the children to his boyhood home in the mountains of New Hampshire. He couldn't go with them because he said he had to stay here to oversee the work at the foundry. But Sarah suspected that David was not well. So, she and the family spent the summer out east, but when they returned to Peoria, it was quite clear to her that David's health was failing.

Sarah's father, Grandpa Storrs, sent for David to come visit them, where all the big-city doctors could be consulted. So David went to Brooklyn. Then, on October 28, a wonderful thing happened. The Proctor's third child, David Gould Proctor, was born.

Sarah wanted to go to David to show him their latest addition as soon as possible, but the doctor said she must wait six weeks before she could undertake such a long journey with three children and the baby so young. The train ride to Brooklyn would take two days and two nights.

She waited until the middle of December but, just a few hours before the family arrived in Brooklyn, her husband died, without seeing his newest offspring.

Some extra help

David's brother John (John C. Proctor of the lumber company) now played an important roll to Sarah and the children. He insisted that Jerry Webb, a black man who worked at the lumber yard, come and live in the room over the carpenter shop and help her with the heavy work at the house. Jerry had been a slave, and all the children in the neighborhood wanted to be with him. He and Sarah got along well, so Jerry came and he stayed with the family for many years.

In the meantime, "Uncle John" also looked after the stove company business for Sarah.

NEXT WEEK - the continuation of the story of "The House That David Built."

Story of the house on Perry continues

This is the second of three parts

Last week we followed the story of David C. Proctor, the cofounder of the Culter and Proctor Stove Co., from the time of his marriage to Sarah Storrs in 1869, through the building of the house at what is now 245 NE Perry Street, until Proctor's death in 1880. He died of heart disease at age 48.

Marv Hult bought the house in 1959 for his advertising agency, and it's still the home of Hult, Fritz, Matuszak and Associates.

David and Sarah had three children, Charles, Julia and little David. The latter was born just before his father died in Brooklyn, N. Y. The older David never saw the baby. He passed away just a few short hours before the family arrived to visit him in Brooklyn, where he had gone to seek medical help for his illness. The following spring David Choate Proctor's remains were brought back to Peoria, and were interred in Springdale Cemetery, upon the hill with an extensive view he used to enjoy.

Proctor-Howe bunch

Charlie and Julie started to school at Mrs. Ellis' house in the next block south on Perry, and Sarah's mother came from back east to help her daughter with the children.

In the autumn of 1884, Sarah's father died in Brooklyn and her mother came to Peoria to live with them. Grandma Storrs would read stories to the children at any time and was ever present to help in hours of trouble. By the following autumn, Charlie and Julie were too big to go to Mrs. Ellis' school, so now they went one block north to the Pettingill Seminary, where their teacher was a Miss Carter.

In October 1885, Sarah remarried, this time to Mr. E. Frank Howe, the minister of her First Congregational Church. He was a widower with two daughters, Grace and Fannie, still at home and two older sons, Clifford and Lewis, who were away at college. Howe and his daughters joined Sarah and her three children at 211 Perry. The busy house was now the home of these two families plus Grandma Storrs, and the "help" included Susie, the cook; Mary, the maid; and Jerry, the handyman. And when the two older boys returned from college, Sarah saw the need for four more rooms.

Adding on

A new staircase, from the upper hall to the attic, was added, and four more fine bedrooms, two on each side of the wide hall, were added to the third floor with a dormer window at each side of the roof. The central heating, which was in a separate building in the rear, would never handle the added rooms, so a second furnace was put in.

Life was happy again at 211 Perry, but not for long. In March 1887, Howe was forced to give up his church because of illness, and a few months later, on August 11, 1887, he also passed away.

Sarah had little time to think of her loss because there were four Howe children to comfort. Their own mother had died in 1882, just as she, Mr. Howe and their family were planning to come to Peoria.

In 1888, Sarah decided that a new barn was needed, and 15-year-old Charlie, who had been raising chickens for several years, was allowed to plan it. The old building, which had contained the carpenter shop and Jerry, the black handyman's room, was too well built to tear down, so Grandma Storrs bought it and gave it to Jerry for his church's parsonage. It was moved to its new location on Monson Street. By now, Jerry had married and was living elsewhere. The new barn was completed in the spring of 1889, with plenty of space for Charlie's prize chickens.

New opinions

Julie joined Charlie in the high school (which became Peoria High) that was, then, one block east of their home on Fayette Street. And about this same time, a 19-year-old Charlie White, who lived across the street from the Proctor-Howe home, often came over to visit Charlie Proctor.

Julie had heard her new stepbrother, Clifford Howe, talk about a newspaper on which he had worked in Washington D.C. called the Public Opinion. She presented the idea of a school newspaper to her high school class, and they voted to call it the High School Opinion. The paper became so successful it was taken over by the entire school, and Peoria High's newspaper is still called The Opinion today.

Charles (left) and Julia Proctor (right) as they appeared in 1877 when the house was built. (Center) Two-year-old Davie in 1882.
(Photos courtesy of Marvin Hult)

Sarah Storrs Proctor Howe on the porch of Charles and Julia White's house at 1118 N. Glen Oak in 1914.
(Photo courtesy of Marvin Hult)

After high school, Charlie was given a trip to Europe, but his friend, Charlie White, continued to visit the house to listen to Julie sing, and he would sit with her on the front porch on warm, summer evenings.

Trip to Europe

Some time later, Sarah took the family on a three-year stay to Europe. A Miss Riggs was taken along to help Fannie and Davie keep up with their studies, and Charlie met their boat when they landed at Antwerp, Belgium.

David Proctor's niece, Etta, had married a Mr. Littlewood, who had two daughters, and the Littlewoods agreed to rent the house while they were away.

After the family had been in Munich, Germany for two years, Charlie became engaged to an Austrian girl. He came home and consulted Uncle John about settling in some kind of business while his fiancee,

Pauline, went with the family to Paris. But Julie stayed in Munich with her violin and voice teacher.

In the summer of 1894, the Littlewoods moved out of the house and the Proctor-Howes came home, after which Julie went to New York to live with Miss Riggs. The following spring, Sarah and her two remaining children also moved to New York, and she rented the house again, this time to the Alexander Tyngs. Mr. Tyng was the son of the family that had earlier lived in the other half of their first little home on North Jefferson.

A return to Peoria

Several years later, Julie visited her brother in Peoria for Christmas, and she and Charlie White rediscovered each other. She announced their engagement on her return to New York, and they were soon married.

The Whites returned to Peoria in the spring of 1901, and found a two-room apartment in a little two-story remodeled house just a block from the Perry home, opposite the high school, and one block from the women's club which Sarah helped start in 1886.

Some time before, Sarah wanted to sell the Perry home but Julie had begged her not to. But after Julie and Charlie had been in their own home on the bluff for five years, she had a change of heart.

So in 1907, when the Tyngs decided to move, it was agreed to sell the house. The man who bought it was none other than Eugene Baldwin, the owner, publisher and editor of the *Peoria Star*.

NEXT WEEK- The house that David built, with its new owners, the Baldwins, and the mystery surrounding the death of Gene Baldwin.

House on Perry: It's not over 'til it's over

Last of a three-part series

In 1907, Sarah Proctor Howe and her younger children were living in New York, so she sold her house at Perry and Fayette to Eugene Baldwin, publisher and editor of the *Peoria Star*.

Her son, Charles Proctor, had married an Austrian girl and they returned to Peoria to live. Her daughter, Julia, had married Charles F. White, the boy from across the street, who was Charlie Proctor's good friend.

The two good friends went into business together. They formed the Proctor & White confection manufacturing company at 318-20 S. Washington Street. White also operated a confectionery shop at 416 Main Street called "The Colonial." The Proctors lived at 807 Hamilton Blvd. while the Whites resided at 1118 N. Glen Oak.

In 1909, Charlie Proctor became 2nd vice president of the First National Bank, where his uncle, John C. Proctor, was president. White operated the candy store for awhile, but later became a special agent of the Northwestern Mutual Life Insurance Company.

Baldwin steps in

Gene Baldwin cofounded first the *Peoria Review* and then the *Peoria Journal*. He sold his interest in the *Journal* before cofounding the *Peoria Star* in 1897. He married Sarah Gove of McLean County in 1866, and they had three children: Ethel, who died young; Frank E., who became a prominent local physician; and Mildred Sidney Baldwin, who became a writer. Her column, "In My Opinion" appeared in the *Star* for many years.

The Baldwins, including Frank and Sidney, didn't move into the house for about 2 1/2 years. It had become shabby and run down since the Proctor-Howes had vacated it. Baldwin bought it primarily to house his large library, which was overflowing his smaller home just a half-block away at 311 N. Perry.

Baldwin had quite a bit of remodeling done. The front porch was taken off and the round one, now there, put on with its pillars. A taller wrought iron fence also replaced the shorter one. Baldwin bought the white frame house next door and had it moved, so he could have a lawn.

Mysterious circumstances

But Baldwin, like Proctor, was not to enjoy the home for too many years. About four years later, he too, died, but with a bit of mystery surrounding the cause of his death.

It was Baldwin's habit to walk to work from his Perry Street home. The offices of the *Peoria Star* were then located at the corner of South Jefferson and Fulton streets, next to the Empire Saloon.

At 8 a.m. on Saturday, October 3, 1914, he was walking down Fayette Street. When he came to the corner of Monroe, he was accosted by an attorney named Giles Keithley, who grabbed him from behind and demanded that Baldwin stop publishing his name in his paper. The *Star* had charged him with perjury in its evening edition the day before. The young attorney was the son of Arthur Keithley, an old Baldwin foe.

What happened next depends on which of the two feuding newspapers, the *Journal* or the *Star*, you read. One report said the attorney slapped the 74-year-old editor, while another said he knocked him down. There were witnesses who saw him on the ground.

In any event, less than seven weeks later, on Thursday, November 19th... Baldwin died.

After Baldwin's death his son, Frank, who was a medical doctor and also directly involved in the story, now charged that he had examined his father after the fight, that his father had told him he had been knocked down and repeatedly kicked, and that his left side had pained him.

The autopsy revealed a large abscess in the region of the left kidney and a pus sack in the prostatic gland. Death was found to be due to uremic poisoning from a diseased kidney. But after only a brief discussion, the verdict of the coroner's jury was "death by natural causes" and with no mention of the fight.

Baldwin's widow, Sarah, became president of the *Star*, and the family continued to live in the Perry house for many years. In 1947, it was sold to the Jewish Center and Hebrew School, and it served the youth of the Jewish community for several more years. Then, in 1959, Marv Hult bought it to house his advertising agency.

Left — **EUGENE F. BALDWIN**, the publisher and editor of the *Peoria Star*, who bought the Perry Street house in 1907. (Photo courtesy of Dick and Marlene Caldwell)

Right — The House That David Built, at 245 NE Perry, shortly after it was painted for the Hult Agency. (A Lee Roten photo, courtesy of Marvin Hult)

Secret hiding places

Sidney Baldwin, who had since moved out east, came back to Peoria in the early '60s for a visit. Elizabeth Belcke brought Sidney by to visit Marv and to see the old house once more.

She told Hult his office had been her father's bedroom, and asked if he had found one of her dad's two secret hiding places there. Hult was unaware of them, so she went into his bathroom, got down on her hands and knees and opened a lower cabinet door. She banged on a board and it fell in, revealing a rather large hiding place.

Sidney said her father had originally created the hiding places to hold highly secret information about some problems between a union and a railroad that he wouldn't even entrust to his bank deposit vault.

Well, the old house has had quite a history over its 115 years, and the other day the students at Father Sweeney School told me of a rumor that the house is haunted. But that rumor was quickly put to rest by Mark Matuszak.

No hauntings here

It all started from a "haunted house party" the agency built around a rather mysterious visit to the home by Julia Proctor White.

One very stormy Sunday morning, Hult was alone in his second-floor office. Between claps of thunder he heard a quiet, sobbing noise downstairs. Looking down the staircase, he saw a little old lady dressed in a lacy, old-fashioned dress and black veil. She was just standing in the hallway wimpering and crying. He asked if he could help her but she wouldn't speak.

Sensing that she must have been a part of this old house at one time, he asked if she would like to look around. She nodded her head and he left her alone. Watching from above, he saw her go from room to room, sobbing and whimpering all the while. It was still storming when she left as suddenly as she had appeared.

A week later, a lady who identified herself as the housekeeper of Julia Proctor White came and handed Marv the book, "The House That David Built." It was written by Mrs. White, who was now living in the Glen Oak Towers. She wanted Hult to have the book as a "thank you" for saving her family's home.

A haunting story, maybe... but, sorry kids, no haunted house!

How about a hall of fame in Peoria?

I've stated in this column many times that I never cease to be amazed at the number of Peoria-area folks who, over many years, have gone on to fame (and often times fortune) in show business... and so many of them did it in the art of comedy.

It has also struck me that just about everyone around our town takes a great deal of personal pride and pleasure in this fact. Yet, Peoria has never made an effort to permanently honor these people. And the question that keeps coming up in my mind is... Why not?

After my 15 years managing the Madison Theater, followed by 25 more in broadcasting, it's become an obsession with me that began even before I retired in 1984.

And during my last year as president of LDX Broadcasting, the parent company of WEEK-TV (which I had previously managed), I had an opportunity to interview one of these local heros I'd heard so much about all my life.

The Plaza hotel in Century City, California, was the meeting place for all three networks, one per week, for three weeks each May. And Flossie and I were fortunate enough to go to the NBC and CBS meetings each year.

The Plaza was built on part of the old 20th Century-Fox Studios lot, right next door to Beverly Hills and the Bel Air district.

In 1984, the CBS meeting was held the week before that of NBC's, and we had about four days between the two. Knowing this in advance, I wrote a letter to Jim Jordan (Fibber McGee), who was living high up in Beverly Hills, telling him I would contact him while on the West Coast.

Me & Fibber McGee

Jordan's first wife, Marian (Mollie), also a Peorian, had died of cancer many years before. Jordan had been remarried for over 20 years and was now 87 years old. So, I called him the Sunday in between network meetings.

We made small talk about Peoria for awhile, and then I asked him to do a TV interview. He said he didn't feel up to going to a studio, so I suggested doing it at his home. He graciously agreed and a couple days later, we met a TV crew at his beautiful home and set up in his living room.

Flossie and I had a nice visit with him while the TV crew rearranged his furniture. Then I interviewed him for about an hour on tape. And since his wife wasn't home at the time, Flossie answered his telephone so it wouldn't disrupt our conversation. We edited the tape down to a half-hour show, and it ran on WEEK.

This was also the year Jim was being honored as Broadcaster of the Year by the Illinois Broadcasters Association.

During the interview, he reminisced about his Peoria days and, at one point, told about he and Marian appearing on stage at the Madison and Palace Theaters, long before their radio success.

The 'little book'

When I retired a few months later, this was all freshly in mind and I got to thinking back to my own experiences while managing the Madison. I decided to write a little book about those days, more for the eyes of my family than anything else.

Well, the "little book" became bigger and bigger. As long as I was doing the '40s and '50s, I felt the need to trace the Madison's history from its beginning on October 16, 1920. Having done that, it seemed only natural to research the theaters that were then in competition with the Madison, plus the Palace Theater, which was being built at the same time across Main Street.

By that time I was really into it, and decided to research the history of all Peoria's theaters, from the first known stage performance in our town in 1838 (in the courthouse of that day), through the various hotel ballrooms and the later halls and music halls that began around 1850.

The little book turned into one that currently stands at 15 chapters, documenting the history of more than 140 different "theaters" in our town. It isn't published yet because the idea for this column got in the way.

While all this was going on, I kept running into more and more names of Peorians who had "made it" in various forms of

Bill and Flossie Adams surround Jim Jordan (Fibber McGee) in his Beverly Hills home in 1984.

Bill Adams interviewing Jim Jordan on TV from Jordan's Beverly Hills home in 1984.

entertainment. I soon collected biographies of more than 40 Peorians, many of whom had been long forgotten, and this list continues to grow, with the entertainers of today like Richard Pryor, Dan Fogelberg and Sam Kinison.

Playing in Peoria

But long before Charles Correll and Jim and Marian Jordan made Amos and Andy and Fibber McGee and Molly household words, local people were making names for themselves in show business. One of the earliest was the internationally known Grand Opera star Emma Abbott, a local girl who began her career back in the 1860s.

Will It Play in Peoria? It not only will, it has for over 150 years.

So, why not a museum... or a hall of fame... or something that would capitalize on a theme that has become known throughout the world?

The first step, in what has become a thousand-mile journey, was to discuss the idea with my friend Jack Brimeyer at the *Journal Star*.

Brimeyer was my very first consultant and suggested that I interest a local organization in becoming the catalyst in this effort. So, having been associated with the Peoria Advertising and Selling Club since 1960, I made a personal appeal to its board of directors, who surprised me. They not only agreed, but several of them joined me in forming an organization called the Peoria Entertainer's Hall of Fame.

But while working on this local idea, it kept occurring to us that just about every art form has an award for special achievement in its field - except for one. Motion pictures have their Oscar... television has its Emmy... Broadway has its Tony. Then there's drama and music, and the list goes on. But the one performing art that has been, so far, ignored is the one that's considered in show business to be the most difficult of them all... COMEDY.

Paying tribute to comedy

So our local hall of fame reorganized and has since expanded into one with a more national appeal. And just this past month we announced that it has become incorporated as the National Comedy Hall of Fame Ltd. This group's current board of energetic people have developed the plan to make Peoria its national home. It will now not only pay tribute to all the Peorians who have made us so proud, it will especially honor those comedians who have excelled in that most difficult of all art forms.

And why not in Peoria? It's the town that gained the show business reputation that, if you could make it here, you could make it anywhere in the country... even the world!

NEXT MONTH: We'll take a look behind the scenes at the people involved in the National Comedy Hall of Fame.

The Bataan Death March remembered

Thursday marks the 50th anniversary of one of World War II's worst atrocities, the Bataan Death March.

Six central Illinois men who were assigned to the 17th Pursuit Squadron of the Army Air Corps and lived through that march, and much more, are Harold Fowler of Peoria, George Brignall of Bartonville, Ralph Forth of Bradford, Merle Lype of Thomasboro, Harold Johnson of Danville and William Wright (recently deceased) of Rantoul. (This group and their spouses have gotten together annually for the past 15 years.)

This is the story of one of those survivors.

Can't find work

In 1939, a couple Canton lads, George Brignall and his friend, John Essex, both recently graduated from Canton High, but couldn't find work. They came to Peoria and applied at Caterpillar and Hiram Walker's, but those companies weren't hiring either. In their search, the two young men saw a sign, "Join the Army Air Corps," and so, with no job prospects in sight, they joined up.

On January 4, 1940, they received their physicals at Peoria's Federal Building, and then were marched in a group down Main Street to the Rock Island Depot, where they boarded a train for Selfridge Air Force Base near Detroit. Later, their group was divided into two squadrons, which separated the friends. Brignall was assigned to the 17th Pursuit Squadron, and Essex went into the 94th.

Brignall's squadron was sent to San Francisco, where they boarded the U.S.S. Etolin to Hawaii. It was the first leg of a top secret assignment to Nichols Field in the Philippines, where they first lived in a tent city, on the outskirts of Manila.

When the squadron was put on alert after the attack on Pearl Harbor, Brignall was assigned to a machine gun pit. On December 10, 1941, the squadron was eating out in the middle of a field when planes began flying over. They discovered it was the Japanese when the planes' began strafing.

Down to Bataan peninsula

Manila was ordered an open city on Christmas Eve, and on Christmas Day, Nichols Field was ordered evacuated. The 17th was moved across Manila Bay by boat to Bataan, and the squadron was reassigned to the Service Command, which was defending the lower third of the Bataan peninsula.

They were sent to Bataan's west coast to rout out Jap snipers, who were shooting at trucks on the road. What was originally thought to be 40 or 50 snipers turned out to be more than 1,000, who had strapped themselves into the jungle's treetops with their belts.

When the Japanese invasion came, Brignall was at Anyason Point, which was one of the enemy's three landing thrusts, but they stopped the invasion on that point. But our forces finally ran out of food and only survived by eating lizards, dogs and tree roots - even making a stew from monkeys. Brignall's weight fell from 155 to 85 pounds.

Surrender

On March 11, 1942, the 17th Pursuit Squadron became part of the Luzon Force, under the direct command of General Wainwright. The surrender came a month later, on April 9.

A physician at Bataan later recalled that our men had lost about a third of their normal weight by the time of the Bataan surrender. Nearly all of them suffered from malaria, beriberi, malnutrition and dysentery. Many had leg sores infested with maggots.

The kid from Canton was captured with thousands of others, and was forced to walk in the atrocity known as the Bataan Death March. Brignall watched his friends drop dead from exhaustion while others were shot to death if they faltered in the march. He watched Japanese tanks run over the wounded who could no longer walk.

During the death march, 30 American and Filipino soldiers were told by their captors they could fill their canteens in a nearby rice paddy. Then, while they were filling their mouths and canteens with water, they were shot to death.

When a marcher next to him faltered, George held him up in an attempt to make the captors think he was walking of his own accord. But a Jap soldier saw the man wasn't walking and rammed a bayonet through his chest.

The death march began at Mariveles at the southernmost tip of the Bataan peninsula, then moved about 70 miles north along the west coast of Manila Bay to San Fernando. There, they were put in cattle cars and moved by rail to within 12 miles of their destination but, again, were forced to march the rest of the way.

Camp O'Donnell was their prison until it became so disease-infected, the Japanese had to bulldoze it. They built a new one, named Cabanatuan, where George was forced to help stack as many as 600 American corpses into a small pit. In their emaciated condition, he and the other survivors were also forced to build a bridge across a river and perform other manual labor.

'Hell ships'

George was one of the first to be shipped out on what later were described as "hell ships." He and the others were kept barely alive, with very little room to lay down in the hot, stagnant hold of a Japanese freighter, the Tottori Maru, bound for Formosa (Taiwan) and then on to Pusan, South Korea. Four hundred people, too sick to continue, were left in South Korea, while the rest were moved by train to bitterly cold Mukden, Manchuria, where they became infested with lice and fleas.

There, British, Canadian and U.S. prisoners were marched daily to a big tool factory where they poured concrete by hand. Finally, they were moved to another camp and forced to march 10 miles to and from work each day in a textile mill, until the war ended.

A 1940 photo of George Brignall, shortly after joining the Army Air Corp.
(Picture courtesy of George Brignall)

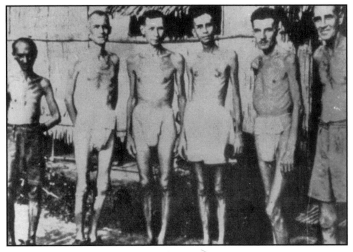

Six of the thousands of American prisoners of war after the Bataan Death March.
(From the "History of the Defenders of the Philippines, Guam and Wake Islands.")

The prisoners were finally liberated by the Russians (our allies in World War II), who escorted them back to Korea, where they were placed in American hands for the first time in 42 months.

Brignall finally returned to the States, but was hospitalized for a year because of the atrocities he had suffered. He was discharged June 10, 1946, as a technical sergeant.

Beating the odds

But the kid from Canton beat the seemingly insurmountable odds. He not only survived the impossible atrocities of the Bataan Death March and the unthinkable treatment in Japanese prisons, he returned to Canton where he met Zelda Fawcett, a nurse at Graham Hospital, and married her the following year.

Brignall returned to Peoria, too, and finally landed that job at Hiram Walker's. He was hired as a security guard in March 1947 and retired in 1978, after 31 years with the firm.

The Brignall's have two sons, Steven and Douglas, one daughter, Georgia K., and five grandchildren, and are retired in Bartonville.

Brignall and the other few from the 17th Pursuit Squadron that made it back are survivors in the truest sense of the word. It's impossible to know the exact number, but of the more than 200 men attached to the 17th Squadron, Brignall estimates that maybe 40 survived the Bataan Death March and the horrors that followed.

The hunt begins for Peorian "Handsome Jack" Klutas

Back in the 1930s, there was a nation-wide manhunt for a Chicago gangleader named "Handsome Jack" Klutas, who got his illicit start in Peoria. That manhunt led to a gun battle at a South Side barber shop, which ended with two dead and two wounded, none of whom was former Peorian Klutas.

In the 1920s, a cultured and well-mannered son of a prominent Sterling, Illinois family, one John E. Klutas, was within a few months of receiving his degree at the University of Illinois when, for some unknown reason, he turned to crime.

After dropping out of school, John came to Peoria and got a job as a fry cook in a downtown restaurant. A few months later, he and several others set up a gigantic still, just a few blocks from City Hall. When the money came rolling in, Klutas began living accordingly.

People who remember him say he spent money lavishly, and it didn't take him long to gain a reputation as "a lion with the ladies," even with some of those in the social register.

In April 1929, Klutas was indicted for auto theft. Then he incurred a temporary setback in the form of a jail sentence after Prohibition agents closed in on his still, which was said to be the biggest ever uncovered by the Feds in this vicinity.

While covering the story, a Peoria newspaper reporter, referring to his uncommonly good looks and gentlemanly manners, described him as "Handsome Jack" Klutas, and the nickname stuck.

Kidnapping business

Jack later migrated to Chicago, where he headed up a gang and went into the kidnapping business. One of his victims was Bill Urban, the proprietor of Peoria's Empire Recreation Parlor.

As previously described in this column, Urban was kidnapped July 1, 1930. It was later determined to be the first in a series of nine abductions for ransom attributed to Klutas and a Chicago-based gang who's co-leader was Frank Souder of Benton. It was believed that Urban was held at a spot near Joliet. He was released without injury, but many think he payed as much as $80,000 for his release.

Meanwhile, another big time gambling boss, James Hackett of Blue Island, was kidnapped and released after paying a whopping $150,000.

But some of Hackett's friends had connections with Al Capone's mob. Capone apparently tried to make a deal with Klutas for Hackett's release. A Chicago newspaper later reported that Handsome Jack and his henchmen covered a Capone gang member with machine guns when he came to their hideout to strike a deal.

Instead, Jack and his clan showed their disdain for Big Al with rude remarks. Klutas was quoted as saying: "You can tell your boss it's no go. We don't deal with greaseballs." It's said that the Capone sources later negotiated for the gambler's release, but Al and his boys never forgot the crack by Klutas.

After seven other abductions, plus the slaying of two peace officers in 1930, Handsome Jack became one of America's most wanted. Like the hunt for John Dillinger in 1934, reports of Handsome Jack's whereabouts cropped up all over the country.

Tracking him down

But Hackett, the Blue Island gambler, was irked by the high ransom of $150,000, and he hired an ace private detective and former Chicago state's attorney investigator, Pat Roche, to track down Klutas. It took

"Handsome Jack" Klutas was the subject of a nationwide manhunt in 1933. He was named the gangleader that kidnapped nine people, including Bill Urban, the proprietor of the Empire in Peoria.

Roche nearly three years, but on November 10, 1933, the following headlines and story appeared in the *Peoria Star*:

"TRAIL PEORIAN AS KIDNAPPER - Predict Klutas Arrest Soon in Kidnap Roundup

"An underworld tip that John 'Handsome Jack' Klutas, former Peorian, hunted as the collegiate leader of an abduction ring that once defied the all-powerful Al Capone, is hiding in a Chicago suburb, sent investigators to nearby towns today.

"Klutas, who is sought as the co-leader of the gang which perpetrated nine abductions in two years with a ransom loot of $500,000 also is wanted as the slayer of two Iowa police officers shot in 1930.

"Pat Roche, P.I., who uncovered the ring, received info that Klutas might be hiding at Joliet. Among the kidnap gang's victims was a gangster friendly with Capone.

"Three other gang members are held: Frank Souder, Benton, co-leader of the gang, Gale Swolley, Peoria (he resided at 915 Blaine St.), confederate of Klutas, and Julian (Babe) Jones, St. Charles.

"Authorities claimed they had confessions from Jones, linking the gang to nine abductions (Jones specifically mentioned Bill Urban's kidnapping). Edward La Rue, Peoria, and Eddie Wagner, were also sought. Two members of the gang were said to have been killed: Ed Nicholson and Ray Nolan.

"The men face death in the electric chair if convicted of kidnapping in Illinois. A formal charge of kidnapping James Hackett, Blue Island, was placed against Souder."

The death-chair penalty for kidnapping came about, not so much because of the rampant kidnapping of gamblers and the like, but the national furor over the kidnapping and murder of Charles and Anne Lindbergh's baby in 1932.

...a time that seems like only yesterday!

NEXT WEEK: The rest of the Handsome Jack Klutas story, and the gun battle his manhunt brought about on Peoria's South Side.

The tale of treacherous "Handsome Jack" continues

Second of a two-part series

John E. "Handsome Jack" Klutas was within a few months of receiving his degree from the University of Illinois when he suddenly turned to a life of crime.

He came to Peoria in the 1920s and got a job as a fry cook at a downtown restaurant. He and several others set up a gigantic still here and he began making bootleg booze.

After the Feds put him out of business, he migrated to Chicago, where he and Frank Souder formed a gang and went into kidnapping, big time. They were connected with nine kidnappings, one of which was Bill Urban of Peoria's Empire Recreation Parlor.

In November 1933, the gang was arrested after a private investigator, who was hired by one of the kidnap victims, tracked them down. Klutas and another Peorian, Edward La Rue, avoided capture. Two other gang members were killed in the process.

Handsome Jack was a bad one. On June 20, 1930, he was being held by the sheriff and deputy after his arrest in Washington, Iowa, for violating Prohibition laws.

The officers took one gun away from him, but they made the fatal mistake of assuming it was the only one. Jack had another one up his sleeve. Enroute to jail he produced the second gun, killed both of his guards, and escaped.

Eventually, on November 10, 1933, a nationwide manhunt for Jack Klutas was put into effect. It was rumored that he might be hiding out in Joliet, but all nearby cities were prime targets for the police net, including Peoria.

A few days later, while the hunt was at a fever pitch, Peoria police received a tip, which led to a terrific gun battle at Lawson's Barber Shop on South Adams Street, near Western Avenue. They were told Russell Hughes, a "buddy" of Klutas, could be found in that vicinity.

On the morning of November 13, Fred Montgomery, chief of detectives, accompanied by detectives Robert Moran and Gay Dusenberry, jumped into a car and began cruising that immediate area.

At about 10 a.m., while passing the intersection, Moran, who had been studying a photo of the suspect, spotted Hughes standing in the doorway of the barber shop. He yelled "There he is...," and with that, Montgomery jammed on the brakes. As the three detectives approached, the suspect stepped inside the shop.

Montgomery drew his revolver and ordered, "All right, Hughes, put 'em up." At that moment, the shop exploded with a hail of bullets. Hughes, who had his hands in his overcoat pockets, came up with two small-caliber revolvers and began firing. The guns of the three detectives blazed back. One of the first shots struck Montgomery, just above his right hip.

The barbers, Arnett Lawson and Charles Hinton, retreated for cover after the first shots, but Alfred Jenkins of 302 Arago Street, who had been talking to the barbers, was struck twice, once in the groin and then in the left hand.

Seconds later, Moran fell after being hit twice. While Montgomery and Dusenberry stopped a moment to aid their fallen partner, Hughes worked his way toward the door. A bullet crashed through the plate glass window and another shattered the glass in the door. He then leaped outside and started toward the alley.

Staggering as he ran, he took time to reload one of his two revolvers and continued firing. Montgomery had reloaded his revolver and emptied it a second time. Dusenberry's was also empty. Calling to the barbers to take care of Moran and Jenkins, Dusenberry grabbed Moran's gun and continued firing at Hughes. Reaching the alley, the bullet-riddled Hughes dropped his pistols in the dirt, and was dead when the officers reached him.

The battle attracted hundreds of spectators who fled for cover as the gunfight came out onto the street. Although he was hit only once, Montgomery's clothing con-

A 1954 photo of Fred Montgomery who was Peoria Police Chief of Detectives at the time of the shooting. He later served as Peoria County Sheriff.

(A *Peoria Journal* photo)

The barber shop on the left was the scene of the 1933 shooting. The pool hall on the corner later became Cookie Blair's Tavern.

(Photo courtesy of Peoria Public Library)

tained four bullet holes. Dusenberry, unhit, had two holes in his clothing. Moran was shot twice, once in the shoulder, and again in the abdomen. He died two days later at St. Francis Hospital.

Ironically, his wife had also been taken to St. Francis to await the birth of their fifth child.

Thousands attended Robert Moran's funeral and a public fund was raised in memory of his bravery. He also became a martyr to the Peoria police department, his

detective shield attached to the tip of the police radio transmitter antenna atop City Hall.

The name Russell Hughes turned out to be an alias. His real name was Guy West, a Connersville, Indiana resident, but he never used his real name in his crime. He went by either "Hughes" or "Harry Stewart," who, the police learned, had connections with the Klutas gang.

His family in Indiana never knew of his criminal background. He left a widow who

was an invalid. The autopsy showed that five bullets had hit him, and that he had been intoxicated at the time of the shooting.

A short time later, Handsome Jack Klutas was found and killed in Maywood, a Chicago suburb. Two of the three men who were originally seized as members of his gang were given prison sentences on charges of kidnapping and extortion.

If you craved excitement, Peoria was as good a place as any, back in those roaring days

...that seem like only yesterday!

Peoria hall of fame dream still out there

About a month ago I wrote in this column about a dream I've had that Peoria should someday have an entertainment museum and hall of fame.

Shortly after I retired from television in 1985, I began to research the idea. The plan was to begin with a local museum and hall of fame.

Early on, I had talked to Bob Armstrong, formerly of WMBD, who had a similar concept of a comedy hall of fame. Both ideas seemed to us to be compatible, and we decided to put the two ideas together: first, create a Peoria Entertainers' Hall of Fame, and then expand the idea into a National Comedy Hall of Fame.

On January 25, 1988, I wrote a letter to Dick Oakford, who was then president of the Ad Club. I asked that the club accept the challenge of being the catalyst for the project.

The board not only enthusiastically bought the concept, but six Ad Club board members, including Oakford, joined me in forming an ad-hoc group to examine the idea and determine recommendations to the club. The other five were Ed Bradley, Bill Burdon, Gary Gresham, Doug Wells and Bruce White. Our first meeting was held on March 3, 1988 at O'Leary's Restaurant.

While all this was happening, I had also been contacting many of the "movers and shakers" around town who had the experience (and, frankly, the clout) to give us guidance in such a project.

The ad-hoc committee soon became our board of directors, and by the end of 1988, it was expanded to include John Parkhurst, who was soon followed by Rebekah Bourland. I was named president, Bradley secretary/treasurer, and Lorri Linthicum of the Peoria Convention and Visitors Bureau became our administrative assistant. On February 1, 1989, we became incorporated.

The following year saw Juliette Whittaker join our board, followed by Gene Holmes and Mike Dentino. Then came Ron Pilon, Gloria Costa, Mary Ann Penn, Joan Janssen, Erma Davis, Jim Wilhelm, Mary Jo Papich, Pat White, Lindsay Wood Davis, Wayne Flittner, Mike McLinden, Gary Clark and Monte Brannan.

Seven have since served their terms or resigned, and we all grieve the loss of Bill Burdon, an original board member who died last year.

In 1991, I passed the presidential torch to Gene Holmes. This year's president is

Bourland, and our current board stands at 16 members.

While we worked on the local idea, we also recognized the fact that the local hall of fame was taking longer to launch than originally intended.

Our ultimate goal, after all, was to acknowledge the field of comedy and those who have excelled in it over the years. Once that was in place, we could then take the time to develop the Peoria Entertainers' Hall of Fame under that larger umbrella.

So the local group reorganized and on March 1st, we announced the incorporation of what is now the National Comedy Hall of Fame Ltd. and our plan to make Peoria its home.

Will it play in Peoria? We firmly believe it will.

Our first fund-raiser was held Friday evening, March 20, at the Bradley Student Center ballroom. Jim Wilhelm came up with the very funny format of inviting local luminaries to come and relate their goofiest gags.

Well, we did just that, and to our utter amazement, 28 local celebs participated.

Picture, if you will, a big ballroom full of people laughing with (and at) this group of brave souls: John Bearce, Jerry Brookhart, Jack Brimeyer, Herb Buzbee, Chaunce Conklin, John Day, Paul Herzog, Henry Holling, Alice Hout, Jay Janssen, Marilyn Ketay, Ray LaHood, Sally Lawrence, Nat LeDoux, Dirk McGinnis, Tom McIntyre, Bonnie Noble, Ron Pilon, Keith Rippy, Mitch Robinson, George

Shadid, Jack Steenrod, Ron Ulmer, Leonard Unes, Lee Wenger, Pat White and Jim Wilhelm. Funny man Mike Dentino and WMBD-Radio's John Williams co-hosted the event and additional musical entertainment was provided by the outstanding Woodruff High School Jazz Band.

I think I can safely say the event was successful beyond our wildest expectations. So much so that similar projects are already being planned.

Well, we're off and running but we obviously have a long way to go. The dream is still out there... a dream of a tribute to all the great ones... the likes of Charlie Chaplin, W. C. Fields, Bob Hope, Milton Berle, Lucille Ball, Danny Thomas, Johnny Carson, Dick Van Dyke, Bill Cosby and yes, former Peoria-area residents such as Richard Pryor, Charles Correll, Marian and Jim Jordan, and Sam Kinison, who recently died in an automobile accident.

If you would like to become a part of the dream, it's not too late to become a charter member.

During the rest of 1992, charter memberships are being offered for $100; individual and family memberships of $25 and $35; lifetime memberships of $350.

This is a not-for-profit organization. But money isn't our most important need. People are the lifeline of any organization and we need good people who have an interest and the desire to see this Peoria dream come true. If you care to join us in either a personal or monetary way, please call or write any of our officers or board members. Or drop me a line at the *Journal Star*.

Who are the possible comedian candidates for the National Comedy Hall of Fame? The movies alone have given us some of the greatest, such as: (Center) Charlie Chaplin (and clockwise) Groucho Marx, Mae West, W. C. Fields, Bob Hope, Laurel & Hardy, Jerry Lewis, Woody Allen, Jack Lemmon, Red Skelton, and Marie Dressler. (Photo from Leonard Maltin's, "The Greatest Movie Comedians")

Editor's note: Since this column appeared in the newspaper, the name of the organization has been changed to the Peoria Comedy Center and Mike McLinden is president.

Former mayor's life a very colorful one

For the past several months, I've been indebted to Dick and Marlene Caldwell, who have loaned me a number of old books in their personal collection on the history of Peoria, Peoria County, and Illinois. These books have been the source for many recent columns dealing with Peoria's early history.

Marlene's mother received the books from David Wead, the brother of Peoria author and playwright Frank Wead.

Wead's grandfather was George C. Bestor, one of our early pioneers who settled in Peoria on August 3, 1835. Bestor's life here was a colorful one, especially during his three terms as Peoria mayor.

In addition to being mayor, Bestor was also in the real-estate business; was a two-term trustee of the Town of Peoria; and was twice appointed Peoria's postmaster, once by President John Tyler and, again, by Abraham Lincoln.

His varied background also included his financial interest in the Peoria & Oquawka Railroad (which named a locomotive after him) and, later, was a director of the T P & W Railroad. During the Civil War, George Bestor and his oldest son, built two gun boats for his friend Abe Lincoln's U. S. Navy.

But an incident occurred during Bestor's reign as Peoria mayor that highlighted his unwavering courage and remarkable ability. He took on a bigger than life character, looking robbers, murderers, and rapists squarely in the eye, and it was said that danger stared more than once into the cool, gray, Yankee eyes of George Bestor... and backed away. He became the first, and only, Peoria mayor to form a group of vigilantes in Peoria's long and colorful history.

This story begins on Columbus Day, October 12, 1850: It was a blustery fall day when a cattle buyer named Harvey J. Hewitt entered the small lobby of the Curtiss Bank at Main and Water streets and withdrew $3,940. While he was counting it, another man - later identified as "Tom Tit" Jordan - was casually observing the transaction.

Jordan, known to the Peoria police as a river boat thief, quietly slipped out of the bank and alerted two more unsavory characters named Thomas Brown and George Williams, who laid in wait for Hewitt.

They followed the unsuspecting cattleman to Spring Street hill, which was then well beyond the city limits. There, they stopped his rig and demanded the money. Hewitt resisted, and one of the thugs struck him on the head with a large rock. They then took a buggy and a fast horse from a nearby livery stable and made a headlong dash for Springfield.

Meanwhile, Jordan fled to New Orleans. But the long arm of the law eventually nabbed him there and returned him to Peoria by river steamer.

News of the robbery and attack of the well-known and liked cattle buyer spread like wildfire.

Using the power of his office, Mayor Bestor formed a posse and they made the long, cold ride to Springfield in pursuit of the dastardly duo. But the posse, which included many businessmen, soon grew tired and returned home.

Bestor, however, was not so easily discouraged. He and one of his possemen, Zenas Hotchkiss, finally caught the two bandits. They clapped them in irons and returned with them to Peoria's flimsy jail. Most of the loot was also recovered.

By then, the whole town was up in arms. Just three weeks earlier, a lynch mob had been formed against a rapist, and whiskey was now once again fanning the flame of lynch talk. The town was, to say the least, in a very ugly mood.

Hewitt had identified his killers before he died and the next day, Judge William Kellogg sentenced both men to be hanged on December 20th.

The ominous cries of lynching grew louder as time passed, but the executions had to be delayed until Jordan's return from New Orleans, so the two could formally identify him as their fellow conspirator.

Fearing that the delay might signal a reprieve for the murderers, groups of angry citizens finally developed into a half-crazed mob and stormed the small jail, while the sheriff was "conveniently absent."

Despite the efforts of Deputy David D. Irons, the mob took both Brown and Williams to a nearby tree. At this point, an unnamed man in the crowd made a plea to the mob, causing their mood to cool.

After that, no one would step forward to place a noose around the neck of either man. They were finally returned to jail and their executions rescheduled for January 15th.

But the lynch mob rumblings persisted, so Mayor Bestor again took matters into his own hands. He issued a proclamation to all the male inhabitants of Peoria, forming a vigilante group for law and order. He also recommended stores and businesses be closed from 12 a.m. to 2 p.m. "during which time the bell will be tolled."

News of the vigilantes' movement and the date of the rescheduled hangings spread throughout the entire area and by January 15th, the town was bulging with a huge crowd of 10,000 people. (This was at a time when Peoria's total population was a little more than 6,000.) Families came from far and wide by horse, buggy, wagon, and on foot, and the event took on a carnival-like atmosphere.

As scheduled, and without incident, the two murderers were hanged at the corner of First and Sanford streets.

Tom Jordan was later sentenced to a long term at the Alton state prison. Ironically, he was pardoned in 1863 after serving 12 years, to serve in the Civil War for the Union Army.

George C. Bestor, Peoria's fighting frontier mayor... another colorful character in our town's exciting Yester Days.

GEORGE C. BESTOR - Peoria's frontier mayor who, in 1851, called for vigilantes to maintain order during the hanging of two murderers.

(Courtesy of Peoria Public Library)

Remodeled Madison brings former contractor to mind

Art Seelye handled painting and decorating for several downtown theaters in the '40s and '50s

When the Comfort family recently had the grand opening of the newly remodeled Madison Theater lobby, my wife, Flossie, and I made it a point to be there.

After all, it's where we first met and spent our dating years and the first years of our married lives. She also weaned our first three children there.

It was a wonderful evening of dining on the Comfort's delicious gourmet fare and dancing to the rhythms of Dave and the Dynamics. Proceeds from the event went to the Peoria Civic Opera Co. and the Peoria Historical Society. It was a very memorable and - for us, at least - nostalgic evening.

Seeing the beautifully redecorated theater lobby with its oval rotunda also brought to mind some of the people I associated with it back in the 1940s and '50s. The remodeling especially reminded me of a man who contracted for all the painting and decorating of, not only the Madison, but all four downtown theaters then operated by Publix Great States Theaters. His name was Art Seelye.

I had known Art for quite some time, but until a friend of our daughter Lesa recently told me, I never knew that Art Seelye also was the leader of one of the local bands that once played around here.

Lesa's friend, Nena Gullette, is Art's granddaughter. Her mother - Art's daughter - was Nan Chianakas, who recently died. (Many may remember her participation in local theater for so many years.)

Arthur Henry Seelye was born in the 200 block of West McClure on June 29, 1901, to William and Lillian Seelye. He was the oldest of three boys and a girl, the others being Jack, William and Josephine. They later moved into the next block on McClure, and then to 307 W. Virginia and Art went to the old Columbia Grade School on Bigelow.

His dad played the violin and Art took up the instrument while still in school. He didn't go to high school but instead took a job at the old box factory at Water and Harrison streets. Then he went on the road as a salesman for an oil company for four or five years.

To augment his income, he formed an orchestra, which varied from five to eight pieces, called Seelye's Sons of Syncopation.

At one time he thought about keeping it at seven pieces so he could call it Seelye's Seven Sons of Syncopation, but decided that might be carrying the idea a little too far. Some of the early members of the group were Rosco Miskeman, Coonie Wagner, Earl Connor and John Mulvaney.

They played for dances all around the area, one of their first engagements being at the new, beautiful Automobile Club in Chillicothe. (It later became the Chillicothe Country Club.) They also played at dance halls such as the Silver Leaf and Fernwood and, later, the Queen's Pantry on Knoxville.

One day Art was walking by a house on McClure when he heard someone playing beautiful piano music. Curiosity got the best of him, so he went up and rang the door bell and asked to meet the person playing the piano. It was Helen Hoffman, who seven years later became his wife.

Art and Helen bought a home at 540 Peoria Avenue, now 1920 N. Peoria. After leaving the oil company, he began painting houses on the side, between orchestra engagements.

He had just joined the painters union in 1928, when the recession came along and wiped out the painting jobs. So the Seelyes hopped into their Model T Ford and headed for California, where Art landed a job painting ships in a shipyard. Both of their children, William and Nan, were born on the West Coast.

In 1932, the Seelye family returned to Peoria. Art returned to painting and started up the old band once again. In 1937, he started his own paint contracting business.

His son, Bill, says that he had no regular customers to begin with, so Art stood

Art Seelye putting the finishing touches on the U.S. War Bond Booth in front of the Madison Theater about 1943.

A 1956 photo of Art and some of his earlier band members. (Left to Right) Rosco Miskeman, Coonie Wagner, Art Seelye, and Earl Connor.
(Photos courtesy of Nena Gullette)

around on downtown street corners, making contacts with local businessmen. I'm sure this must be how he met Great States Theaters' city manager, Len Worley, and got a start contracting for the theater work.

Son Bill went to work for his dad in 1954, and when Art retired in 1969, he took over the business. Bill later incorporated, and A. H. Seelye Painting and Decorating became A. H. Seelye and Son.

By the time I started working at the Madison in the early 1940s, Art Seelye was already firmly established as our painting contractor.

While talking with his son, Bill, the other day, he remembered a time when his dad received a call from Len Worley to paint the Apollo canopy. It was a rush job and Art agreed to paint it the following day. But it was raining the next morning so, obviously, Art and his crew didn't show up.

Len called him and raised the roof because the work wasn't being done. Art tried to explain that it shouldn't be painted

under those conditions, but Worley was so adamant Art brought his crew down and they painted it in the rain.

The next day, of course, the paint had all washed away and the job had to be redone. But that's the way Len Worley was. A deal was a deal and, right or wrong, he almost always had his way.

But, right or wrong, those were great times at the Madison and remembering Art Seelye makes it... seem like only yesterday!

Peoria just one stop in Al Larson's life

Some time ago I received a call from Mrs. Mildred Burr of Peoria, who was interested in a column I'd written on the Tiny Hill Orchestra. Burr's close friend, Mary Woodrow Larson, is married to Al Larson, whom I'd mentioned as a vocalist with Tiny Hill. She wondered where she might find some old recordings of his. I had a couple of his old 78s, so I taped them and sent them to her, along with some other Tiny Hill recordings.

A while later, I received a voice tape from Larson himself, who now lives in California, personally thanking me for providing the tapes for her. Now that I had his address, I wrote to Larson, asking for his biography, and the other day he sent it to me. I knew of his Tiny Hill background but, until he sent his bio, I was unaware of his Peoria connection.

Larson had been a nightclub performer for several years, booked by agents in Chicago and Kansas City. He started professionally in radio at WROK in Rockford, Illinois, followed by staff jobs at WALA in Mobile, Alabama, and KFA in Montgomery, Alabama. From there, he went to Peoria's WMBD.

While here he also sang with the old Palace Theater pit band, conducted by Cary Robards, Sr., whenever that 12-piece group had an outside date.

Larson remembers it was May 5, 1935, when WMBD-Radio first became a CBS affiliate, because he sang with the Robards band that night on a half-hour program carried on the CBS network to celebrate the event.

A short time later, Larson was featured on a 13-week broadcast called "Hollywood Previews," sponsored by Loewenstein's Furniture Co. The show also featured Florence Pierson and the Bob Black band. Each week, Publix theaters showed a current musical motion picture, and Larson sang the hit songs from these films. Florence (who later married Harry Luedeke) did the Hollywood Reporter bit. Al also did a morning show from the Madison Theater with Gomer Bath playing the Madison's "Mighty Hinners Organ."

In 1937, Larson moved over to WOW in Omaha, Nebraska, where he sang with Freddy Ebner's band on radio, and at night was the master of ceremonies at the famous (or infamous) McDonald Club, owned by Omaha's bootleg queen, Louise Vinsqueira. Many dignitaries frequented the club, including Father Flanagan of Boys Town. Larson did several benefits at Boys Town and kept in touch with Flanagan until the priest's death.

After Omaha, Larson played supper clubs all over the midwest, including a summer on the "borscht circuit" in northern Wisconisin, where Pappy Walton's band (which wintered at Peoria's Talk of the Town nightclub) went for the summer.

He recalls that he and Dick Coffeen, who played trumpet for Tiny Hill, were close friends. The first time he met Coffeen was in summer 1940, at the Roth Hotel in Oshkosh, Wisconsin. Larson was appearing as the singing master of ceremonies in the hotel's supper club. Coffeen caught his show and brought Tiny Hill, who was looking for a vocalist, over to hear him.

The Hill band was doing a split week at the local theater. Hill's vocalist, Allan DeWitt, had just left the band to go with Jan Savitt, and Columbia Records was insisting that Tiny get another singer for some upcoming recording sessions.

DeWitt didn't get along well with Hill. His specialty was romantic ballads, and he didn't like Hill's style of music. (Larson personally thought DeWitt was one of the two or three best vocalists in the business).

Larson says, "Pappy - I always called Hill Pappy - asked me to audition for him the next day, with Don Fairchild playing for me. We spent a couple hours doing some of Allan's old numbers, and at the end of this time, Hill asked me to join them in Chicago a week later."

Shortly after he joined the Hill band they went on location at the Aragon Ballroom in Cleveland, Ohio, after which they rehearsed every day for two weeks for their opening at Chicago's Oriental Theater, where Duke Ellington had played the previous week. The audiences must have liked Tiny Hill's band; they were held over an additional week.

For this appearance, the band worked out a production number using flashlights on a darkened stage, while the piano and bass played "Stardust." It was very effective, but the guys in the band hated it.

To make the band appear bigger, they were set up on three tiers, with music stands lit up by electric wires running across the floor. On the bill was a knock-about act that used smoke pots, which were activated by the musicians on cue. Larson, as vocalist, was seated on the top tier.

When Al was announced on the very first show, he started down from his third-tier seat to a microphone that automatically rose up from the stage floor. He accidentally stepped on one of the smoke pot buttons, filling the stage with smoke. Then he tripped on one of the wires, sending him headlong toward the orchestra pit. Only the rising microphone saved him from serious injury. The audience, thinking it was part of the act, loved it.

The manager jokingly asked the band to keep it in but they told him they didn't have enough smoke pots to last the week (not to mention enough vocalists).

AL LARSON - as he appeared as vocalist with the Tiny Hill Orchestra. He was also a former WMBD-Radio personality.

On the same bill was Ruth Lowe, who also wrote the big hit, "I'll Never Smile Again", which Frank Sinatra made famous with Tommy Dorsey. Also on the bill was Dorsey's former vocalist, Edythe Wright.

Whenever the band played theaters they would set up a huge scale near the ticket booth. Anyone who weighed more than Tiny Hill would get in free. But as Larson recalls, not many did.

MARY FRANCES WOODROW - former WMBD-Radio receptionist. She and Al Larson were married in 1942, and, this year, are celebrating their 50th wedding anniversary.

NEXT WEEK: The rest of the Al Larson story, with and without Tiny Hill.

Continuing on with Tiny Hill

Second of Two Parts

Last week we told the story of former Peorian Al Larson. Larson not only had an interesting Peoria connection, he was also vocalist with that great Tiny Hill big band back in the early 1940s. So, let's pick up his story after the the band's very successful appearance at Chicago's Oriental Theater.

The band was so well received at the Oriental, it was held over for a second week. Then they went east for a memorable engagement at Donahue's Restaurant on the Pompton Turnpike in Mountain View, N. J., just a mile from Frank Dailey's Meadowbrook, where Jimmy Dorsey's band was appearing.

Hill had a Mutual network broadcast each night from Donahue's, while Dorsey had one on CBS. Hill played and broadcast from there for three months. At this same time Alvino Rey and the King Sisters were at the Rustic Cabin in nearby Westchester (the place where Frank Sinatra sang with Harry James). The musicians would visit each other on their nights off.

Jimmy Donahue was a unique character who began at this location with just a hot dog stand, until his buddy, Babe Ruth, urged him to expand. He did so by adding a beautiful restaurant onto the stand.

But Donahue always stayed out in the stand, wearing his old white apron, dispensing hot dogs to the drive-in trade. Larson once asked him why he never came into the dining room. He replied, "It's too high class in there for me."

After Donahue's, came a series of 42 one-nighters, most of them in February and March, in upstate New York, Pennsylvania, Virginia, Illinois and Wisconsin. Having just come off of three months on radio, the band drew big crowds everywhere.

A young woman even started an Al Larson fan club. Larson first knew about it when groups of young girls would cluster on his side of the bandstand. One (usually the local chapter president) would come up and introduce herself.

Some of the one-nighters the band most enjoyed were the university dates, including Cornell, Indiana University, Northwestern, and the University of Wisconsin at Madison.

After the band finished the one-nighters, Hill and Larson agreed to part company and, after playing the Playmore Ballroom in Kansas City, Larson returned to Chicago and was booked to open the season at Waterloo, Iowa's famous Tavern-on-the-Green. After this he returned to Peoria. He then went to work for Caterpillar on the "graveyard shift," and also went back on staff at WMBD.

His Cat shift ended at 7:30 a.m. and his first broadcast was at 8:30 a.m., followed by another at 3 p.m. Then, three nights a week, he did a show at 7:30 p.m. with Bob Black, Ozzie Osborne and the WMBD band.

Osborne had left Tiny Hill's orchestra shortly before Larson had joined it in 1940, so he didn't really know him before coming back to the station. But Larson says he doesn't believe there was anyone more liked or admired than Osborne.

During this second time around at WMBD, Larson was courting the station's beautiful receptionist, Mary Frances Woodrow. Between his personal life and two jobs, he wasn't getting much sleep.

A few months after he and Mary were married, Larson developed a bad sinus condition and his doctor advised him to go to a dry climate. So the newlyweds packed up and moved to Burbank, California, where Larson worked in a defense plant. But having two brothers in the service, he felt the need to enlist, and he joined the Air Force.

Two other WMBD alumni had also moved to the coast: Jack Sherman was at KNBC in Hollywood, doing sports and a variety of other broadcasts, while Bill Ewing was doing remotes from the Hollywood Paladium. Larson appeared on the "Borden Show with Ginny Simms," with the Sportsmen Quartet, and Frank DuValle's Orchestra.

After the service, MCA signed Larson to a contract and sent him to Detroit for two weeks at Leon & Eddy's nightclub, with Zero Mostel and Bobby Burns' band, followed by a week in Cleveland.

After a year as a talent scout, he left show business and became a salesman for Nesbit

DICK COFFEEN played trumpet for Tiny Hill's band, and introduced Al Larson to Tiny, who hired him as vocalist.
(Photo courtesy of Marian Coffeen)

fruit products, where he became a district manager.

After a couple years, the Larson's moved to San Francisco, where Al later entered the auto business.

The couple fell in love with the Napa Valley region, so they bought a place in the little town of Calistoga, California where Larson still plays golf.

They've also spent many years preparing the cuisine of different countries, which they learned from their travels, and they cater many of their community's group activities (for fun, not profit).

But it seems like only yesterday that Al Larson was doing the vocals with Tiny Hill and his orchestra!

TINY HILL "fronting" for the band, with Dick Coffeen on trumpet at right. The radio audience couldn't appreciate Tiny's antics, he was broadcasting over the Mutual radio network.
(Photo courtesy of Marian Coffeen)

Story of "The Tonight Show" began 38 years ago

I was affiliated with NBC during all of my 25 years in the television business, so naturally I've been a close observer of "The Tonight Show."

Johnny Carson joined the show two years after I started as promotion manager at WEEK-TV. So his recent retirement gives me a a a good excuse to take a look back at the show from the beginning. "The Tonight Show" was already eight years old by the time Johnny took over.

"Tonight" (one word) began on the NBC network on September 27, 1954, with Steve Allen as its first host. Allen actually originated the program 15 months earlier as a local show on NBC's flagship station, WNBT-TV in New York City, and remained the show's host when it moved to the network.

Allen's regulars on the show were announcer Gene Rayburn and Steve Lawrence, Eydie Gorme, Andy Williams and Pat Marshall. The original band was Skitch Henderson and his Orchestra. Pat Kirby and Hy Averback joined the group in 1955.

Allen would open each show seated at the piano, chatting and playing some of his own compositions, one of which was his most famous "This Could Be the Start of Something." He also used guest stars along with the regulars, but the show's emphasis was on Steve and his ad-lib comedy, including his hilarious man-on-the-street routines.

Allen began his own prime time comedy-variety series, "The Steve Allen Show," in the summer of 1956. On this show, in addition to the "Tonight" show carry-overs of Gene Rayburn and Skitch Henderson, its original regulars were Don Knotts, Tom Poston, Louis Nye, Marilyn Jacobs and Gabe Dell.

Steve Allen remained on "Tonight" Wednesday through Friday until the following January. A number of guest hosts appeared on Mondays and Tuesdays until October 1, 1956, when Ernie Kovacs took over as permanent host those two nights.

Kovac's permanent cast included announcer Bill Wendell and regulars Peter Hanley, Maureen Arthur and Barbara Loden. Music was furnished by LeRoy Holmes & his Orchestra.

Kovacs featured most of the zany antics of his prime time shows, including blackouts, satires and slapstick comedy routines.

When Steve Allen left the show in January, 1957, the name changed to "Tonight! America After Dark," and its format changed completely.

Jack Lescoulie, the former "Today Show" veteran, hosted from January 28 until June. Then Al "Jazzbo" Collins hosted its last two months of June and July.

The program featured several regulars including Hy Gardner, Bob Considine and Irv Kupcinet. These columnists reported from New York, Chicago and Los Angeles with live coverage from all three cities and elsewhere, via remotes. It included interviews with personalities in the news, in politics, or in show business, interspersed with live visits to night clubs, Broadway show openings and the like.

"Tonight! America After Dark" had not been successful with either the viewers or the critics and NBC decided to return to a format closer to the original.

So, on July 29, 1957 - just six months after Steve Allen left the show - Jack Paar, a young comic raided from CBS, became the new host of "The Jack Paar Show," and he held reign over the late-night audience for the next five years.

Hugh Downs became Paar's announcer and sidekick, and music was provided by Jose Melis & his Orchestra. Paar's original regulars were Tedi Thurman and Dodi Goodman. Over the five years came a parade of semi-regulars: Elsa Maxwell; the Bil Baird Puppets; Betty Johnson; Genevieve; Cliff Arquette, as Charley Weaver; Pat Harrington, Jr., as Guido Panzini; Hans Conried; Peggy Cass; Alexander King; Joey Bishop; Hermione Gingold; Florence Henderson; Buddy Hackett; Renee Taylor; and Betty White.

While Allen had depended on a frenzied pace and comedy sketches, Paar was at his best as an interviewer. He was incisive, witty and highly emotional. He would often get so emotionally involved with his guests and their stories, he'd often cry on the air.

JACK PAAR (left) listens to Cliff Arquette (as Charley Weaver) read one of his letters from Momma, on "The Jack Paar Show."
(An NBC photo)

STEVE ALLEN - the creator and first host of NBC's "Tonight."
(An NBC photo)

Both presidential candidates, Kennedy and Nixon, were his guests on separate occasions.

Many controversies surrounded Paar's emotional outbursts.

When he first took over the show, it was being done live. But it soon began taping in the early evening of the night it was to air, and NBC would often edit the tapes before airing them. This precipitated Paar's famous on-air tearful walkout, the night of February 11, 1960.

A "water closet" joke he had told the night before was considered in bad taste by NBC's censors, and it had been removed. Paar didn't think the joke was offensive and he left the show for a month.

He later feuded with Ed Sullivan over the fees paid to guest stars. Sullivan paid several thousand dollars to Paar's $320. Paar also feuded with other newspaper columnists, including Dorothy Kilgallen.

But taping the show eventually enabled Paar to work only four days a week. Starting July 10, 1959, the Friday show was retitled "The Best of Paar," and was made up of excerpts from previous shows. Jack Paar's last late-night show was March 30, 1962.

Johnny Carson, a new, young comedian who was currently hosting ABC's daytime game show, "Who Do You Trust?," was signed to host "The Tonight Show," but first he had to fulfill his ABC contract. So, for six months, beginning April 2, 1962, the show aired with a succession of substitute hosts.

All this happened in the first eight years of "The Tonight Show" ...and before Ed McMahon first uttered the words, "Heeeeere's Johnny!"

NEXT WEEK: The Tonight Show starring Johnny Carson.

1962 marked start of Carson's reign

Second of Two Parts

Last week we followed "The Tonight Show" from its beginning in 1954 with Steve Allen, through its various formats and hosts, including Jack Paar, who left the show on March 30, 1962.

Johnny Carson, a young comedian who was then hosting ABC's daytime game show, "Who Do You Trust?," had been signed to replace Paar, but he had to fulfill the remainder of his ABC contract. So, beginning on April 2, 1962, "The Tonight Show" began a six-month run through September 28, using substitute hosts.

These various hosts represented a wide range of personalities; Art Linkletter, Joey Bishop, Bob Cummings, Merv Griffin, Jack Carter, Jan Murray, Peter Lind Hayes and Mary Healy, Soupy Sales, Mort Sahl, Steve Lawrence, Jerry Lewis, Jimmy Dean, Arlene Francis, Jack E. Leonard, Hugh Downs, Groucho Marx, Hal March, and Donald O'Connor.

During this time, the show also had three different announcers; Hugh Downs stayed on a short while, followed by Jack Haskell and Ed Herlihy. Allen's original band, headed by Skitch Henderson, also returned to the new show.

Then on October 2, 1962, a very young Johnny Carson took over and no one could have predicted that he would hold forth for the next 30 years. He brought with him his daytime game show announcer, and Ed McMahon also became his "Heeeeere's Johnny" sidekick for all those years.

The Skitch Henderson Orchestra continued to provide the music for Carson's first four years. Then Milton Delugg's band handled the music for the 1966-67 season. Doc Severinson and his Tonight Show Orchestra took over later in '67 and continued until the very end of Carson's reign. Tommy Newsom began fronting the band in 1968 whenever Doc was away.

By the way, you may be interested to know that the show's theme song was written by Paul Anka and Johnny Carson, and is titled "Johnny's Theme."

Although both men were funny, Jack Paar and Johnny Carson were at opposite ends of the spectrum when it came to personality. The emotional Paar was apt to blow up at a moment's notice, while Johnny was calm and unflappable.

Other than his durability, Carson's biggest asset was his knack for salvaging disasters and turning them into funny pieces of business. Two of his bits that became the most durable over the years were his "Mighty Carson Art Players" and "Carnac the Magnificent" sketches.

Until his closing show, the most watched and celebrated telecast was probably that of December 17, 1969, when Tiny Tim married Miss Vicki.

Carson's first shows originated in New York and were taped on the same evening they aired. He was on all five nights and began the monolog at 10:15 p.m. (CST).

In February, 1965, he refused to do the first 15-minute segment. He left that up to McMahon and Henderson because many of the local stations carried local news until 10:30, preempting the first 15 minutes. Carson wanted to save his monolog until the full network was watching. Two years later, this opening segment was dropped altogether.

In March 1967, Johnny walked out on the show in a dispute with NBC over money. He was lured back after several weeks with a contract for a reported $1 million per year.

"The Tonight Show" moved permanently to Burbank, California in May, 1974. Carson also had begun cutting back on his appearances and after July, 1971, he no longer appeared on Mondays. By 1978, he was working only three nights a week, but earning $3 million a year.

I've had the opportunity to be in the audience of "The Tonight Show" both in New York and California. One night in the early 70s, I was in New York on a buying trip with the buyers for Carson Pirie Scott's Peoria department store.

I invited one of the buyers to be my guest to see "The Tonight Show." It happened to be a night when Carson was not on and the guest host was Don Rickles, who would always go into the audience so he could heckle the people.

My guest, who could have been a stand-in for Erich von Stroheim, had a shaved bald head. He also had the bull-neck build and features of the famous actor/director. I had intentionally seated my guest on the aisle, in case of any audience participation and, after a commercial break, Rickles headed for the audience.

He came up our aisle, and the first person he saw was my guest. He ran up the stairs, did a double-take and said:

"Wouldn't you know it... the first night they give the little Jew boy a break, they bring in the Nazi general." The show went up for grabs and my guest was the hit of the show that night!

But my best memory came later, after the show had moved to California.

Flossie and I were attending the NBC annual meeting in Hollywood. All the affiliate representatives were invited to see the show and attend a post-taping cocktail party with Carson and Ed McMahon. The cocktail party preceeded a sit-down dinner on one of the main sound stages at Universal Studios and virtually every star in Hollywood seemed to be there.

A line formed to meet the show's host and, naturally, we got in it. He was standing shaking hands with everyone, with a cocktail in his left hand, while McMahon stood next to him but sort of back-to-back, almost as if he were protecting Carson. It's said that Johnny is uncomfortable in large crowds.

Just as we got to the head of the line, someone behind us gave a push. I was shoved forward into Flossie, just as she was

The very young Johnny Carson and Ed McMahon surround the Tonight Show's original band leader, Skitch Henderson.
(An NBC photo)

reaching out to shake Carson's hand. As she lunged forward, her little finger on her extended hand went right into Johnny's drink. He gave her that now-famous dead-pan glare, looked down at his drink, then back up at her again.

Without cracking a smile he said, "What's your name, Cool Hand Luke?" Flossie found out first "hand": Johnny Carson is one of the fastest in the business with a one-liner.

...and it all seems like only yesterday!

Riding Peoria's old "rails"

Some of my fondest childhood memories are of "riding the rails" on Peoria's old street cars.

It doesn't seem possible but it's been 46 years since my last ride. The very last Peoria street car pulled into the N. Adams Street car barn at about 12:45 a.m. on October 3, 1946. It was car #360, and had just completed its last run on the Peoria Heights line.

The only way I know to recapture those memories today is to pick up a copy of Paul Stringham's wonderful book, "76 Years of Peoria Street Cars." It's a complete history of an era, from the first mule- and horse-drawn cars to the end of the old orange electric cars that I remember. But it's more than that.

It's also a trip through our town's historic past, with nearly 100 photos showing street cars in every nook and cranny of Peoria's old business sections and neighborhoods.

Although buses were first put into service in Peoria in 1924, they were only used to serve areas that had no street car service. It wasn't until 1927 when they first replaced any street cars, and that was only because of the poor condition of the Second-Sixth Avenue line and the cost to rebuild it.

As an experiment in the summer of 1927, one of the double-truck electric street cars was fitted with a treadle door, allowing the discharge of passengers at both the front and rear of the car. It proved so successful that most cars were equipped with them the following year.

Then, on March 1, 1928, cash fares were raised to 10¢, or three tokens for 25¢. Fares had been 10¢, or seven tokens for 50¢. (A token increase of about a penny.)

After the closing of Al Fresco Amusement Park and the advent of the automobile, the company dropped the single street car on the Galena Road line and replaced it with a bus in the fall of 1930. On November 22 of that same year, the Illinois Power & Light Co. moved its general offices from State and S. Adams to the newly completed Illinois Terminal Railroad station at S. Adams and Walnut. (This is the building that currently houses Peoria's police department.)

Then, in 1931, new electric trolley buses were introduced in Peoria on the Monroe Street line. These ran from Abington Street, down Monroe to Hamilton, looped around the business district, and back to Hamilton.

By the time I entered Woodruff High School in 1940 we had moved to 1512 N. Perry and my best friend, Gil Crotty, lived at 1601 N. Monroe. During those days (before Dad let me borrow his car), Gil and I spent many hours bouncing along on those huge-tired Monroe trolley buses, but I missed the old street cars.

The last change in street car fares took place on October 30, 1932, when a $1.00 weekly pass was inaugurated. It was good for unlimited riding by the purchaser, or anyone he or she wished to let use it. The pass became very popular, and did more to hold riders than any other plan.

On August 31, 1938, the prettiest stretch of track in the entire system was terminated: the Country Club line.

This was an extension of the Peoria Heights line that ran east from the Peoria Heights business district along Seiberling Avenue, then on a private right-of-way across a high fill, through dense woods, and then through a deep cut to the Peoria Country Club. The closing of this extension was attributed to the popularity of the automobile.

World War II brought on a great local shortage of gasoline and tires. The street car company was hard pressed to find enough equipment to handle the crowds who were using their service while conserving their auto travel.

Many of the larger Birney cars lost several of their seats for the duration, to make room for more standees, especially during rush hours.

The company's franchise was due to expire in April 1946, and the death knell of Peoria's street cars sounded after an incident that occurred the morning of April 2.

Street car #354 leaving the end of the Country Club line at Grand View Drive. (Photo by Paul H. Stringham)

Street car #448 rounds the curve from Main onto S. Adams, while #434 passes the Apollo Theater on August 4, 1946. (Photo by Paul H. Stringham)

Car #354 had just come out of the shop after a complete overhaul, and was inbound from Peoria Heights. The motorman called the barn with a complaint that the brakes weren't working properly.

No defects were found, but the motorman was instructed to not attempt Knoxville hill without help, if he was unsure of the brakes. (If brakes should fail, the cars could also be controlled by "bucking the motors," similar to controlling an automobile by leaving it in low gear.)

But with no apparent attempt to buck the motors, he started down the hill and then suddenly shouted to his passengers that the car was running away. It left the rails at a sharp curve at the bottom and crashed into a steel trolley support. The car's front platform was badly damaged and several passengers were injured but none seriously.

That evening, in view of the "unsafe" conditions, the City Council granted the franchise to the Peoria Transportation Co. for an all-bus system.

When street car service ended in October 1946, there were 70 cars in revenue service. They were scrapped on the property, and a large number of bodies were sold for various uses. I've often wondered if any are still around today in one form or another?

Those wonderful old Peoria street cars... the end of an era

...and it seems like only yesterday!

Sweet Adelines still singing in harmony

I was hooked on barbershop singing at a very tender age.

As far back as I can remember, when my folks got together with their friends and relatives for picnics and parties, the men would sing barbershop. Some were good and some bad, but over time, four of them - Dad included - would "perform" at these affairs. The songsters were: Walt Heintz (my uncle), baritone; George Heintz (his brother), tenor; Henry Paetz, bass, and Virg Adams (my dad), lead.

By the time my voice had changed, I was filling in for Dad whenever they'd let me. I learned the words to just about every old barbershop song I ever heard, and the very first one was "Sweet Adeline." I'm still an avid fan of this type harmony and my first song describes a group of lady barbershoppers who are still around today.

This Thursday, the Sweet Adelines celebrate their 40th anniversary.

Also known as the Belles of Harmony, the local chapter is even older than that, and what they love to do most is get together to sing and perform in harmony and (if you'll pardon the expression) "barbershop."

Although they were first incorporated into the Sweet Adelines, International on July 16, 1952, the local chapter of the organization actually got its start in September 1948, when nine wives of the male members of the SPEBSQSA (the male barbershop singers) got together and decided to have their own night out to sing.

Ten more wives joined them for their second meeting, then two more ladies joined, to expand the charter membership to 21. They enticed one of the men, Floyd Connett, to be their director. Connett headed up the group for the next 15 years, until he passed away in 1963.

The group incorporated as the Belles of Harmony on February 9, 1949, and Billie Myers (wife of another male singer, Rollie Myers) became its founder and first president. Three of its charter members are still active singers in the group: Verna Eichorn, Marg Hochstrasser and Vera Hillers.

Connett was also instrumental in expanding the group by forming three more chapters - Chillicothe in 1949, followed by Fort Madison, Iowa 1950 and and Canton, Illinois in 1951. All four chapters sang under the Belles of Harmony name.

But the ladies wanted a chance to compete with other groups, as the male organization did, so on July 16, 1952, they joined the international organization known as the Sweet Adelines.

Peoria women had competed with the Adelines even before the Belles. A local group - known as the Keystone Barberettes (which included Vera Hillers) - placed third in the first Sweet Adeline international quartet competition in 1947.

Local quartets have competed very well ever since.

In 1952, the first year as an official member of the Sweet Adelines, a local quartet, the Pitchpipers, won first place internationally. The Big 4 quartet from Chillicothe placed first in 1954, and the Junior Misses were second in 1955 and first in '56.

In regional chorus competition, the Nautical Notes placed third in 1958, second in '59, and first in '62. Then, in 1963, the Sugar Tones took third place.

And over the years in regional chorus competition, the local Sweet Adelines took first place in 1955, '58, '60, '62, '76, '78, and '81.

Sweet Adelines International now has 29,000 members, representing 600 chapters in 17 countries.

The Belles of Harmony gals have many memories as members over the years. But the high point had to be their appearance in Royal Albert Hall in London, England, the scene of the 1977 international competition, and they placed in the top ten. They also competed internationally in St. Louis in 1980, and in Minneapolis in 1982.

The Belles of Harmony's first local show was performed in 1950 at the Shrine Mosque, and they have continued there (except for 1967 and '68, when they moved to Manual High School) ever since.

The group's current officers are: Jan Borror, president; Jo Ann Lambie, vice president; Sandy Adams, treasurer; Pat Miller, corresponding secretary; and Jeri Dubois, recording secretary.

October 10 is the date set for the group's 42nd annual show, which will again be held at the Shrine, under its current

The combined group of the Sweet Adelines from Peoria, Chillicothe, Canton, and Fort Madison, Iowa as they appeared on the Shrine stage on Feb. 8, 1953.   (Picture courtesy of Verna Eichorn)

director, Joy Pautler. This year's theme will be "Wheels," and some of the songs in rehearsal are: "Round and Round," "King of the Road," "On the Road Again," "Little Old Lady from Pasadena," and "Beep Beep."

Each year the Sweet Adelines select a charity to which they donate a portion of the show's proceeds. This year, they've selected Seniors in Need.

But don't get the mistaken impression that Sweet Adelines is just for older women. To the contrary.

Colleen Dunham, a charter member of the Chillicothe chapter, says the current group has participants ranging in age from 18 to 80, with more than half of the current membership under 50. And they're looking for new members. Anyone interested should contact Jan Borror or Jo Ann Lambie.

I can tell you first hand that their annual shows are vibrant and exciting. We had the pleasure of seeing several, including the one last year. If you enjoy good music, you can't help but get caught up in the great harmony and the intricate performances

that are a treat to the eye as well as the ear. And "Wheels" should roll 'em right out into the aisles again this year.

Barbershop harmony always brings back fond memories of those times when Dad let me stand in for him in his old quartet. Invariably, I'd start them off with Sweet Adeline

...and it seems like only yesterday!

Kidnapping capers not just for gamblers

Local kidnappings in the early 1930s were not necessarily restricted to gamblers. One of the more interesting ones in Peoria occurred the evening of March 14, 1932, and this time the victim was a prominent physician. It was also considered to be one of the most blundering criminal efforts ever recorded here.

The 65-year-old Dr. James W. Parker left his home at 508 Bradley Avenue about 7 that Monday night to go bowling at the Creve Coeur Club. He never arrived at the club.

His wife, Donna (also a physician, who held offices with her husband in the Commercial Bank Building), noticed nothing unusual until after 10 p.m., when he failed to return home.

It was Parker's habit to return from bowling shortly before 10, and the possibility of a motor accident had crossed her mind.

She was debating calling the police when the phone rang around 10:45. An unfamiliar male voice said, "Doctor Parker will not be home tonight. You will hear from him in the morning. His car is parked on Laramie Street near Madison Park." Mrs. Parker asked who was calling, but the man hung up.

Donna Parker notified the police and Mr. & Mrs. Rex Post, friends of the family, were called to the home to be with her. Rex Post also assisted the police in the search for the car, and it was found where the voice on the phone had indicated.

A search of the yard indicated that Dr. Parker's heavy car had hurdled a small cement coping, which led the police to believe an unfamiliar hand had been at the wheel.

Parker had once been a wealthy man but recent severe financial reverses indicated that a personal enemy - rather than ransom - might be the reason for his kidnapping. One angle was checked Monday night, but it produced no definite clues. A thorough search of the terrain where the car was found failed to turn up Parker's body, which dispelled the theory of suicide.

The day after the kidnapping, a special delivery letter came in the mail, asking for a $50,000 ransom. Details as to how the ransom was to be paid were so sketchy and obscure that Mrs. Parker, and her relatives and friends, decided to ignore it.

On the day after the first ransom note was received, an attorney, Joseph Pursiful, appeared at the Parker home and stated that the kidnappers were willing to accept $35,000. On subsequent calls, the figure was reduced in rapid stages, until it finally got down to $5,000.

The case was easily solved, beginning with the involvement of a Peoria attorney (Pursiful), and a former Peoria policeman, Virgil Betson, who had become intermediaries in the case.

When the police finally rounded up the nine gang members responsible for the kidnapping (in addition to the attorney and former police officer), they found most of them to be farmers, and some with minor criminal records.

During the 18 days that Parker was held captive, Chicago's famed "Secret Six," an organization of businessmen formed to combat gangland activities, got involved in the Peoria case. They used such things as secret dictaphones and wire tapping. The investigation reached a ludicrous high point when a "mind reader," an attractive brunette who was playing a vaudeville act at the Palace Theater, was called in.

Parker was released from an automobile a short distance from Fondulac Drive in East Peoria on the night of April 1, 18 days after his abduction. He told the police his abductors were actually two men, one of whom carried a machine gun, and they ordered him into the back seat of the car. A blindfold was placed over his eyes and the car sped away.

Parker estimated it was about a half-hour later, when he was placed in what appeared to be the bedroom of a farmhouse. He was kept blindfolded or forced to face a blank wall most of his waking hours. At night he was chained to his bed, but at no time did he see any of his captors. The "cawing of blackbirds" and the incessant pounding of a pump convinced him he was in a rural area.

His deductions were later proved correct.

It was determined the hideout was a farm house in the Illinois River bottom lands near Banner, with a noisy farmyard pump and cawing blackbirds nearby.

Both the lawyer and the ex-cop had quaint alibis. The attorney said he was forced to act as an intermediary on threat of his life. The ex-policeman said he was "repaying a favor" to a man who had once given him a bribe.

The wife of the defendant at whose home Parker was being held, told authorities she was prompted several times to call the police. She said she'd grown tired of cooking his special meals and taking care of his bed and room.

Apparently completely discouraged in their efforts, the abductors finally gave up in despair with no ransom money for their efforts. Eight of the 11 people arrested in the plot went to the penitentiary for terms ranging from five to 25 years.

In November 1937, more than five years after the kidnapping, the typewriter used to write the ransom notes was found in a 40-foot cistern at 97 W. McClure Avenue - the one-time home of Betson, the former city policeman

...and it seems like only yesterday!

DR. JAMES W. PARKER, Peoria kidnap victim of a gang of eleven amateur abductors in 1932.
(*Journal Star* photo file)

Peoria Bicycle Club got its start in 1881

More than a hundred years ago, Peoria was a national hub of bicycle manufacturing in the United States.

This Illinois city had no less than five bicycle manufacturing plants and one tire company. They were: Rouse, Hazard & Co.; Ide Co.; Seiberling Co.; Luthy Co.; Patee-Simpson Co. and Peoria Rubber & Mfg. Co.

It took two young men from the predecessor firm of Rouse, Hazard to capitalize on Peoria's - and the nation's - bicycle craze, by forming the Peoria Bicycle Club.

This club was also later instrumental in putting Peoria on the map in another exciting way. Our town became the host city to some of the nation's top bicycle racing tournaments in the late 1880s and early '90s, bringing national and international fame to Peoria.

The Peoria Bicycle Club was recently revived in 1989 by Eric Carlson, just 108 years after its founding.

And this year's big Peoria bike race is being sponsored by Proctor Hospital, Caterpillar, CILCO, Illinois Heart Institute, AT&T, Tru-Value, Panasonic/Matsushita and Ruppman Marketing Technologies Inc. The August 9 race, called the Proctor Cycling Classic, is now affiliated with the U. S. Cycling Federation.

Carlson estimates there are at least 5,000 active cyclists in Peoria today.

He says:

"Americans are beginning to rediscover that the bicycle is so much more than the child's plaything it has become over the past 60 years... Once again, the United States may be balanced on the brink of a cycling boom not seen since the 1890s... Once again, the Peoria area is home to multitudes of recreational cyclists nearing the proportions of a century ago... Soon this city will host an event which will, with a continuation of support it already has, draw racers from around the world."

The numbers back up his statements.

In five short years, the Proctor Classic has grown to be one of the Midwest's most challenging and prestigious cycling events. This year's 11 categories will feature races from eight laps on an .85-mile criterium race course to a 100-mile race on a 6.5-mile road course. The start/finish line for all races will be at the downtown corner of Hamilton and Jefferson.

The Proctor Cycling Classic is a revival of a great Peoria Bicycle Club tradition.

It was Saturday, January 22, 1881, when Harry Rouse and Fred Patee, two young friends and business associates, were discussing the rapidly growing sales of bicycles in Peoria.

Rouse's father was the owner of George W. Rouse & Sons, Peoria's largest retailer of farm implements. Two years earlier, the firm, located at 110 S. Washington St., had gone into the bicycle distribution business. It became the first company in America to sell bicycles through a no-interest installment plan. In 1895, Rouse, Hazard & Co. built a large factory in Peoria Heights and became Peoria's first bicycle manufacturer. (The building still stands near the railroad crossing on Prospect Road.)

Charles Duryea came to Peoria and became a bicycle designer for Rouse, Hazard, and he also became a member of the Peoria Bicycle Club. (In 1893 he and his brother, Frank, completed the first American gasoline-powered car, in Springfield, Mass.)

Harry Rouse worked for the company and Fred Patee was its top salesman. As they looked over the sales figures, they got excited about the city's cycling phenomenon and they were right in the middle of it.

They were discussing the social aspects of cycling when one of them said, "Let's form a cycle club!"

They invited some of their cycling buddies to a meeting the next day at the Rouse store.

Stephen H. Tripp and Will Gulick attended the first meeting with them on Sunday, January 23, 1881. N. H. Tallman and George Willcox were unable to attend, but became members later. After considering many different names, they settled on the "Peoria Bicycle Club," and the first officers were: S. R. Henderson, president; Tripp, captain; and Rouse, treasurer.

As was the fashion of the elite bicycle clubs of England, France, Boston and New York, the local club had special uniforms, badges and awards. Their outfits were of gray corduroy knee breeches, gray hats, blue flannel shirts, gold whistle cord and blue stockings.

Its membership was an affiliation of educated, well-bred young men who believed in having a good time, but they always conducted themselves in a manner acceptable to polite society.

Club picnics, dances, pie-eating contests and Halloween stag parties were sources of great fun and the club opened its doors to ladies on Thursday evenings. This courtesy to the women cyclists was very progressive and set a good example for other men's clubs. They helped women learn to ride, which eventually inspired the ladies to organize their own cycling clubs.

In October 1881, the Peoria Bicycle Club joined the national League of American Wheelmen (LAW), which grew to more than 100,000 members by 1898. Then LAW experienced a drastic decline in the 1900s, with the advent of the automobile. The national organization was revived in the 1960s by members in the Chicago area and, as mentioned, the Peoria Bicycle Club was revived in 1989 by Eric Carlson.

(Source: The book, "Bicycle Fever" by Steven Streight.)

NEXT WEEK: The national cycling races in Peoria a century ago.

HARRY ROUSE AND HIS FIRST BICYCLE

Harry Rouse, co-founder of the Peoria Bicycle Club, on his first cycle, a high wheel "Ordinary."
(Photo courtesy of Peoria Public Library - Historical Collection)

Peoria Bicycle Club's heyday

Second of Two Parts

Last week's column described Peoria and its bicycle manufacturing business before the turn of the century and the founding of the Peoria Bicycle Club by Harry Rouse and Fred Patee in January 1881.

At its peak, the club had more than 450 members. Its first meeting rooms were in the old Baptist Church on the 300 block of Hamilton Boulevard.

The meetings were later moved to rooms above the Peoria National Bank at Main and Washington, followed by the Jack Building at 215 S. Adams, the old library building at Main and Jefferson (the later site of the Lehmann Bldg.), the Norton home on the 100 block S. Jefferson, the Frazier home on Fayette and N. Jefferson (where the YWCA now stands) and, finally, in the Lightner Mansion at N. Jefferson and Hamilton.

"Chicken Runs" became a club tradition that survived long after the club became inactive. These were annual bicycle trips that ended with a chicken and mashed potato dinner, first up Galena Road to Crawl's Hotel at Mossville and later to Webb's Inn at Chillicothe.

Five years after the club was founded, Charles Albert "Bert" Myers joined. Myers began riding bikes in Toulon when he was 16, and went on to become one of the club's most famous members. He was the world champion unicycle rider at age 25, and he and his brother, Edward, became bicycle dealers at 209 S. Madison.

When the club began in 1881, the high-wheel bicycle known as the "ordinary" was in vogue, but by 1885, the "safety bike" was on its way to becoming preferred. This is the one that's still in style today, with both wheels the same size and with a chain-driven rear wheel. It opened the door to the joys of cycling for women, children, short men and older people.

In 1887, the P.Bi.C. held its first major race in the Illinois division of the national League of American Wheelmen. Then in 1889, it hosted its first national bicycle tournament, followed by national tourneys in 1890, '91 and '92. These races were held at the old Lake View Park, a half-mile dirt track with grandstand, at the foot of Grant Street in Averyville. These prestigious races attracted international cycle stars, distinguished American and foreign journalists and thousands of excited spectators.

Peoria's second national race was called "The Greatest Bicycle Race in U.S. History" and was held on September 12 and 13, 1890. There were more record-breaking cyclists in Peoria's Lake View Park then, than had ever gathered together in a single spot in the history of cycling.

Cycling history was changed forever at the Peoria track that year. Louis Masi of the Peoria Bicycle Club and England's Willie Windle won the two heats in the quarter-mile dash.

Then international cycling news was made when America's August Zimmerman of New York defeated Willie Windle by two feet in 36 seconds, in the final quarter-mile heat. This made Zimmerman the first racer to ever beat the "unbeatable" Windle. Then, in the 10-mile race, Zimmerman beat Windle again and won the national championship.

After each evening's racing events the Peoria Bicycle Club sponsored a "ball and smoker" at Rouse's Opera Hall.

But by the turn of the century the demand for bicycles fell sharply, due to the oncoming domination of the automobile.

By November 1900, the club membership had dropped from 450 to 117, and interest in cycling had diminished. The cycling club entered into negotiations with the newly formed Creve Coeur Club, which offered to take in no less than 50 bicycle club members without payment of initiation fees. One hundred members transferred to the new C.C.C. and the bicycle club became officially inactive in January 1901. In effect, it became a club within a club, and it enabled the Creve Coeur Club to ascend to social prominence.

Bicycle racing remained a popular spectator sport until the 1930s, when baseball, basketball and football began drawing bigger crowds. By World War II, bicycle racing in America was dead and it was not until the mid-1970s that competitive cycling in this country came back to life.

Waiting for the finish of a 10-mile bicycle race before the turn of the century at Peoria's Lake View Park.
(Photo coutesy of Peoria Public Library Historical Collection)

In 1982, Nevada's Greg LeMond took the silver medal at the professional world championships. He then captured the gold in 1983. The United States won four out of eight Olympic cycling events in 1984, their first Olympic medals since 1912.

By 1988, an estimated 88 million cyclists - one of every three people in the United States - said they rode for recreation, exercise, transportation, or competition. Cycling is now considered the second most popular recreational activity in the nation.

Greg LeMond has become the modern day August Zimmerman, and his racing style exemplifies the greatness of top American athletes.

Locally, interest in the revitalized Peoria Bicycle Club and its Proctor Cycling Classic has been building fast. And its president, Eric Carlson, may be right. Someday Peoria just may, once again, play host to the world's top racing stars in our nation's top cycling events... just as it did more than a century ago.

(Source: The book "Bicycle Fever" by Steven Streight.)

A barber and a performer

After serving in the Navy for a couple years, I came back to my old job as manager of the Madison Theater in the spring of 1946.

By 1947, Flossie and I had our first child, a daughter, Kim, and we rented a little house on Butler Street in the "south end," across the street from the Palmer House. The house was owned by my dad's mother, Beulah Adams Bowman, who was then married to Milt "Shorty" Bowman. We rented it for $23.50 a month, which was about all we could afford on my $45.00 a week salary.

Milt ran a barber shop near the side doors of the Palace Theater in the 100 block of SW Madison. I don't remember ever having my hair cut by anyone but him from the time I was born until September 1947, when he dropped dead ringing up a sale at his cash register.

A short time after that, I struck up a friendship with a man who came to the Madison to see the movie every week. His name was Paul LaRocca.

LaRocca was a barber whose shop was in the 400 block of Fulton Street, just across from the old Alcazar. It was on the second floor of an old building just east of City Hall. I was in need of a good barber, and started going to him. Paul's brother, Roxy LaRocca, operated the Fulton News Stand across the way, at the corner of Fulton and Jefferson.

Paul loved to tell a story about a time during the early 1940s, when he had a customer who played the piano between orchestras for a number of weeks at the Hotel Pere Marquette. His name was Walter Liberace. This was before the future star dropped his first name and became a hit on TV with his baby grand piano and candelabras.

Now, Paul was an excellent barber and a wonderful man but he had one failing: he would talk your ear off. If you were in a hurry (which I usually was), forget it. Paul finished your haircut when he finished his conversation, and at times that seemed like forever.

But I learned a lot of things about show business from Paul. He played the violin and had been a vaudeville performer in his younger days, as was his older brother, Roxy, who became a star and traveled with his own show throughout the world. Roxy was a master of the harp.

I always felt there was a deep-seated jealousy between the two brothers. Paul had his vaudeville career cut short when he suffered a nervous breakdown as a young man, while Roxy went on to become a headliner on the stage. But Paul loved to talk about those wonderful vaudeville days and - when I had the time - I loved to listen to them.

Paul LaRocca also was proud of his songwriting ability. He claimed he wrote much of his own vaudeville material, including a favorite song he had written about his old home town, Peoria.

This story became a fetish with Paul. He claimed that a song about Peoria that later became a hit, was actually one he had written in those early vaudeville days which he had featured in his act. He said he was the victim of plagiarism.

Paul said it wasn't uncommon in those days to not publish songs that were used in many of the stage acts. He had been lax in not copywriting his song and because of it, it became published by someone else. The song he referred to was one we've known, hummed, and sung around here for many years, "I Wish't I Was in Peoria."

Paul never claimed (at least to me) that the song that later came out under the names of Billy Rose, Mort Dixon and Harry Wood, was actually lifted by any of them. He did tell me, however, that he remembered a guy who used to come around backstage and watch the various acts. He thought this man probably copied the song, made a few changes in it and the title, and then sold it. This was a common practice in the publishing business during those Tin Pan Alley days.

Whether or not my friend was correct about his song, I don't know. But I do know that Paul was an honest man and I never

Although neither Paul nor Roxy were in this orchestra, it's the "LaRocca Orchestra" in 1924, made up of brothers and cousins.

Joe LaRocca is standing with the harp, brother Frank is standing at right with the violin. Cousin, Frank "Dud" DeNufrio is seated between them.

(Photo courtesy of Marian Coffeen)

knew him to make up stories about other things, so why this particular one? And something later happened that made me believe his story even more:

One day, when I came in for a haircut, he showed me some old manuscripts of a number of songs he had written over the years. Among them was his "Peoria" song. As I recall, it wasn't titled "I Wish't I Was in Peoria," but it was similar, and the words and music were slight variations of what I knew to be the published version.

Several years later Paul LaRocca's barber shop suffered a disastrous fire. All his memorabilia, including his prized old violin, were either destroyed or badly damaged. Most of his songs were stored in an old trunk that barely survived the fire.

He asked me if I would store what was left of the trunk and its contents until he could find a place for them, which I did.

His Peoria song was in that trunk, and all that was left of it were charred bits and pieces. Suddenly, all he had left were memories... and a story.

Paul is dead now, but until the end he was still trying to come up with another song to commemorate his old home town. Unfortunately he never did.

"I Wish't I Was In Peoria"

...and it seems like only yesterday!

Three Peoria murders in gangland style

Near the end of Peoria's wide-open gambling era, a series of gangland-style murders occurred around our town.

As described in past columns, Bernie Shelton, the younger brother of Carl and "Big Earl" Shelton, was assassinated on Farmington Road in 1948. And in 1946, there were three gang-related murders - one of them on the very same road.

The first murder took place the evening of February 20, 1946. Frank Kraemer, a local tavern operator, was reading a newspaper in the sunroom at his 3900 Farmington Road residence, when a car moved into the driveway.

A moment later, there was a crash of glass and a bullet whistled over Kraemer's head. He yelled to his wife, who was sitting nearby, to take cover as he headed for the adjoining living room.

After he took a few steps, five more shots rang out and he dropped with three slugs in his body. The other two were imbedded in furniture and a wall. One of the shots hit his wrist watch, which stopped at exactly 7:31.

Frank was still alive when Peoria County police arrived. One of the deputies asked him if he knew the identity of his assailant, but his answer was, "Just get me to the hospital."

Kraemer died just before 9 p.m., enroute to St. Francis Hospital, and if he knew anything, he was either unwilling or unable to tell.

Police were at a loss to explain the murder. Kraemer owned The Spot, a tavern at 1712 N. Knoxville, and he was also a partner with George Parks in the operation of the Par-K Club at 419 Hamilton. Parks said if Frank had any enemies, he was unaware of it.

Questioned by police shortly after the incident, Kraemer's wife said she knew of no motive for the crime. Her husband had never expressed the slightest fear for his life.

Coroner William B. Elliott said the gunman broke a pane of glass with the weapon and sprayed the victim with bullets.

Sheriff Charles L. Swords conducted the preliminary investigation and said six shots were fired. Three entered Kraemer's body, one above and another below the heart, and a third in the abdomen. The newspaper he was reading had three holes in it.

A curtain on the window, through which the murderer fired, was scorched, indicating that a part of the gunbarrel had been pushed through the glass.

Police theorized the first shot brought the victim to his feet and the death shots were fired as he attempted to flee to the other room.

The next day, Peoria County officials agreed that Kraemer was murdered with a 30-caliber carbine, a semiautomatic rifle of the type issued to U. S. paratroopers during World War II. State's Attorney Roy P. Hull said one of the shells found at the scene was manufactured in 1942, and the other five in 1943.

Although Kraemer had been a member of a slot-machine syndicate at one time, the machines had since been removed from the city.

The Kraemer home was a rather large house about 500 feet from the entrance on Farmington Road. At one time Kraemer operated a tavern in a building at the rear of the home. It was a beautiful area, deeply shaded with large trees, which afforded the assailant an opportunity to make his way to the residence undetected.

The shooting might have been averted had Kraemer's three dogs been loose in the yard, but they had been locked up in a shed.

Frank Kraemer was a lifelong resident of Peoria and a veteran of World War I, having served in the U. S. Navy, and was a member of the American Legion.

If the Kraemer home area described here seems familiar to you, maybe its because you may have frequented it in past years. It was later purchased by Jack

Rosenak, who turned it into a very popular eatery known as the Shady Oaks Restaurant.

But the Kraemer murder went unsolved, as so many did back in those "Roaring Peoria" days, with the coroner's jury returning a verdict of murder by "parties unknown."

Kraemer's death was the first of three gang-related murders in 1946. Just seven months later, the bullet riddled body of Joe Nyberg, a known Peoria police character, was found on the golf course of the Lacon Country Club.

Then, on October 25, Phillip Stumpf, an ex-convict, was shot to death in his car after leaving a tavern on Big Hollow Road, where he had answered a call to fix a slot machine.

There is reason to believe the three murders were related, and may have even been connected with the later shooting of Bernie Shelton. We'll revisit those next two murders during the next couple of months.

... *and it seems like only yesterday!*

FRANK KRAEMER, local tavern owner who was assassinated on February 20, 1946.
(*Journal Star* photo file)

Second gangland slaying discovered at golf course

Last month I wrote about the slaying of tavern operator Frank Kraemer at his home on Farmington Road on February 20, 1946. It was the first of three gang-related murders that year. The second one occurred just seven months to the day after Kraemer's death.

Joel (Joe) Nyberg's bullet-riddled and battered body was found on the Lacon Country Club golf course at 7:30 a.m. on September 21, the victim of a beating and shooting the night before.

Police said Nyberg and Kraemer were known to have been friends. The 32-year-old Nyberg was known to Peoria police, having been in and out of trouble for the past 15 years, and was usually armed with guns or knives.

Five slugs from a .38-caliber revolver had entered his back, with several emerging from the right side and another had fractured his left arm. His face and head had been badly beaten with a blunt instrument.

His body was taken to the Lentz Funeral Home in Lacon and first identification was made by O. F. Brinkman, a *Peoria Journal* reporter who knew Nyberg from his frequent appearances in police court. Peoria County Sheriff Charles L. Swords and inti-mates of the deceased later corroborated the identification.

Peoria police theorized that the murder was probably the result of the resumption of gangland warfare in Peoria County.

Lacon Marshal, William Blackburn, saw Nyberg about 4:30 the previous afternoon. Nyberg had gotten out of an automobile to inquire about the location of the Lacon Country Club. Another man was driving the car.

But the victim must have returned to Peoria after that because he was known to have been in Peoria as late as 10:30 that night.

It was presumed that he left for Lacon about 11 p.m., where he and two companions were seen drinking in Craig's Tavern there about 11:30 p.m. Owen Baker of Lacon told authorities that, as they left, Nyberg (again) inquired as to the location of the Lacon Club.

Nyberg's body was found about 400 feet from the clubhouse by groundskeeper Belvie Turpin as he started his early morning tour of the golf greens. An investigation of the death scene indicated that Nyberg probably struggled with his slayers, who drove him to the club's parking lot and then continued on toward a tool shed at the end of a narrow lane. The men apparently walked another 300 feet before Joe was felled by a blow from the rear.

The investigation also disclosed the victim probably raised his left arm to ward off a second blow. He fell to one knee, as indicated by marks on his trousers, and was presumed to have fallen face downward and then shot through the back.

Marshall County Sheriff Zenas Grieves' theory was that Nyberg was accompanied by two "friends" who steered him to his death through a ruse of robbing the clubhouse or storage shed.

Deputy Coroner Dr. R. L. Eddington of Lacon established the death at around midnight. He said death was due to a bullet that pierced the heart. Coroner J. G. Johnson of Varna said the victim was beaten about the head and face with a heavy instrument and was badly bruised about the right temple and right eye.

A stenciled cleaning mark in a trousers pocket bore the name "P. Egan." Friends immediately linked the name to Nyberg's girlfriend, Phyllis Egan, a waitress. Nyberg had been arrested on numerous occasions on complaints filed by Miss Egan for assault, carrying concealed weapons, and on peace warrants.

Nyberg had been one of the most indicted people in Peoria County. In January 1944, he was indicted for manslaughter in the death of Thomas Dalrymple, who was said to have argued with Nyberg at the St. Elmo club in the 200 block of Hamilton Street.

At 12:45 a.m. on July 9, 1945, he shot and critically wounded Jack Nahas, a Peoria gambler, in the Oak Hall Tavern at 501 S. Adams. Nahas lay ill in the hospital for several weeks but recovered. During this shooting an innocent bystander, Guy Wixin, was shot in the eye by Nyberg. He also recovered but lost the sight of his eye.

The feud between Nyberg and Nahas apparently started after Nyberg was severely beaten by Eli Cupi, a former nightclub operator.

On January 24, 1946, Joel Nyberg was convicted of assault with intent to kill, and was subsequently sentenced to four to 14 years, but was granted a stay of sentence, and released on a $10,000 bond pending an appeal to the supreme court.

In the early morning hours of November 28, 1945, Nyberg allegedly assaulted Floyd Bartelmay of Morton, a discharged World War II veteran, in the 100 block of First Avenue.

Nyberg, his girlfriend, Phyllis Egan, and two other men, one of whom had on an army uniform, had just alighted from a taxi as Bartelmay and two sailors were walking to their car. The Egan woman had a dog on a leash, and a remark was apparently directed to the woman and her dog. A fight broke out and Nyberg alledgedly stabbed Bartelmay.

Rita Douglas, a hat check girl at the Talk 'O the Town (strip-tease club), testified that a party entered the club after the

 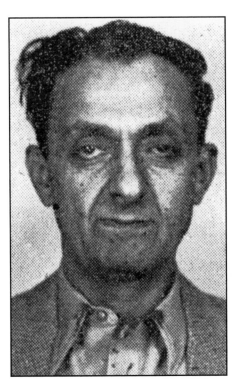

JOE NYBERG　　　　　　　　　　**JACK NAHAS**

(*Journal Star* photo file)

alledged fight, and a soldier attempted to check a government issue knife, which was blood-stained, but she refused to check it.

After these and many other run-ins, Joel (Joe) Nyberg died as he had lived, in the second of three gang-related slayings in 1946. We'll take a look at the third one next month

...and it seems like only yesterday!

Architect Frederic Klein left his mark on Peoria

Shortly after World War I, when Dee Robinson was making plans to build the Madison, his new 2,000-seat "dream theater," he hired a young architect named Frederic J. Klein. Although Klein was only in his mid-40s, Robinson wasn't hiring an unknown or untried theater designer. Klein had already created an impressive list of local theatrical edifices, and had worked for Robinson before.

Klein had created the Hippodrome (which later became the Rialto), the Apollo (the balcony of which is still with us), and the Duchess (where the First of America Bank building now stands). And he would go on to design Rockford's "wonder theater," the beautiful 2,400-seat Coronado.

Although none of his entertainment emporiums were similar in style, they all had one important quality in those early days of silent motion pictures: opulence. They all reflected a luxury that denoted wealth and affluence to the public. A public who's only association with it was a trip to a grandiose movie house, where Hollywood gave them a taste of that "other" lifestyle, if only for a few short minutes each week.

The variety of styles Klein chose for his theaters is evident in two of his larger ones.

The Hippodrome, which opened in 1913, probably reflected its owner's desire for a circus theme. The proscenium arch featured a frieze of performing elephants, with a large elephant head displayed on each side of the stage.

The Madison, on the other hand, featured a classical-style, bas-relief plasterwork to decorate the auditorium's high-domed ceiling.

An oval dome also opened from the inner lobby up through the mezzanine promenade, with Italian Renaissance-designed balconettes decorating the east facade of the building's exterior.

But Klein's genius as an architect was not limited to theaters. Another of his creations was the National Building in the 200 block of N. Adams, part of which still stands. We knew it later as the Packard Building. Bud Grieves had it recently remodeled, and the Packard Plaza is now a part of his Mark Twain Hotel complex.

Other local Klein creations are impressive school structures, including Peoria Central High School and Washington and Franklin schools. Another of his public buildings was the South Park Pavilion. He also designed the Labor Temple, which has once again received a new face-lift; the old First National Bank building (at 210-12 S. Adams); and the old factory buildings for the Stuber & Kuck, and Carr & Johnston companies.

But of all of Klein's works, maybe his greatest lasting memorial is Grand View Drive, which he helped develop. He also designed many of the drive's early homes. In addition, he helped develop and lay out Glen Oak Park, while the beautiful doors of the Springdale Cemetery Mausoleum were also of his design.

Some of Klein's most memorable Peoria residences were those of Milton Newman, Charles Wilson, A. W. Wilson and the McDowell apartments.

Another of his imposing out-of-town structures was the Beta Theta Pi fraternity house on the campus of the University of Illinois at Urbana-Champaign.

By now, I think you'll have to agree that Frederic Klein was a true genius in his field who left a great imprint on Peoria. But what makes his record even more impressive is the fact that he never went to architecture school... he was a *self-taught* architect.

Frederic John Klein was born in Detroit, Michigan on June 11, 1874, the son of John and Emma Best Klein, who came to Peoria when he was a mere infant. He married Barbara (Bessie) Eckley here on October 30, 1902. They had two daughters, Jane and Mary Louise.

Klein developed a desire for architecture as a youngster and left school at an early age to become an apprentice in an architect's office. His natural talents soon developed and after serving his apprenticeship in several prominent companies, he went into business for himself.

I know of three different locations for his offices over the years. In 1915, he was located at 127 S. Jefferson. By 1920 (when he designed the Madison), he was in the Pinkney Building at 331-33 Main Street (where the new Janssen Building is now under construction). By the 1950s (after he retired in the 40s) he reopened offices at

103 N. Madison, in the upstairs offices in the Madison Theater building that he designed.

Klein and his family lived at 4017 N. Grandview Drive (naturally), overlooking the Illinois River valley. Its lived-in comfort included a living area and dining room, which were joined by a large center hall.

The Klein's two daughters had many young friends, who affectionately called Mrs. Klein, Bess, and they were always welcome in the Klein home.

Fred Klein was always tolerant of all the young people who invaded his domain, and during his many years of practice he assisted many young aspirants along the road to success in the field of architecture.

Frederic J. Klein died at Methodist Hospital on January 3, 1957, where he had been a patient since the previous Thanksgiving Day.

I never knew Klein nor, during my Madison Theater days, knew that he designed the theater I managed. But as I reflect back, I wish I had realized that the man who created the "Magnificent Madison" was holding forth just above my office. I would surely have made it a point to have stopped in to say hello and offer him my heartfelt thanks

...and it seems like only yesterday!

The auditorium of the new Madison Theater, designed by Frederic J. Klein, as it appeared for its grand opening on October 16, 1920.
(Photo courtesy of the Peoria Public Library)

Several radio stars called Peoria home

The golden age of radio was a wonderful but all-too-brief time that began when it was discovered that advertisers would pay big money to have their products and services mentioned on the air.

A program format evolved and by the late 1930s and early 40s, it had developed to such an extent that the ear of our nation was glued to radio set speakers, both day and night.

During those years, four former Peorians played major roles in three of the top ten prime-time programs, "Amos and Andy," "Fibber McGee and Molly" and "The Bing Crosby Show." The four Peorians were Charles Correll, ("Andy" of Amos and Andy), Jim and Marian Jordan ("Fibber McGee and Molly"), and Ken Carpenter (who was Bing Crosby's announcer on his Kraft Music Hall program and later became Bing's "second Banana" on the show).

The success of "Fibber McGee and Molly" may have surprised even its creators. I recently listened to a tape of the very first program, which aired April 16, 1935, and it was a far cry from the hit program it later became. Jim Jordan used an "old man" voice he originally created for his Luke Gray character on his earlier "Smackout" program. That first, "McGee" show was a mixture of vaudeville slapstick and jumbled words that lacked polish (except for Johnson's Wax).

But by the time the Jordans were preparing to leave Chicago for Hollywood in 1939, the program was showing signs of development, primarily at the hands of the Jordans and their producer, Don Quinn.

Marian was the one who wanted the program to get closer to reality. Her feeling was, "What couldn't happen back home in Peoria, shouldn't happen on 'Fibber McGee and Molly.' "

One of Jim's many great assets was his ability to do tongue-twisters without muffing a word. Here's one of his best:

"Pretty Please McGee I was known as in them days. Pretty Please McGee, proclaimed by the press and public the peerless prosecutor of pilfering pickpockets, political parasites and persons performing pretty peccadilloes, putting prison pajamas on poker players preyin' on poor punks with peculiar pasteboards, pleadin' with passion and pathos for poor people in pretty pickles - a peppy personality with a capitol P!"

Marian used an Irish brogue for her strong, faithful but long-suffering Molly character. She had originally used it for the part she played on radio's very fist soap opera, "The Smith Family." In addition to Molly, she also developed a little girl character on the show. Teeny was a little neighbor girl who could, and usually did, drive McGee crazy.

The half-hour program consisted of a series of skits that highlighted a parade of characters who visited the McGee home at 79 Wistful Vista. Harlow Wilcox was not only the program's announcer, he was also one of the show's characters who visited them each week, which allowed him to weave his Johnson's Wax commercials into the actual program instead of going to a commercial break, which never failed to raise the ire of Mr. McGee.

The versatile actor with the greatest voice flexibility was a young man named Bill Thompson. He's best remembered for two of his voice characterizations: the Old Timer, who always started his tall tale with, "That's pretty good, Johnny, but that ain't the way I heard it!"; and Wallace Wimple, the wimp of a husband of Sweetie Face, his "big old wife" (who was never heard on the show).

But Thompson also portrayed Horatio K. Boomer, a con man-type character who sounded like W. C. Fields; and a Greek restaurant owner named Nick Depopulous.

And long before Gale Gordon appeared on TV with Lucille Ball, he was Mayor LaTrivia on "Fibber McGee and Molly." Each week Fibber would go out of his way to give his honor apoplexy.

Arthur Q. Bryan (who was also the voice of Elmer Fudd in the Bugs Bunny cartoons) became Doc Gamble on the McGee show on April 6, 1943. He became Fibber's friendly enemy and the two exchanged verbal abuses whenever they met.

Two women portrayed female characters on the show. Shirley Mitchell played Alice Darling, a scatterbrained, man-crazy war plant worker, who began renting the

GALE GORDON who later became Lucille Ball's TV sidekick, was "Mayor LaTrivia" on radio's "Fibber McGee and Molly."
(An NBC photo)

Left to right: Freeman Gosden (Amos) and Peoria's Charles Correll (Andy) became instant hits when "Amos and Andy" went on the NBC radio network in 1929.
(An NBC photo)

McGee's spare room on October 5, 1943.

Isabel Randolph became the snooty Abigail Uppington, referred to by Fibber as Uppy. Mrs. Uppington became one of the better long-lasting personalities on the show.

But another female character wasn't a female at all. Beulah, the McGee's black maid, was portrayed by a white male actor, the handsome Marlin Hurt. The studio audience would go into convulsions of laughter when Hurt would cry out, "Somebody bawl for Beulah?" She was the only one on the show who appreciated Fibber's corny jokes and would laugh riotously at his worst ones, then pause and sigh, "Love that man!"

One of the show's strongest characters was one of its early ones. By 1939, Harold Peary had developed a number of roles on the show, all named Gildersleeve, and by 1940, Throckmorton P. Gildersleeve had become the McGee's next door neighor. Living that close, he and Fibber were always at the point of doing mortal combat.

The Gildersleeve character became so strong, in the summer of 1941, Harold Peary was offered his own program, and Gildy left Wistful Vista to become water commissioner in the town of Summerville on his own new show, "The Great Gildersleeve."

Spinoff programs are common on today's TV sitcoms, but Gildersleeve was the first one to do it back in those golden radio days

...and it seems like only yesterday!

St. Bernard's alumni could fill a Peoria "Who's Who"

Yesterday St. Bernard's Catholic Church held an Alumni Homecoming and Open House. The church and school, located at the northeast corner of Kansas and New York avenues in Peoria's East Bluff, has an alumni roster that reads like a section out of Peoria's "Who's Who."

Pete Vonachen was chairman of the event, and the alumni list included such prominent Peorians as Father Robert Livingston, longtime pastor of St. Vincent De Paul's; Father Bernard Render, now retired and living at St. Augustine's Manor; Ray LaHood, assistant to Congressman Michel; the prominent Becker family, including brothers Paul, Bill, Chuck, John, Ray, Jim and Ed, and their sister, Joyce Cover; and former Peoria mayor Bob Lehnhausen.

There's also *Journal Star* columnist Jerry Klein; WEEK-TV sports director Lee Hall; John Blasek, president of Peoria Flag and Decorating; and the Cusack family's 11 children, five of whom still live in Peoria: Dan is an attorney, Bill a dentist, Tom a physician at St. Francis Medical Center, Jerry's in sales and their sister, Delores Rettig.

This open house and homecoming kicked off a year-long celebration at St. Bernard's, commemorating 90 years of service to its East Bluff residents and members.

Coincidentally, St. Bernard's Class of 1942 celebrated its 50th reunion with a dinner the night before Sunday's homecoming.

It was January 4, 1902, when it was first announced that a new church of Romanesque design would be built on the East Bluff that spring, under the direction of Father Francis J. O'Reilly, then pastor of St. Mary's Parish, and his assistant, Father Maurice P. Sammon.

On May 17, 1902, a building permit was issued for the new church, which was being designed by the architectural firm of Reeves & Ballie. The main structure would be 46 by 100 feet, with a wing of 39 by 44.

The dedication for the new $26,000 red brick and Bedford stone church was held on September 27, 1903. It had frescoed ceilings and walls, stained glass windows, three wooden altars and theater-type seats.

Monsignor Sammon became its first pastor in 1903, and served there until he died in 1957. Sammon was born in Bloomington on January 10, 1873, and was ordained on June 16, 1899.

The dedication's High Mass was sung by Monsignor Legris. The Very Rev. Michael Weldon was deacon, assisted by Father John Powers of Spring Valley and Father James Shannon. Bishop Spalding gave the sermon.

The first rectory in 1903 was a small cottage at the corner of New York and Nebraska. Then, a two-story house on New York was rented until a permanent rectory was completed in 1906.

On January 3, 1904, the church bell, made in St. Louis and weighing a ton, was donated by George and Mary Kanne and dedicated by Bishop Peter J. O'Reilly.

The convent was also built in 1904, across from the rectory, for $20,000. School also started in the wing of the church that year, consisting of two rooms of double-desks, with three grades to a room. It was later expanded to the sacristy, to accommodate all eight grades.

A bucket of drinking water with a cup was provided in the back of each room but, unfortunately for the kids, the restrooms were out-houses!

Three Dominican Sisters (two teachers and a housekeeper) also came from Sinsinawa, Wisconsin, in 1904. One of the most remembered was Sister Mary Sienna, who taught manners, helped the poor students, favored unpopular children, and convinced all the students that she had eyes in the back of her head when she wasn't facing them.

The parish was extended in 1904 from Glen Oak, north to St. Peter's in Averyville, and from the East Bluff beyond Knoxville to the west.

At this time, a large area near Knoxville was a pasture, with a large windmill and water tank. Both sides of Wisconsin were hills and fields, with few houses and wooden sidewalks. There was also a streetcar line on Wisconsin, but all the streets were either muddy or dusty, depending on the season. During bad weather the kids would have to walk in the wagon tracks to get to school.

The rectory was built in 1906, and on Sunday, September 23, 1909, Bishop E. M. Dunne confirmed the first school class. A new $25,000 school, with a capacity of 600 students, was dedicated on September 3, 1911, and the first graduation in the new school was held in 1912.

In 1925, parish donors gave the church new marble altars and a communion rail. A pipe organ was donated by the William Brown family. A parish hall and upper class-rooms were also erected then for $70,000.

New pews and kneelers replaced the theater seats in 1948, and a front addition to the rectory was built. Since then, many improvements and remodeling projects have occurred.

After Monsignor Sammon died in 1957, he was succeeded by Monsignor James B. Reidy, who served until he passed away in 1967. Monsignor Murray V. Haas then served until 1978, when Father Robert Gilles took charge. Father Thomas Miller, St. Bernard's present pastor, succeeded Father Gilles in 1988.

So, Happy 90th Birthday to St. Bernard's Parish! I'm sure all the alumni enjoyed yesterday's celebration, and it should have given them all an opportunity to reminisce about those earlier, happy times

...that seem like only yesterday!

St. Bernard's, the Peoria Parochial Basketball Champs of 1933, placed second in the state. L to R, back row: Rev. Barnard Rank, Asst. Coach Jim Larkin, Coach Jack O'Hearn. Middle row: John Cardinal, Phil O'Connell, James Kelly, Charles Schlink, Buddy McLinden. Front row: Ed Stacy, Ed Larkin, Capt. Bob Livingston (now pastor of St. Vincent De Paul's), Don Plack and John McGrath.
(Photo courtesy of Phillip O'Connell)

Sigma Phi an historic fraternity at Bradley

One of Bradley University's most prominent local fraternities ceased to exist back in 1949, when it became a part of Sigma Chi's national organization. I'm speaking of Sigma Phi.

The fraternity holds a special place in Bradley and Peoria's heritage, since many of its members came from our town's families. But it will never die as long as some of its men are still around.

Next Friday and Saturday, Sigma Phi will hold its seventh reunion, a tradition that began back in 1961, when Bill Ridgely organized the first one. Members will return from all over the country, and upwards of 100 members and their wives are expected to show up. Among those expected is Leo Yap from Hilo, Hawaii. He always attends and donates orchids from his home state.

The Sigma Phi fraternity was founded at 11 a.m. November 11, 1911 (the 11th hour of the 11th day of the 11th month of the 11th year), at then - Bradley Polytechnic Institute - by Homer S. Jacquin and Eugene M. Harsch, both of Peoria, and George F. Coriell of Green Valley.

Its very first pledge was Bruce B. Lackland, and its five other members that first year were Elmer Seaburg, Mercer Francisco, Leonard Wyckoff, Robert Moore and Richard Graner. And for many years Sigma Phi's honorary member was Dr. Charles Truman Wyckoff, dean of the college.

The main function of Sigma Phi wasn't in its house's bricks and mortar, or its secret ritual and handclasp. It was in the bond of fellowship for its 852 men who were initiated during its span of 38 years as an active fraternity. Its colors were maroon and gold and its flower was the American Beauty rose.

Brothers of Sigma Phi come back at reunion times to share memories, "shoot the breeze," make new friendships and renew old ones.

The Peoria reunion committee consists of 13 men, headed by its chairman, Bob Carkenord, and officers Bob Runkle, Chuck Anderson and Bob Whitcomb.

This week's event will begin with an informal get-together on campus Friday night, followed on Saturday by golf for the men at Kellogg Golf Course and lunch or shopping for the wives. Saturday night's banquet will be in the Cotillion Room at the Hotel Pere Marquette, which has become a tradition.

Between 1911 and 1949, when each member was initiated, he witnessed a ritual that included "The Legend of Sigmon" of medieval days. This legend has been brought down through the generations by one of the founder's families.

Each man signed a parchment scroll with his name and initiation date. This scroll has been well preserved over the years and is now housed in Bradley Library. Six scrapbooks of clippings and pictures have also been preserved in the library.

Many of the fraternity's members have gone on to make great contributions to society, both locally and nationally. Here are a few examples:

Gen. J. Randall Holzapple, military aviation hero; Louis Skidmore, architect of world fame; John Brewer, medical surgeon & pioneer in cancer research; Herbert White, banking and investments; David B. Owen, former president of Bradley University; Robert D. Morgan, former Peoria mayor and senior federal judge; Fred King, author of high school text books; Clarence Noe, executive vice president of Eureka College; Albert Siepert, Jr., NASA executive; and Marvin Hult, business executive & philanthropist.

Also, Jack Pearl, insurance and auto dealership executive; Bob Leu, insurance executive and former voice of Bradley sports events; and Charles (Chuck) Orsborn, former member of Bradley's Famous Five, Bradley coach and athletic director.

The other Famous Five members, Dar Hutchins, Ted Panish, Carl Schunk, Les Getz and Kenny Olson, were also members, as was Bradley's legendary coach and athletic director, A. J. Robertson's son, Jim.

Three Peoria families have been represented by four of their members: the Jacquin family by Homer, Eddie,

The Sigma Phi fraternity house at the corner of University and Main St., as it appeared in 1925.
(Photo courtesy of Charles Anderson)

A 1939 Sigma Phi stunt show, written, directed, produced and acted in by Joe Hession, in the fall of 1939. Standing L to R: (Mahatma Gandhi) Kline Richardson, (Neville Chamberlain) Carmen Dixon, (Joseph Stalin) Dick Bodtke, (Benito Mussolini) John Knezovich, (Adolph Hitler) Harris Blomeyer and seated: (F.D.R.) John E. Heisel.
(Photo courtesy of Charles Anderson)

Wentworth and Lucien; the Morgan family by Robert, Donald, David and George; and the Hession family by Tom, Joe, Bob and Dick.

For the first several years, the fraternity met in a classroom in Bradley Hall and then a vacant store building at the corner of Bradley and University. They then moved to a location on N. Elmwood, and around 1925, they purchased a home at 97 N. University at Main (where Avanti's Restaurant is now). The house was razed in 1953.

Sigma Phi's first faculty advisor was A. W. Jamison and its last was Loyal G. Tillotson.

During the 1930s and 40s, Sigma Phi issued "The Sigmon" annually, which listed all activities of the past year, with photos. It was cancelled during the war in 1943, but was revived in 1947.

Also during the war years, three Peorians - Tom Greer, Auren Muir and Max Bass - wrote a special song titled the "Sigma Phi Sweetheart Song" (not to be confused with "The Sweetheart of Sigma Chi"). It was played at most fraternity functions and in later years, orchestra leader Tiny Hill used it as his theme song.

The house mother for many years was Hazel Stuart Hunt, who did the cooking and gave motherly advice, and was beloved by all. She died in 1984, at the age of 95, and a Bradley University scholarship was set up in her memory.

The fraternity's main activities between 1911 and 1949 were "The Annual Sigma Phi Follies," which featured the famous "Glowworm Chorus," the annual house decorations and the parade downtown. The 1935 stunt show was so good, it played the Palace Theater for two days and nights.

Can it be 43 years since the Sigma Phi held forth on the Bradley campus?

...it seems like only yesterday!

The Madison's second life begins as dinner theater

It's finally happened. After a nine-year hiatus, the Madison Theater is entertaining audiences once again. And no one is more pleased to see it happen than me.

I must confess, there have been many times during those past nine years that I would have given odds that it would never happen... that the Madison would become just another parking lot.

Thanks to two people, Jim and Josephine Comfort, that never happened. Instead, the 72-year-old auditorium is once again hearing voices of laughter. But the entertainment isn't in the form of the old silent movies it featured when it opened October 16, 1920. Nor is it the "all-singing, all-dancing, all-talking" movies that came along seven years later.

No, the grand old lady is now a dinner theater, and this form of entertainment should be warmly welcomed as a part of Peoria's new downtown scene.

It was certainly welcome news to us. Flossie and I were at the grand opening Friday, September 25, when the two-man play, "Greater Tuna," became its first, ever, dinner theater offering. We were joined by attorney John Parkhurst and his wife, Harriet, along with *Journal Star* features editor Dennis Dimond and his wife, Marion.

In addition to an entertaining evening, thanks to the acting abilities of two very talented young men, the food was excellent, and it was quite a pleasant surprise that it wasn't the usual buffet format you normally expect at a dinner theater. We were served at our table and given a choice of three entrees. Cocktails and wine were also available.

"Greater Tuna," written by three native Texans, Jaston Williams, Joe Sears and Ed Howard, is a play about Tuna, the seemingly smallest town in Texas. Its director is David Mink, a 29-year theater veteran who is currently associated with the LaSalle Street Management Theatre in Chicago.

The show's two strongest points are its stars: Dan Frick and Sam Patterson. Patterson is well known in Chicago, and his favorite roles include Dead Scrooge in "A Christmas Carol," Sylvestro in "Scapino," and Soliony in "The Three Sisters." He performs no fewer than ten roles in "Greater Tuna," portraying residents of this little Texas town.

Frick has performed in four countries with such stars as Sally Rand, Jack Kelly, Kathryn Grayson, Kirk Douglas, Steve McQueen, Placido Domingo and others. He's appeared seven times with the Lyric Opera of Chicago and has also performed at the Goodman Theater, Drury Lane, and Drury Lane Oakbrook. Frick also has done numerous radio and TV commercials, as well as film work.

The Comforts are being assisted with their new dinner theater concept by a local boy and a favorite here for many years, Tom Joyce. Joyce is supervising the plays and talent being selected for the Madison. He's currently affiliated with the Drury Lane Theater in the Chicago suburb of Evergreen.

His interest in the Madison goes much deeper than that, though. He's most interested in helping restore the grand old theater as well as developing talent for it locally. The Madison is currently Illinois' only Actor's Equity theater outside of Cook County, but the plans are to also utilize the better local actors here as well.

After the opening performance, Jim Comfort told me that they had purposely opened conservatively by using simple sets. It's also one of the reasons they selected a two-man comedy to begin their season.

The first ten rows of theater seats have been removed from the front of the

DAN FRICK (left) and SAM PATTERSON, the stars of the two-man show, "Greater Tuna." It's the first offering now playing at the new Madison Dinner Theater.

The Madison Theater's side exit doors have, since, been remodeled, with a canopy added, and are now the entrance to the new Madison Dinner Theater.
(Photo courtesy of the Peoria Public Library)

Madison auditorium to make room for the dinner tables and chairs. The stage has been extended out over the orchestra pit, which brings the live presentations closer to the audience.

"Greater Tuna" will play the first six to eight weeks of a planned 37-week season. The next production will be a musical, Comfort reports.

Barry Cloyd, who's been closely involved with Peoria theater, is the new public relations director for the Madison Dinner Theater. It's his job to build a pro-

motional campaign, work on group sales and advertising campaigns for future events.

Cloyd says the Madison is being well received by the riverboat management as well as all the downtown hotels. The Par-A-Dice is currently preparing a brochure to send to their out-of-town customers, which will include a calendar of Madison Dinner Theater shows.

Tickets for dinner and a show at the theater range from $20 to $25 per person. Show only tickets are available for $13.50.

To encourage local theater goers to check out the new theater fare, the Comforts are offering a special grand opening special this month: for each full theater dinner ticket, they are offering the second ticket at half price.

Yes, dinner theater is now playing in Peoria. Just being in the grand old theater again makes it

...seem like only yesterday!

Janssen and Becker bring beauty back

Two self-made Peoria men are mostly responsible for transforming the downtown corner of Main and Jefferson into a thing of beauty. Although they are in totally unrelated businesses, in a sense, they did it in tandem.

And both, developer Ray Becker and attorney Jay Janssen, can justifiably be proud of their two new buildings, which came together simultaneously at this corner.

It's also a near duplication of the feat that occurred back in 1920, a block up Main Street, when the Madison and Palace theaters were being built at the same time, and across from one another.

Janssen has already moved his law offices into one of the plushest interiors ever seen in our town.

The rich cherry wood paneled lobby with matching cherry wood and green verde marble double staircases leading to the second floor are, well, breathtaking. The lobby floors are white carerra marble and brass, and everything is trimmed in brass and beveled glass.

The beautiful red and mauve granite used on the building's exterior was mined in Norway, but was cut and and finished in Italy. It was then shipped from Italy to Canada, through the St. Lawrence Seaway, and came from there to Peoria via truck.

This all began three or four years ago, when Becker's company purchased the corner property and decided to put up an office building there, in addition to their other one across Jefferson Street.

Jay Janssen was looking for more space for his law offices at the time and talked to Becker about leasing two or three floors of the new building. But Jay had very definite ideas about the design of his offices. So much so that Becker suggested Janssen buy the property and put up his own building. He did.

Architects Gordon Burns and Associates had already planned the six-story building for Becker, and Janssen retained the firm. The interior design is by David Haase.

Although Janssen's staff has relocated and Jim's Steakhouse is operating in the building's lower level, the interior isn't completely finished.

Janssen is planning a grand opening for Saturday night, December 12, complete with a sit-down dinner catered by Jim's and a big-band orchestra. Proceeds for this black tie affair will go to the Crisis Nursery of the Crittenton Care & Counseling Center in celebration of the center's 100th Anniversary.

The new Janssen Building is just the latest link in a long history on that corner, dating back to at least 1834. It was on May 28 of that year that county commisioner Aquilla Wren and two others authorized a divided platt of Peoria, which included this corner.

Then on August 3, 1835, John Coyle and two other commissioners deeded the 72 by 171-foot corner to William Sillman, who probably became its first owner since the French claims were settled. On May 3, 1844, Sillman deeded the property to Elihu N. Powell and William F. Bryan.

Powell and Bryan apparently subdivided the land, because on March 25, 1851, Bryan deeded over to Powell the corner portion of the lot measuring 36 by 74 feet. On July 26, 1853, a mortgage by Powell was deeded over to Richard Hebdeb, and the mortgage was released July 8, 1854.

On November 19, 1856, Powell leased the corner to Joseph D. Bacon and William Hughes, and by then a building with a storeroom had been erected.

On March 13, 1866, Mr. & Mrs. Powell sold the corner property to two brothers, Richard M. and Theodore Pinkney, which led to the erection of the Pinkney Building in 1866. That building graced the corner for the next 120 years and its history included at least three restaurants.

THEN - The corner of Main & Jefferson as it appeared around the turn of the century. The Pinkney Building is just left of the old courthouse monument.
(A postcard photo, courtesy of Peoria Public Library)

NOW - The new Janssen Building at the same corner where the old Pinkney Building stood.
(Artist's rendering by Rice Associates of St. Louis)

Many Peorians will remember the last two, "The Bee Hive" in the 1930s and 40s and, of course, "Jim's Steakhouse," which was there in 1986, when it was destroyed by fire.

But it was March 1866, when the Pinkney brothers purchased the old frame building and corner lot, which then housed the photo studio of T. J. Luccock. The old building was moved to Hancock Street, to make way for the new Pinkney Building. Work progressed rapidly on the new 36 by 74 foot, three-story structure that summer, and by September 1866, the final touches were completed. That November, the new brick sidewalk on Main Street was also completed.

On December 5, William B. Goodwin opened its first eating house in the basement, and that same week, N. B. Little moved into the corner store. Then the week before Christmas, Luccock moved his photo gallery into the third floor.

It was also noted in the newspapers that many years later (in 1901) the main floor was remodeled for the Northwestern Railroad's ticket office.

Over the years, several businesses maintained stores or offices in this grand old building. Some of them were: Israel C. Pinkney (a nephew to the owners) and William G. McRoberts, for their Pinkney & McRoberts law offices; J. B. Profitlich

Furriers; and architect Frederic J. Klein (who designed the Hippodrome, Madison Theater and Packard Building).

But in July 1986, Jim's Steakhouse, which then occupied the main floor caught fire. The entire building and part of Potter & Anderson jewelers next door were destroyed.

The corner is now reborn, with the beautiful Janssen Building, a big, bright jewel in the crown of what is now Peoria's new downtown.

But I'll never forget the Bee Hive, with its intimate balcony. A great place to take your date after the game or show

...and it seems like only yesterday!

(Names and dates for some of the facts were supplied by Peoria County Recorder, Dirk McGinnis, and Peoria historian, Paul H. Stringham.)

Becker brothers did parents proud with business, new building

Last Monday I talked about the new Janssen Building and the history of that corner location at Main and Jefferson, dating back to 1834. This new building was begun by Becker Brothers and sold to Jay Janssen, who completed it.

Now, let's take a walk across Jefferson to the 400 block of Main Street and visit the new Becker Building, which is also currently being completed. It should be noted that both the Becker and Janssen buildings were recently awarded Orchid Awards by Peoria City Beautiful. The awards honor businesses and organizations that have worked to beautify the city.

The new Becker Building will be the downtown location of Ray Becker's Community Bank, which is now in the Central Building.

While we're looking at the Becker Building, it's interesting to take a closer look at the Becker family, itself. It's one of Peoria's pioneer families that began here in 1881 when Nicholas and Justine Augusta Margis Becker moved their family here from the Alsace-Lorraine area of Germany.

Nicholas Becker was a stone mason in the old country and became a naturalized citizen in Peoria in 1886. The Beckers lived in a house at the corner of East Armstrong and (then) White Street, and Nicholas continued in the business of stone and brick masonry, constructing many of Peoria's early street curbs, manholes and brick sidewalks.

The Beckers had eight children, the youngest of whom was William Nicholas Becker, who went to White School until the fourth grade. William then quit school to go to work, which was not uncommon in those days.

William later joined his father in his N. Becker Co., which became N. Becker & Son around 1918. William began making his own cinder blocks, and later purchased the Stever gravel pit at Sterling and Farmington Road.

William married Florine Martin, whom he first met while ice skating at the Glen Oak Park lagoon. They, too, eventually had eight children, seven boys and a girl: Paul William, William Nicholas Jr., Charles Joseph, John Martin, George Raymond, James Anthony, Edward Bernard and Joyce Ann (Cover).

(In later years Ray donated the land in the 3300 block of Richwoods Boulevard to the Peoria Park District for the John Martin Becker Park, in honor of John, who was killed on Okinawa during World War II.)

This large Becker family also resided on East Armstrong, first at 258, then 262 and, later, 260. Former Caterpillar president, Bob Gilmore, and his brother, Jack, were next-door neighbors.

When Grandpa Nicholas Becker died in 1938, his company was dissolved, after which William went to work for W. G. Best's home construction company as a cement finisher. Ray also started working for Best during summer vacation in 1946.

When World War II broke out, the four older brothers left for service, and it wasn't until Paul returned that he and Ray formed the new business we know today as Becker Brothers. That business began January 10, 1949. Bill came home in the fall of that year and joined the new family company.

Becker Brothers became a concrete subcontractor for Best Homes doing basements, stoops, and porches. Paul moved to California around 1953, and Best Homes left Peoria the following year.

Also around 1954, the company opened a Bloomington branch and brother Bill ran this operation. Ray also began his G. R. Becker Lumber Co. on

Farmington Road in 1954 and he lured his brother, Chuck, away from his regional sales job with Minneapolis-Moline to manage the lumber company. Chuck came aboard and is still running that operation today.

It was about this same time that Becker Brothers (under the name of the Acme Co.) began building small brick houses (for the same price as frame houses). Ray estimates that they built between 400 and 500 of them here and in Bloomington.

Paul later moved back to Peoria to work with the company and is now retired, while Jim and Ed have been very active in the company over the years, and still are.

Since those early days, Becker Brothers have done more projects in Central Illinois and throughout the country than we can possibly mention here, but back when Ray was putting together his twin tower, mall and office complex, he bought the closed Palace Theater. He razed the theater and used part of the land for that complex and its underground garage.

Then, after the Lehmann Building fire, he purchased it and the remaining properties along Main Street and began planning for the new Becker Building, which is now being completed.

Now, you might think that the name on the building is for Ray or the Becker brothers, but that's not the case. The

A family picture of Grandma and Grandpa Becker and their eight children. William Nicholas Becker, Sr., father of the Becker brothers and sister, is the youngest child, sitting on his father's lap.
(Photo courtesy of Bill Becker)

"Becker" name on the building is in memory of their father, William N. Becker Sr., who died in 1983 and their mother, Florine Martin Becker, who passed away in 1989. Ray says its most fitting, since their dad was a cement contractor all of his working life and this building, other than its glass windows and frames, is entirely constructed of concrete.

And directly below the Becker name over the building's Main Street entrance will be a monument to their father, with the following inscription: "Dedicated to the memory of William N. Becker Sr., a Peoria pioneer in concrete construction. His finisher's trowel was as a brush to the artist."

The new Becker building, as seen from the Court House corner of Main and SW Jefferson streets.
(Photo courtesy of Becker Brothers, Inc.)

Around the corner on Jefferson Street, the garden area containing the "Peace" and "Harvest" statues will be named the Florine Anna Martin Becker Plaza, and the monument in her memory will read: "Her peace and harvest were in her family and in the care she gave to others."

As I look around downtown today, I can't help but take pride in Peoria's new look... and a large part of it has happened through the efforts of Ray Becker and his family. A pioneer family that's had its roots deeply planted in Peoria for more than a hundred years.

NEXT WEEK: Part two of the Becker family and Becker Brothers, Inc.

Just a few of the projects Becker Bros. worked on

Second of Two Parts

Paul and Ray Becker formed their fledgling Becker Brothers company on January 10, 1949, and a young accountant named Chuck Ginoli was soon counseling Ray on many of his early decisions.

Ginoli recommended a young lawyer named John Parkhurst to Ray, and "Parky" came aboard in the early 1950s. In later years, Ginoli's younger brother, Gene, became associated with the firm.

Now, Peoria's new "Becker Block," which contains the new Becker Building, Twin Towers mall, and condominiums , underground garage and office building complex, would be enough for one man, one family or even one company, but this just scratches the surface of Becker accomplishments.

Here are some of the other major Becker Brothers projects that have further changed our downtown the past 28 years:

Their first downtown project was the Sears building and parking garage in 1964. Then came the 200 Main St. office building, Ramada Inn, Illinois Mutual Building (old Peoria Dry Goods Store), 330 SW Adams St. office building, Continental Regency Hotel, the new Central Fire House, VA Clinic Building, Methodist Hospital's professional building and parking deck, Jefferson Building (now River Valley Plaza), Heartland Building and the Peoria Rescue Mission.

In addition, there are the Amkor Building (later Union Sangyo, now USA Technologies), Central Building parking deck, Illinois Central College downtown campus, Orthopedic Building, State of Illinois Employment Office and the beginning of the Janssen Building.

But that, too, just scratches the surface of Peoria-area projects. I've personally counted at least 43 more.

Here are some major ones: Sheridan Bank, East Peoria Shopping Center, Galena Park Homes, Northwest Bank, Eurocor Cabinets, Peoria State Hospital.,Big Hollow, The Institute and Touchstone Alcohol Treatments Centers, Grandview Drive Pavilion and Bradley University Art Center, Library, Student Union, Becker Hall, Coaches Office Building and other permanent and temporary dorms.

There also are the Wal-Mart's and Sam's Clubs in Peoria, Bloomington, Washington, Rockford, and Joliet, two East Peoria Community Bank buildings, the Landmark complex, Sterling Towers, Lexington Hills, Pennsylvania Towers, Lexington Ridge, Knoxville Clinic, PJS Publishing, University Shopping Center, Neil Norton Cadillac, Prairie Farms Dairy, Off-Track Betting Parlors in Peoria, Aurora, LaSalle, Joliet and Maywood and the Kerasotes theaters in Peoria and Bloomington.

Also the Franciscan Elderly Apartments, monastery, and complex, Carver Community Center, John Bearce Auto Mall (in East Peoria), Mt. Hawley Court Shopping Center & Community Bank, Eureka College dorms, Proctor Hospital Heart Surgical buildings (additions 1 & 2), the Boys & Girls Club, and the Illinois Air Guard Security Building & Operations & Training Center.

Is that all? Well, no.

We haven't even talked about the 90 plus nursing homes built around the country, from Illinois to Michigan, Virigina and West Virginia. And the Beckers either operated, staffed, directed, or otherwise participated in 49 of them. This was an area where Bill Becker became very instrumental with his degrees in clinical psychology and his administrative ability.

Nor have we mentioned Becker Brothers' participation in junior college programs, which began at Illinois Central College in 1982. Ray developed a new concept of pouring the slab, erecting the outside walls and roof, then tiling the entire floor area before installing the interior walls. This allowed for the total interior to be very simply revamped as school requirements changed. This "instant school" concept has been incorporated by the firm on 16 campuses across the country.

Back in late summer of 1981, Bradley's increased enrollment found the university short of dorm space. They contacted Ray about leasing 50 rooms in his Continental Regency Hotel. Ray visited the campus to assess their acute problem. The next morning, he contacted then Bradley president Martin Abegg, and promised to build a temporary dorm in a campus parking lot in one month.

Ray had the plans drawn up in one day and his crews began work on August 1. He handed over the keys to the completed 50-room dorm (to house 100 students) on August 24, a week before his month was up. But that isn't his record. He later built a temporary dorm in just 14 days.

I asked Ray what personal comment he'd like to make. The quiet man replied: "Peoria has been very good to me and, along the way, I've tried to give back a little of what I've received." But he won't elaborate on the many charitable things I know he's done. When I asked him if he

THE BECKER FAMILY - (L to R) Bottom row: Edmund, G. Raymond (Ray), James. Middle row: Paul, Joyce, William N., Sr. (father), Florine (mother). Top row: John, William N., Jr. (Bill), and Chuck.
(Photo courtesy of Bill Becker)

was justifiably proud of his achievements, he, again, gave a brief reply: "I'm not proud... I feel humbled."

Then, I asked what one project gave him his greatest pleasure and, to my surprise, it wasn't one of his monumental projects. It was his long association with the Boys and Girls Club.

The club recently came to him with a mere $6,000 budget to enlarge and remodel the club's facilities. But, rather than say it couldn't be done, with the help of eight inmates from the Hanna City Corrections Center and a warehouse full of materials accumulated over the years, a $120,000 facility was developed, using only $1,700 of the club's original budget.

And yes, it was a humble beginning back in 1946, when a junior at Woodruff High joined his dad, a cement finisher, working on Bill Best's pre-fab homes.

...but it seems like only yesterday!

Taking a walk around yesterday's downtown

I've thoroughly enjoyed writing about downtown's new Janssen and Becker buildings the last three weeks. They're not only impressive, they also bring home to me just how much the loop area has changed over the past few years.

As I walk around downtown today I think about many of the old landmarks, but I have a hard time remembering their exact locations. For instance: What was the exact location of the Rialto Theater? The Jefferson Hotel? The Central Firehouse? The Majestic Theater? The Jefferson Bank? The Empire? Kresge's and Woolworth's dime stores? The B & M Store? and the "old" First National Bank?

And while describing the new "Becker Block" last week, with its Twin Towers, mall, office complex and new Becker building, my mind went back to the 1940s, and I tried to remember some of the businesses that occupied that four-block area of Main, Jefferson, Fulton and Madison streets back then.

I've done a little homework since then, so, just for fun, let's go back now and take a nostalgic "walk" around that old block once again.

The year is 1941 (the year I began ushering at the Madison Theater) and we'll start at the corner of Main and Madison, just across from my old place of employment:

On the corner in what was the Hull Building at (441 Main) was the Sutliff & Case Drug Store. Walking down Main toward Jefferson we'll pass (439) Fuegar Jewelers; (435) the Palace Theater (where the entrance to the new Becker Building is now); (433) Fannie May Candies; (431) McKee Jewelry, Rushford Optometrist, Hartung Massage & Dar-Meene Beauty Shoppe; (429) Stavropoulas & Green, shoe repair & shine; (427-1/2) Idlehour Social Club; (427) Rooney & Eagan, liquors; (425) The Pantry restaurant; (423) Loveridge Florists.

(421) Webb's Bank & Pawn Brokers; (rear) the Puff Lounge; (419) Delphia Hosiery Shop; (417) Picadilly Liquors; (415) Hardy Shoe Store; (413) The Nut House; (411) Thom McAn Shoes; (409) Main Street Flower Shop; (407) Two Legs Clothing Store; (405) Lehmann Building entrance, with Henry J. Ziegle Printers (in the basement); (403) Rex Camera Shop; and (401) United Cigar Store.

Turning the corner, we'll walk down Jefferson toward Fulton, past (103 S. Jefferson) Nine Cent Shoe Repair; (105) Sam Keltner, barber; (107) People's Federal Savings & Loan and Traders Realty; (109) Saratoga cigar store, bowling & billiards & Charles F. Swords, contractor; (113) O'Brien-Jobst, men's clothing; (115) Austin Engineering, Henry Koch, architect, Graphic Arts Co. & three dentists; (117) John B. Profitlitch, Furs; (123) Jefferson Trust & Savings Bank; (125) *Peoria Journal*; (127) Ware-Andreen, men's clothing; (129) Oscar Moehn, ladies clothing; (131) Knupp's Luggage; (135) E. F. Scott, tailor; (139) the Empire, cigars & liquor (home of the baseball pool); (143) Pierson's Grill; and (145) Fulton News Stand.

Now we'll turn the corner again and walk up the 400 block of Fulton to Madison, past (402) Forcom's Shoe Repair; (404) Fern's Furs; (406) Bill Webster's Barber Shop; (408) Wm. F. McDaniel, justice of peace, and Zoe Hartquist, tailor; (410-12) Peoria Barber Supply; (414) Alcazar, cigar store (home of the "little" baseball pool); (416) Jack Adams' Clover Club; (418) Metzger Apartments; (420) Northwestern Beauty Academy; (422) Johnnie's Restaurant; (422-1/2) Herman Bridegroom, justice of peace (not a pun), John Lane, constable, and Charles Slack, office; (424) Natural Food Shop; (424-1/2) Plaza Hotel & Thomas Driscoll, justice of peace; (426) Hamburger Inn (5¢ hamburgers, six for a

Left — Part of the
400 block of Main St.
as it appeared in the
1960s.
(From the Grassel
Photo Files of the
Peoria Public
Library)

The 100 block of SW Jefferson in the early
1920s. That's the Dime Savings Bank (which
later became the Jefferson Bank), to the right
of the *Peoria Journal-Transcript* building.
(From the Grassel Photo Files of the Peoria
Public Library)

quarter); (428) L. C. Smith-Corona Typewriters; (430) NuEnamel, Glos Paint Store.

And now to complete our walk, we'll turn the final corner and walk toward Main Street in the 100 block of S. Madison, past (134) Moy Sing Laundry; (132) Venard Film Co., Peoria Fo-Dax Photos & Edgar Salzenstein, tailor; (130) Wilson's Appliances; (128) Bill DeGaris' Tavern; (126) Helene Beauty Shoppe; (120) Kett Watson's 120 Club; (118) Palace Arcade; (114) Bowman's Barber Shop (Milt "Shorty" Bowman, my step-grandad); (108) Hull Apartments; (106) Madison Beauty Shop; and (104) Palace Cafeteria (downstairs).

Well, did you remember some of those old places? If you did, you may have had a little trouble with their exact order or location. But where were some of those others mentioned at the beginning of the column, that weren't in the "Becker Block" area?

The Rialto Theater was about where the Jefferson Street entrance to Carver Arena is now and the Jefferson Hotel was at the corner of Jefferson and Liberty streets (although Liberty doesn't continue above Jefferson any more). The Central Fire House was at Liberty and Franklin and the Majestic Theater was across from the Rialto on Jefferson, connected to the Jefferson Building (now River Valley Plaza).

Kresge's 5 & 10 was in the middle of the 100 block of South Adams, just up from Block & Kuhl's (which is now Bank One, formerly the Jefferson Bank, which was originally on Jefferson. Who's on first?) Kresge's also had a dollar store across Adams Street, near Woolworth's 5 & 10, which is now Illinois Central College. The B&M was on the corner of South Adams and Fulton (but in a building that was razed to build the Grant Store, which is now the closed World Drug). And the "old" First National Bank was in the middle of the 200 block of South Adams, just down from Bergner's Department Store.

Well, it was a nostalgic walk in that wonderful year of 1941

... and it seems like only yesterday!

"Paid executioners" did Stumpf in: police

I've recently written about the rash of gangland murders that occurred in Peoria back in those wide-open days of the 1940s. The most sensational one was that of Bernie Shelton of the infamous Shelton Gang in 1948. No fewer than three gang-style slayings had already occurred in 1946; I've already covered the first two.

Frank Kraemer, a local tavern operator, was shot down in his Farmington Road home on February 20 of that year and Joe Nyberg, a well-known Peoria police character, was killed seven months later. Nyberg's battered and bullet-riddled body was found the morning of September 21, 1946, on the Lacon Country Club golf course.

Then, a little more than a month later, Phillip L. Stumpf, a former convict and slot machine operator, was murdered in his car on Friday night, October 25, while returning to town from a tavern on Big Hollow Road. A companion in the car, Charles Logsdon, was also wounded.

All this caused county and city police to continue searching for what they believed to be a "gang of exterminators," a group they were sure had murdered all three men. The three victims all had some association with gambling.

Stumpf was known to be a handy man with dynamite, who had allegedly "muscled" into Peoria's slot machine rackets with the use of blasting powder.

After the shooting, Logsdon told city chief of detectives Fred Nussbaum that he was in a south end tavern earlier in the evening when Stumpf stopped in and asked him to take a ride. Stumpf then drove out Big Hollow Road to the Stork Club, which was operated by Zelma Halsted. (It had formerly been the Big Hollow Inn.) Mrs. Halsted had called Stumpf to repair a nickel slot machine that was out of order.

Logsdon was thought to be a slot machine mechanic but he denied it, saying that he drank three bottles of beer and played "That's How Much I Love You" five times on the juke box, while Stumpf repaired the machine.

Mrs. Halsted said only neighborhood customers were in the tavern at the time. She also said that Friday was not a regular collection day for the slot machines.

The two men left the tavern around 9 p.m. and headed back to Peoria. Stumpf was driving his 1938 black four-door Buick sedan. Logsdon said another car began following them as they crossed the railroad bridge in the "hollow." About 400 feet west of the junction of the old Big Hollow Road and U.S. Route 150, they attempted to shake off the pursuit of the other car by cutting across a field from the old road toward the new one.

As they entered the field, gunfire from the second car riddled the back of the Buick. Logsdon said he heard one shot when he was struck. He asked Stumpf what was happening and he replied, "How the hell do I know?" Then Stumpf was shot in the top of the head, the left arm and in the back. He was killed instantly.

Nine bullets were fired through the rear of the car, with five going through the front windshield. The bullets were later determined to be carbine ammunition.

Mrs. Ralph Hoerr, who resided nearby, told county police she was at a service station on Big Hollow Road when Logsdon walked in and said he'd been shot and another man had been killed. He was bleeding from a head wound and asked her to call him a taxicab. Then he made a phone call. A short time later, he was getting into a dark blue coupe when a Kupper cab driver, George Reese, arrived.

Phillip L. Stumpf (left) was killed and Charles Logsdon was wounded when the two were shot in gangland fashion on October 25, 1946.
(*Peoria Star* photos)

The bullet-riddled and bloody auto in which Phillip Stumpf was killed in 1946. The victim's hat (right), with a hole in the crown, lies on the front seat.
(*Peoria Star* photos)

Reese headed off the car and demanded payment for answering the call; he was paid.

Later that night Logsdon was taken into custody after being treated for a scalp wound by Dr. Herbert Williams of Bartonville.

The next day, coroner Chauncey Wood said a .38-caliber revolver, the same type used in the slaying of Joe Nyberg five weeks earlier, was found in the glove compartment of Stumpf's car.

Phil Stumpf was first arrested here on February 1, 1929, on a charge of robbery. He was later arrested in Ottawa by the FBI and was sentenced to two years and fined $3,000 for violation of the Prohibition act. He was paroled from the federal penitentiary in Leavenworth, Kansas on January 3, 1930. Then on February 7, 1933, Chicago police arrested him for safe robbery and the shooting of two policemen.

Stumpf became suddenly active in the local slot machine syndicate about two years before his death, following the bombings of the homes of two Peoria gamblers. He was arrested but was never prosecuted for the bombings.

During their investigation, police theorized that this third 1946 gang-style murder might be the act of an outside gang interested in moving into Peoria, or "paid executioners" brought into town by some other groups.

But these murders, as well as that of Bernie Shelton a couple years later, all wound up the same way so many others did back in Peoria's wide-open era... "murder by party or parties unknown"

...and it seems like only yesterday!

Pottery synonymous with town of Morton

Greater Peoria has had its share of major businesses over the years... agricultural and heavy-duty equipment, tractors, wire products, distilleries, breweries, watch manufacturing, auto and truck manufacturing and even the making of peanut roasters.

Peoria also had its Peoria Pottery, but until a few short years ago, Morton was the home of one of the largest pottery businesses in the country. The town and pottery became so synonymous that Morton High School went so far as to name their athletic teams the Morton Potters.

During most of the industry's 99 years, there were several potteries in Morton, operated by two generations of the same family.

The Rapp Brothers Brick & Tile Company was founded in 1877 by Andrew and Barthol Rapp, two brothers from Burgberg, Germany, who could trace their family tree back to a Clemens Rapp in 1665. A few years later, four more brothers joined them in the Morton business.

The company originally manufactured bricks for chimneys and cistern walls and field tile for draining farmland around the area. The company later turned out a variety of items, including spitoons, kerosene lamps, bed pans, bed and foot warmers, water pitchers, ashtrays, statuettes, ceramic tile and many other variations of pottery.

When local clays started to diminish, the company began using yellow burning clays from Indiana to manufacture large jugs and jars for storing water and food products. Demand brought about the making of earthenware mixing bowls, tea pots, baking dishes, flower pots and other clay products.

After the original Rapp Brothers company, there were the Morton Earthenware Co., the Cliftwood Art Potteries and Midwest Potteries (all at the same location); American Arts Potteries and Morton Pottery Company.

And on August 15, 1930, Mathew Rapp and his sons opened the Cliftwood Inn as a showroom for their Cliftwood Art pottery. It has since been operated by various owners but few today associate it with the pottery company.

By the 1950s, the Morton Pottery Co. had become the largest in the Midwest and the third largest of its kind in the United States. Beer steins had now become their biggest selling item and they made some 300,000 a year for Anheuser-Busch, Schlitz and many other breweries throughout the country. They also owned a subsidiary, Morton Ceramic Tile Co., for which they manufactured a ceramic tyle called Mor-Tile, turning out 30,000 tiles a day.

During these peak years, the plant employed from 130 to 160 people, about 75 percent of whom were women. Its products became nationally known and plant tours were conducted regularly.

Senator Everett Dirksen of Pekin became a valued customer during his political days. The Rapps, who were Republicans, produced GOP elephants for him, and Dirksen even had special Delftware ashtrays made. He distributed them at a political convention.

During World War II, Gilbert Rapp trained as a co-pilot with President John F. Kennedy's older brother, Joe Jr., and President Kennedy later had the pottery make a brown glazed donkey for his campaign.

By 1966, the Japanese were making large inroads into the ceramic tile business. Although the novelty and art lines were doing well, the Rapps decided to sell Morton Pottery Co. in May 1969.

But by 1971, the company - under new ownership - had filed for bankruptcy. Morton Pottery Company's payroll had dropped to 80 employees, and to only 15 at the end. In March 1971, the bankrupt firm was sold to Addison, Illinois-based A.K.F. Industry.

In October 1972, A.K.F. sold the firm to Rival Manufacturing Co. of Kansas

The original office of the Rapp Brothers Brick & Tile Co. (Photo courtesy of Geraldine (Rapp) Carius)

John W. Rapp in the glazing room of the Cliftwood Art Potteries. (Photo from the R. C. Conibear Collection, Morton Public Library)

City. Employment was back up to 85 and A.K.F. had been primarily making crock pots, one of Rival's most important products.

Rival finally leased the plant to the Lincoln Stonewear Co. of Wellsville, Ohio in January 1976. The company continued to make Rival products.

The end of Morton's pottery business came on September 8, 1976. Lincoln Stonewear called the employees together in the morning to tell them that the business was closing permanently at 3:30 that afternoon. Morton's 99 years of pottery manufacturing had come to an abrupt end.

But it was a fascinating business during all those years, and in 1982 a Morton couple, Burdell and Doris Hall, authored a wonderful history and product guide on the business titled "Morton's Potteries: 99 Years."

Burdell Hall, who had actually worked at the pottery as a high school student, retired from teaching history at Morton High in 1980. In addition to outlining the city's pottery-related history, the book features reprints of catalog pages and photos of pottery manufactured during all the various periods of the companies.

Whether you are a pottery enthusiast or just a history buff, the Hall's book makes for enjoyable reading. Limited copies are still available for sale at East Peoria's Pleasant Hill Antique Mall.

The Rapp family contributed greatly to Morton's history and much of their later years of operation

... seems like only yesterday!

Rolla Spaulding left authorities hanging

It was a hot, humid afternoon on July 10, 1922. The quiet of the Peoria County sheriff's office was suddenly broken by the jangle of a telephone. Wiping the perspiration from his forehead, chief deputy Grant Minor picked up the receiver. There was a long pause as Minor listened to the voice at the other end, with a few answering remarks of his own.

Hanging up, he turned to several other deputies and newspaper reporters sitting in the office. "It looks like some of the boys are trying to kid me," he said. "Some guy over at the Jefferson Hotel says he's Rolla Spaulding and wants me to come over and get him."

It wouldn't have sounded any more incredible if someone had called and said he was John Dillinger. Spaulding was a reputed member of the dreaded Purple Gang in Detroit, and for the past month had been sought here in connection with the brutal killing of a local constable named Arthur Smith.

On the night of June 12, Smith and his partner, Joseph Turner, stumbled onto four men, who appeared to be about to strip an automobile on Easton Road behind Bradley Park. The car had been stolen earlier on North Perry.

As the two constables approached, a shot came from behind a second car, a Buick that was later identified as Spaulding's. Smith drew his gun and then three more shots rang out. One struck Smith in the lower right breast, and another went through his heart, killing him instantly. The four men leaped from the roadway into an adjoining field and disappeared.

When Minor received that phone call a month later, police were still checking on the mysterious disappearance of a teenager named John Schorr, who had frequently been seen with Spaulding.

Grant Minor grinned as he reached for his hat. "Maybe they're playing me for a sucker but I can't afford to take a chance. We'll know in a few minutes."

About a half-hour later the deputy sheriff strolled back into the office with a tall, dark-complexioned man at his side.

"Sit down, Rolla," he said. "You'll have a nice cot tonight in jail. Hope you sleep as good as you did at the Jefferson."

"Maybe," Spaulding replied, "but it won't be for long." He didn't know it at the time but he was about to bid farewell to freedom for the rest of his life.

Less than 24 hours later, two hunters were trudging through a timbered area near Havana when their feet sank in a patch of newly turned earth. A moment later they discovered a human foot. Sheriff's deputies later found the body of a man whose head, face and upper body was eaten away by quicklime. A bullet had torn a gaping hole in the skull.

During the hunt for Schorr, Peoria County states' attorney Ernest Galbraith received a note from Mason City, bearing the supposed signature of Schorr. In illiterate terms it stated that he, Schorr, had killed the constable to "get even with the cops who beat me up." It also stated he had borrowed Spaulding's car that night and had had an accident.

At the bottom of the note were several smudgy fingerprints which, when checked, appeared to be those of Schorr. Still, Minor was unconvinced.

"This looks like a plant to me," he said. "I can't imagine Schorr doing this voluntarily." There was also no explaination for the second car at the death scene. His doubts were confirmed with the finding of the body in Mason County.

Schorr's mother was called in to try to identify her son's body. All she could do was shudder and shake her head. It wasn't until sometime later that she did identify

An early postcard photo of the Jefferson Hotel. (Courtesy Peoria Public Library)

the body through a toenail injury on a foot that hadn't been destroyed by the quicklime.

Mrs. Schorr had also asked to be taken to the makeshift grave because she had consulted a spiritualist and the medium had informed her that she had made a mistake and would discover what it was at the gravesite.

Another search of the grave brought forth nothing but, while there, a deputy decided to check the debris of a nearby cabin that had recently burned down. While walking through the ashes, Mrs. Schorr suddenly came upon a pair of charred trousers and broke into sobs. "They belonged to Johnny," she cried. "He wore them the day he left home."

On the basis of evidence now piling up, Mason County authorities issued a murder warrant against Spaulding for the murder of Schorr, but Peoria states' attorney Galbraith had already had a warrant charging him with the slaying of constable Smith. A Peoria County grand jury also had returned a quick indictment against Rolla Spaulding.

Through his attorney, Spaulding asked for, and received, a change of venue to Stark County, where a lengthy trial was held. It ended in a conviction and he received a life sentence on September 22, 1922.

But Rolla Spaulding wasn't destined for a long incarceration. He had served less than two years in the Illinois state pen when his body was found hanging from a noose, fashioned from a blanket in the hospital ward. A coroner's jury called his death a suicide.

Spaulding's death left several questions unanswered. It was generally thought that he took his young "friend," Schorr, for a ride and killed him after forcing him to write a note of confession to the killing of Smith. This, however, was never conclusively established.

Isn't it strange how some men with good backgrounds turned to a life of crime back in those gangland days? Rolla Spaulding was purported to be a successful inventor, a musician of unusual ability and had also traveled in high social circles in Detroit... all before his car theft days back in Peoria's roaring 20s.

(Part of this column is from an anonymous Peoria Journal or Star reporter.)

Ruth Jackman left quite a legacy

On Sunday, January 26, 1992, an 84-year-old lady named Ruth Haag Jackman died quietly at Proctor Hospital. What hospital officials didn't know at the time was that it would be willed the bulk of this multimillionaire's estate.

And last Wednesday night, during the Proctor Foundation Chairman's Dinner at the Peoria Country Club, it was announced that the hospital would receive $9 million with the specific understanding that it all be used for Proctor's cardiac programs.

With that in mind and at the same dinner, the hospital announced its plans to dedicate its new heart surgery center the Haag Heart Center.

You will readily understand the reason for its name when I tell you that Mrs. Ruth Haag Jackman was the only child of one of the twin brothers who founded the Haag Brothers washing machine company in Peoria back in 1912.

The Haag twins, George A. and Albert R., were born at Rock Falls, Illinois on March 30, 1879. Their parents were native Germans named Edward and Caroline (Enterley) Haag. Their father died while they were youngsters, forcing them to quit grade school and go to work to assist their mother in providing for a large household of children.

The twins learned the blacksmith's trade, which didn't pay much. A few years later, they moved to Peoria in hopes of earning more money. The two became mechanics and for 12 years helped their struggling mother and family. But they weren't satisfied with meager wages and they began planning to start a business.

Both men were inventive and they dreamed of building something mechanical. Being very aware of the hard work and drudgery their mother had to go through, they put their minds to the task of devising machines that would reduce the workload of the housewife.

Finally, around 1910, they decided that a power washing machine would give the most satisfactory results. They devoted all their spare time, night and day, to design a washer that operated on either a gasoline engine or a tractor's flywheel. It was designed with the farm housewife in mind, at a time when farms didn't generally have electricity.

In 1912, the two mechanics, who had helped build the old P&PU railroad bridge, rented a small corner of a building at 812-16 N. Commercial St. in Peoria, which was then occupied by the Western Stove Works. They soon realized that a small electric motor, rather than the big, noisy, cumbersome gasoline engine, would be more practical.

The new electric model was presented to the public and in a short time they were swamped with orders for washing machines from all over the country. Forced to expand, they eventually took over the entire two-story building. Their success was nothing short of phenomenal!

By spring 1919, they had bought an East Peoria site, built a $300,000 plant and were manufacturing 75 to 80 washers a day while employing about 100 workers.

The business began to decline during the Depression, and their plant was sold to Caterpillar in 1940, while parts for Haag washers continued to be manufactured until 1947.

George Haag married Daisy Lulay and they had one daughter, Ruth, in 1908. (She's the one who willed the money to Proctor.) The other twin, Albert, married Anna Gogele, and they had one son, Albert Jr., in 1919 who, I'm told, still resides in El Paso, Texas.

Ruth Haag Jackman was a 1930 graduate of Bradley Polytechnic Institute, a member of First Methodist Church and St. Augustine Manor's board. She was also a member of the Peoria Country Club, where she was active in their women's golf league.

It seems that Jackman lived a very low-key life, with no close relatives and few friends in her retiring years. She had divorced long ago and resided alone, except for a housekeeping companion, at the old family home at 2405 N. Linn Street.

Out of curiosity, I recently visited Curtis White of the Herbert B. White & Co. investment firm that handled Ruth Jackman's affairs. His father, Herb White, had started working with Ruth back in the early 1950s, when she was still trying to manage her own finances.

Over the years, he not only handled her business affairs, he became her personal confidant. Since that time, whenever she had any problem, big or small, business or personal, she'd always come to Herb for his friendly counsel. He became her buffer, her equalizer... her best friend.

Curtis took over her account when his father retired in 1987, but Herb remained available for Ruth's personal counseling until he had a stroke and died December 9, 1991.

The loss of her old friend devastated Mrs. Jackman, who was now in failing health and suffering greatly with arthritis. She died the following month.

Now, what may surprise you as much as it did me, is the fact that, in addition to the $9 million she left Proctor, Mrs. Jackman also left more than a half-million dollars to many other local institutions.

She left $100,000 each to St. Francis and Methodist medical centers, St. Augustine Manor and Bradley University; $50,000 to the Children's Home; and

Haag washing machines were still being manufactured in March, 1940, shortly before the plant was sold to Caterpillar.
(Photo courtesy of the Peoria Public Library)

$10,000 each to the American Heart Association, the local Easter Seals program, St. Jude's Mid-West Affiliate, First United Methodist Church, the Peoria Association for Retarded Citizens, South Side Mission and Youth Farm.

But why did this very wealthy lady leave most of her estate to Proctor Hospital? No one is sure, including the hospital.

Her parents had been significant Proctor contributers in the past. She had been in and out of Proctor several times

RUTH HAAG - an early photo of the beautiful young daughter of Mr. & Mrs. George Haag of the Haag Brothers washing machine company.
(Photo courtesy of Curtis White)

during her later years, but she always paid for her hospital care with no special considerations. She did indicate to several people, however, that she was very grateful for the very special care she received at Proctor over the years.

Ruth Haag Jackman... one of the last remaining heirs of one of our town's many interesting old manufacturing firms

...and it seems like only yesterday!

Pabst celebration one of area's biggest

For quite some time now, much of the Pabst Brewery in Peoria Heights has slowly succumbed to the shuddering force of the wrecking ball. Happily, however, the main administration building has been preserved.

And while passing this landmark in my car the other day, it occurred to me it couldn't have been all that many years ago that this building, along with a new modern brewhouse, had been built. Actually, it was dedicated in 1949, and it turned out to be one of our biggest local events, ever.

Radio was at its peak at the time, just before TV made its big impact on broadcasting. And one of its biggest stars was Eddie Cantor, whose popular NBC radio show was being sponsored by Pabst Blue Ribbon Beer.

The brewery pulled out all the stops to publicize its newest brewery, by bringing Cantor and his entire radio show to Peoria for a full week's celebration.

Cantor and his Hollywood crew stepped off the Santa Fe Super Chief in Chillicothe at 11:45 a.m. Monday, March 21, 1949, and were greeted by hundreds of fans who turned out to meet their train.

With Cantor were movie and radio star Mitzi Green, who would be a guest on his show that week, along with Bert Gordon who was "The Mad Russian" on the show, Pabst Blue Ribbon announcer Harry Von Zell and Cookie Fairchild and his orchestra.

As it turned out, the effervescent Cantor was probably the busiest star to ever visit our town. At 1 p.m. that first day of a week designated "Blue Ribbon Week," he joined Illinois governor Adlai Stevenson for a dedication luncheon at the new Pabst Blue Ribbon Hall, followed by the dedication ceremony at 2:30, with the governor cutting the blue ribbon (the traditional red ribbon was changed to blue for obvious reasons). Cantor assisted, as did Peoria mayor Carl O. Triebel and Peoria Heights mayor, Guy Yates.

In his opening statement, Stevenson said, "We are witnessing an agricultural and industrial marriage at its best." He was referring to the making of beer here in Illinois, using grain that was also grown here.

The second day (Tuesday), leading scientists and chemists of the Peoria area were invited to inspect the new plant, and WEEK-Radio's general manager, Fred Mueller, hosted a luncheon for Eddie Cantor and his cast at the Creve Coeur Club, where the radio star received a special citation for his services to the radio industry.

After the luncheon, he bounced down the stairs of the Hotel Pere Marquette to sign autographs, and also used the occasion to give Coach Fordie Anderson of Bradley's Braves a little tip. He suggested that he (Cantor) would be a great running mate for Squeaky Melchiorre during the next basketball season, indicating that Melchiorre would have to really move to keep up with him.

Each day was filled with appearances and luncheons by the Hollywood star, one of which was a talk at the Lions Club luncheon at the Pere Marquette, where he spoke on Americanism.

Wednesday night was the first of three in which Cantor presented a two-hour show to 4,500 people at the Peoria Armory. These shows included warmups for his Friday night radio program, which would be broadcast direct from the Armory over the NBC network, via WEEK-Radio.

At the Thursday night show, former congressman Everett M. Dirksen presented Cantor with a plaque from 14 Peoria and Peoria Heights service organizations for his fine work in the entertainment field in peace as well as in war.

Visibly touched, Cantor thanked the veterans for the scroll, but modestly pointed out that his success was just an example of how one of humble begin-

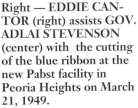

Left — A 1938 photo of Eddie Cantor with one of his show's most famous characters, Bert Gordon as the "Mad Russian." (A CBS photo)

Right — EDDIE CANTOR (right) assists GOV. ADLAI STEVENSON (center) with the cutting of the blue ribbon at the new Pabst facility in Peoria Heights on March 21, 1949. (A *Journal* staff photo courtesy of the Peoria Public Library)

nings may become somebody "in this, the most wonderful country in the world, the United States."

Eddie Cantor (real name Edward Israel Iskowitz) was born January 31, 1892, in New York City's East Side, to Russian parents who died when he was a toddler. He was raised by a grandmother but quit school at an early age. He sang for change on street corners and eventually got a job as a singing waiter in a Coney Island beer garden where Jimmy Durante played piano.

He later played in vaudeville, where he did an act in blackface, which became his trademark until Chase & Sanborn made him a radio star. He also played with a group of juveniles with Gus Edwards, which included Walter Winchell, George Jessel and Bert Gordon. (Gordon later took the part of the "Mad Russian" on his radio show.) Cantor then became a Ziegfeld Follies star and embarked on a movie career.

But his biggest success was in radio. Cantor's first radio show was on Sunday nights, but he was later heard on various nights of the week. He was on Wednesday nights in 1946 when he started with Pabst Blue Ribbon. He then moved to Thursday nights from 1946 to '48. The show was moved to Friday night in the 1948-49 season, which is where it was when he came to Peoria to dedicate the new brewery.

And do you remember his closing theme song? "I love to spend each Friday with you. As friend to friend, I'm sorry it's through. I'm telling you, just how I feel. I hope you feel that way, too."

Well, after a full five days and nights of celebrating the opening of the new Pabst plant, the entire Peoria area must have felt that way about the one and only Eddie Cantor. It was truly a "Blue Ribbon Week" in our town back in March 1949

...but it seems like only yesterday!

Harry Von Zell was a radio great

Last Monday I mentioned Harry Von Zell as the announcer on Eddie Cantor's Pabst Blue Ribbon Beer radio program when it visited our town back in 1949.

It brought back a flood of memories to me of all the great radio announcers who were not only accomplished actors and comedians but handled the commercials on many of those old programs, as well. Von Zell was one of the best, and he became almost as popular as the stars he worked with.

He, and a handful of others, were so good they not only did the announcing but also became characters on the programs.

One was a former Peorian I've written about before, Ken Carpenter. Carpenter not only handled the commercial duties on Bing Crosby's "Kraft Music Hall" and, later, "Philco Radio Time," his talent also allowed him to become Bing's "second banana" on the show. He became one of the better ad-libbers, which complimented Crosby's casual style on the show.

Harlow Wilcox did the same thing for two other former Peorians, Jim and Marian Jordan on their "Fibber McGee and Molly" program. Wilcox became so synonymous with the show's sponsor, Johnson's Wax, he became one of the regular characters that visited 79 Wistful Vista each Tuesday night. So much so that Fibber even nicknamed him "Waxy."

The great Jack Benny had his second banana, too, and a large one he was - Don Wilson. Wilson also made the transition with Benny with more than one sponsor. He became so closely related with Jell-O and, later, Lucky Strike cigarettes, that listeners knew the product as soon as they heard his voice.

But the one who probably developed his talent in acting and comedy the most was that same Harry Von Zell who visited us when the Eddie Cantor show came here to dedicate Pabst's new administration building and brew house in Peoria Heights on March 21, 1949.

While he was here, Von Zell did an interview for the *Peoria Journal*, and he recalled how he got his start during radio's infancy. The stocky, slick-haired announcer and comedian had an infectious giggle and his spontaneous witticisms never failed to add to the humor of the show.

He recalled that, as far back as he could remember, he wanted to get into the entertainment business as an actor and comedian. But vaudeville was going on the rocks at the time and he wasn't able to crack the movies, so he decided to try the only field open at the moment, radio.

He recalled, "It was no trick to get on the air in those days. If you could play a tune on a hairpin, you were in. Anybody could do it."

He landed a job as a part-time announcer and entertainer on KMIC, a small radio station in Inglewood, California. As was often the case then, he first worked this job while holding down another on a railroad.

Von Zell gradually worked his way up in radio. On September 2, 1931, he had the honor of introducing Bing Crosby on that crooners first nationwide radio show, "Fifteen Minutes with Bing Crosby." (I have a tape of this first program.) He also became the "voice of time" on radio's "The March of Time" in the early 1930s.

He left this show when Fred Allen gave him a chance to fill in for his regular announcer, Allen Reed, who was loaned out temporarily for a road show playing in Boston.

Von Zell grasped the temporary opportunity on a comedy show, even though he had become closely related to "The March of Time" program. He became so well-liked on the Allen show that he was asked to stay as his full-time announcer.

Harry Von Zell, one of old radio's top announcers and comedians.
(An NBC photo)

Don Wilson as one of Jack Benny's gang. (Left to right) Eddie "Rochester" Anderson, Dennis Day, Phil Harris, Mary Livingstone, Jack Benny, Wilson, and Mel Blanc.
(An NBC photo)

"The March of Time" executives held long conferences over releasing him from his contract, but a substitute was finally found, and Von Zell went to his first love, comedy.

Fred Allen gave Von Zell his first opportunity to expand as an actor and experience in the art of ad-libbing, which was a strong point of Allen's radio humor.

This all boded well for Von Zell, who blossomed as a comedy actor when he joined the Eddie Cantor show. (Cantor actually took over the old CBS spot formerly held by Allen and Von Zell came along with it.)

In addition to handling the announcing chores, he also became Cantor's chief foil on the show.

"Then I got the chance to do everything, from playing the part of a wardrobe trunk (anything was possible on radio) to that of a little boy in long pants. Eddie made me much more a part of the show."

This led to other fields that Von Zell had his eye on for a long time, namely the stage and motion pictures.

All this experience helped Von Zell do the same thing for George Burns and Gracie Allen, not only on their radio pro-

gram, but also later, on their television show. He can sometimes still be seen on cable reruns as their "bumbling friend" on the TV show, which aired from 1951 to 1958.

When Gracie retired from show business, George continued the TV series from October 1958 to April 1959, keeping on the one and only Harry Von Zell

...and it seems like only yesterday!

Madison shows the McCaddon touch

While researching some recent stories on the Pabst administration building, I ran across a name of the contractor that did all its plasterwork: H. B. McCaddon and Son.

It rang a bell because a few weeks ago Nanette Meals wrote to me about this same firm. She informed me that the firm was also responsible for all the beautiful ornamental plasterwork in the Madison Theater.

Mrs. Meals' grandfather was Fred McCaddon (the "son" in the firm) and when she was a young girl he told her many fascinating stories, especially about the Madison project.

Ever since I managed the Madison in the 1940s and '50s, I've often wondered who did all the sculpting of its beautiful decorative artwork and especially the "dancing lady" that is still the symbol of that beautiful old theater.

Her great-grandfather, Horace B. McCaddon, was born on August 14, 1851, in Livermore, Pa. As a young man he became acquainted with Mary P. Bruce of Cumberland, Maryland, and they were married February 7, 1877 in Pittsburgh. They had six boys and a girl, but twin boys died in infancy and another son died in 1920.

After learning the plastering trade in Pittsburgh, Horace McCaddon went to St. Louis in 1875 and the following year came to Peoria by boat. He came here to work on the Peoria County Courthouse - the structure before the present courthouse - which was then being built. He worked at his trade for $1.80 a day; then in 1877 he took over the contracting firm, Stillwell Brothers, for which he previously had worked.

His first contract was a house on South Glen Oak, owned by an attorney, Nick Ulrich. His firm's first lime yard was between Main and Hamilton, where Globe Street later would be formed, and its water supply came from an old sulfur well on what later became Glen Oak Avenue.

With the opening of Globe Street, the lime yard was moved to the 800 block of Main. Still later, it was on the former site of the Inglaterra Ballroom, where Methodist Medical Center's Atrium Building now stands.

McCaddon built the family home at 333 N. Elizabeth (now N. Sheridan) in 1882. It still stands at the corner of Sheridan and Columbia Terrace.

H. B. McCaddon and Son had its offices in suite 301 of the Masonic Temple at the time the Madison was built. It had the contract for all the plain and ornamental plastering in the theater, and the first thing the firm did was to send to New York for the best and most skilled workers in ornamental plastering. These artists were brought to Peoria and were housed in a building at Main and Glendale, where they worked day and night.

At the time, Horace McCaddon stated: "I am safe in saying that this is the most artistic piece of art-workmanship ever consummated in Peoria.

"When we went into it, we did not expect that we would find it so difficult. But in a building of the nature of the Madison Theater, the work was so complicated that it went forward very slowly.

"We used 65 tons of cement in the walls and three whole carloads for the moulding and plaster-Paris relief figures.

"There are 80,000 feet of channel-iron in the domes and ceilings, and it all had to be bent to the proper shapes. We put in our hardest efforts on the proscenium arch and on the stage. Over 6,000 yards of metal lath was used to cover the form work in the entire building.

"The entire plastering contract cost more that $50,000 (which, in 1920, was about one-tenth of the entire building cost).

"The motif in the work is the famous 'Adams style' and is the first of its kind in a theater costing under two-million dollars."

Mrs. Meals knows that one of the sculptors was an H. T. Steinmetz because he did a signed bas-relief of her mother, Marjorie McCaddon, in 1920, when her mother was 16-years-old.

But one of her favorite stories was told to Mrs. Meals by her grandfather, Fred McCaddon, when she was a child.

He told her he took her grandmother to the Madison to see the wonders of the beautiful domed auditorium ceiling. He took her up on the scaffolding to the very top to get a close-up look at its intricate artwork. Going up was fine but once there, Grandma froze and wouldn't (or couldn't) come back down. She finally did come down but only after a considerable length of time and much persuasion.

The Madison and Pabst were just two of many magnificent efforts on the part of this old firm. It did hundreds of public buildings and fine residences throughout Illinois, Iowa, Michigan, Arkansas and Mississippi during its 72-year existence.

Other local buildings featuring its work include the Apollo Theater; Bartonville state hospital's 12 buildings; eight schools, including Manual Training High; six churches, including St. Mary's Cathedral; the Niagara, Fey, Harold and Majestic hotels; Proctor Home (now St. Augustine's Manor); Proctor Hospital (on

HORACE B. McCADDON - The founder of the firm that created the decorative plaster artwork in the Madison Theater.
(Photo courtesy of Nanette Meals)

Horace McCaddon's sons (left to right) Fred (Mrs. Meals' grandfather), Hartley and Frank.
(Photo courtesy of Nanette Meals)

Second Street); the Pekin Courthouse; the Peoria Star Building (downtown); St. Joseph's Home; Dime Savings & Trust Bank; the Woolner Building; Block & Kuhl's; Peoria Country Club; Masonic Temple; the old Shrine Temple; the Coliseum; the Union Depot; the old Peoria County Jail; and Holt Manufacturing Co.

I, for one, am happy to know that every one of those beautiful Madison figures, including the "dancing lady," was made right here in Peoria by Mr. H. T. Steinmetz and his fellow craftsmen

...and it seems like only yesterday I admired them, while managing the Madison Theater!

Madison show based on the legendary Fats Waller

Doing last Monday's column on the ornate plaster work in the Madison Theater reminded me that I haven't as yet gone to see "Ain't Misbehavin." It's the stage musical based on the life and music of one of my all-time favorites, Fats Waller.

December was too busy a month for me but, thanks to Jim and Josephine Comfort, the musical is being given an extended run, after a hiatus this past week, and is now scheduled to continue through the middle of February.

From all I've heard from the public and critics alike, it's an outstanding show with a great cast doing those great Fats Waller tunes... one not to be missed.

I got hooked on Fats Waller very early on. My dad was a big Waller fan and I grew up listening to his stride piano and warm, happy and sometimes wacky singing style on our old wind-up Victrola. Later, when electronic record players came along, I was old enough to collect my own records, and his were some of my first, and I still have many of them.

Thomas "Fats" Waller was born in New York City on May 21, 1904, to the Rev. Edward and Adeline (Lockett) Waller. His father was an Abyssinian Baptist minister and, at one time, he had one of the largest Protestant congregations in the country.

Waller's musical talent came from his Grandfather Waller, who was a violinist, and his mother, who sang and played the piano and organ. But his father thought jazz was "music from the devil's workshop" and wanted him to become a minister.

By the time he was ten, Waller was playing piano and organ at student concerts and playing the organ at his father's church. He was also playing in his grade and later, high school orchestras, where he said he "had a mind full of music."

While attending DeWitt Clinton high in 1918, he was asked to play the big Wurlitzer grand organ at New York's Lincoln Theater, which he recalled as one of the biggest thrills of his life. He was later called back to become the theater's regular organist at $23.00 a week, and he dropped out of school.

It was about this time that he met the dean of Harlem piano players, James P. Johnson, who taught him ragtime and piano style in general. The following year, while in Boston as a pianist for a vaudeville act, he wrote his first tune called "Boston Blues." After he changed the title to "Squeeze Me," it became a well-known jazz piece.

Under Johnson's teaching in the 1920s, Waller became one of the most prominent pianists in Harlem, playing at parlor socials (known as "rent parties"), and also in cabarets, night clubs and vaudeville. It was there he met many of the nation's outstanding composers, including Irving Berlin and George Gershwin.

Also during this time, he cut his first piano rolls for player pianos for the QRS company for $100 per roll. A short time later he made his first records as accompanist for Sara Martin. He also recorded with Clara and Bessie Smith and toured in vaudeville with Bessie in 1926, the same year he married Anita Priscilla Rutherford.

Waller returned to the Lincoln Theater in 1927, but this time with his own band. In 1928, he was writing show music and with his teacher, Johnson, he composed "Keep Shufflin'." For a long time he collaborated with lyricist Andy Razaf, who became a close personal friend.

In 1929, Fats did the score for the "Hot Chocolates" stage revue, which featured his biggest hit, and the name of the current show at the Madison, "Ain't Misbehavin'." In the late '20s and early '30s, he also wrote "Honeysuckle Rose," "Keepin' Out of Mischief Now" and "I've Got a Feelin' I'm Fallin." Waller toured Europe in 1932 and appeared at London's Kit Kat Club and Paris' Moulin Rouge.

In 1933, he was broadcasting a program over WLW in Cincinnati and was later heard over New York's WABC and the Columbia radio network. He also played with other groups, sometimes under his own name and other times under the pseudonym, "Maurice," the name of his second of two sons. In 1935, he appeared in two Hollywood movies, "Hooray For Love" with Ann Sothern, Gene Raymond, Bill Robinson, and "King of Burlesque" with Warner Baxter, Jack Oakie and Alice Faye.

Fats Waller had a nasal baritone voice and he sang with an exuberant "jive" patter. He could play serious piano with a band, but he's best remembered for his light comedic vocals and a driving piano style with his small band that made him a favorite on into the early 1940s.

In the summer of 1938, he made a second European tour, drawing record crowds. He was even held over for a second week at London's Palladium. He also probably became the only jazz musician to ever play the organ at Notre Dame Cathedral in Paris. The following year he again toured Scotland and England.

THOMAS "FATS" WALLER (front center) starred in Frank Sebastian's New Cotton Club Revue.
(Photo from the book, "*Big Band Jazz*")

Fats earned his nickname. At 5 feet, 11 inches tall, he weighed around 300 pounds and was often billed as a "girthful of blues."

In 1943, Waller did his war-time bit for Uncle Sam by appearing at service camps around the country. He was ill when his train left Los Angeles near the end of the year, and when the train arrived in Kansas City on December 15, he had already died of pneumonia.

But some of my favorite records of this great entertainer's many hits are, "Two Sleepy People," "I'm Gonna' Sit Right Down and Write Myself a Letter,"

"It's a Sin to Tell a Lie," "Hold Tight," "Your Feet's Too Big," "By the Light of the Silvery Moon," "Handful of Keys," and of course, "Ain't Misbehavin'" and "Honeysuckle Rose."

Well, now I've done it! With memories of all those great Waller hits running through my head, I've got to find the time to go see the Madison Dinner Theater's version of the show

...it seems like only yesterday I was spinning his old 78s on our old Victrola!

Eckwood Park's name has history

Former mayor, public works commissioner had impact on area

Have you ever wondered about the name Eckwood Park?

I'm referring to that river front area at the foot of Main Street we now know as The Boat Works. It's still park-like in a sense, although much of the area is now parking space for those who come to gamble on the Par-A-Dice or to eat at the River Station.

The name was fashioned from the first syllables of the names of two men who served in our town's government many years ago. It received its original improvement as a park in 1912 and was named in honor of Sherman W. Eckley, Peoria's commissioner of public works and Peoria mayor, E. N. Woodruff, hence the name Eck-Wood.

In August of that year, the park was the site of the Peoria Water Festival which included sail boat, motor boat, rowing and swimming races. But the park wasn't formally dedicated until June 1915, on the same day the eight-foot waterway bill was ratified, and the steamer "Peoria," of the Eagle Packet Co. was christened.

The park was earlier known as Levee Park and contained about ten acres which was redeveloped at a cost of $100,000. It had an amphitheater located near the foot of Hamilton Street, which was used during the various water races and such.

By the 1950s, Eckwood Park was allowed to deteriorate to a low state of decay, becoming the city's most prominent eyesore and a haven for derelicts and winos, who slept on its broken down benches.

Its original trees, shrubs and flower beds had long-since disappeared and in their place were broken bottles, trash, and a tangle of untended grass and weeds. A once artistic drinking fountain in the center of the park had fallen into a pile of rubble. About the only original thing remaining was a bronze plaque installed in 1912.

In 1957, Peoria city fathers began a plan to clean up and dress up the area for a new Eckwood Park that would give travelers arriving at the Rock Island Station a much more favorable first impression. The parking area was increased from 300 to 526 spaces. Additional area was gained by erecting a seawall of steel pilings about 45 feet out from the old shoreline. They filled the area with dirt from the right-of-way of the new Illini expressway and the Murray Baker Bridge.

But what about the men for whom the park was named?

Sherman W. Eckley was born in Peoria in 1866. His father was a senior partner of Eckley & McKinzie building contractors. After leaving Peoria High School, Sherman went to Cole's Business College and then became a brick contractor. After 15 years of that, he operated a jewelry business at 1305 S. Adams Street. He had also attended the Horological School of Peoria.

Eckley became well known in Republican political circles and his knowledge of bricklaying secured him the job of sewer inspector under mayor Woodruff. After later being named commissioner of public works, a great amount of street work was done under his direction, including the asphalt paving of Harrison, Madison and Perry streets and he did more to beautify and clean Peoria than any of his predecessors. Bridges were also under his care and he was deeply involved with the development of Eckwood Park.

Edward Nelson Woodruff went by his initials, E. N. but he was also nicknamed "The Little Napoleon." He was born in the family home at the corner of Pecan and S. Washington streets on February 8, 1862. His father, Nelson Woodruff, built the first canal boat used on the Illinois River between Peoria and Chicago and he operated the river boat, "Fort Clark," until 1855. He then established an ice business in Peoria, which stayed in the family for 70 years.

One of seven children, Ed went to Peoria grade schools and attended Peoria High for three years. When he was 14, his parents moved into a new home at 1025 N. Jefferson and after he married, he built another home across the street. After his father's death he spent a year on a New Mexico cattle ranch, but returned here to learn every phase of the ice business.

His political career began as an alderman in 1899. After two terms, he ran for mayor on the Republican ticket in 1903 and served a one-year term. He threw his hat in the ring again for mayor in 1907 but didn't win the nomination. But in 1909 he was again elected mayor and remained in office for 11 consecutive years. He failed to receive the nomination again in 1921, but that didn't stop him. Altogether he served 16 terms as mayor.

Over the years, Woodruff became a skillful politician and much of his strategy was done during leisure hours up the river near South Rome. He converted the hull of an old river boat into a friendly rendezvous for his close political cronies and renamed it "Bum Boat."

It should also be noted that Woodruff High School was named in his honor in 1937.

Woodruff was mayor during Peoria's wide-open days of gambling and vice, the

SHERMAN W. ECKLEY - Former Peoria commissioner of public works and one of the two men for whom Eckwood Park was named.
(From *"Peoria of To-Day"*, 1915, Peoria Public Library)

Mayor E. N. Woodruff (right) enjoying a day in the sun at South Rome with some of his cronies.
(Photo courtesy of Peoria Public Library)

profits of which were shared by the city. In fairness to him, however, the money went into the city treasury and not for any personal gain. Woodruff was almost 83 when he turned over the mayor's gavel to Carl O. Triebel, who became known as the "reform mayor," on May 2, 1945. Woodruff died two years later.

And it seems like only yesterday that The Boat Works was prominently known as Eckwood Park!

She more than held her own

Riverboat namesake experienced horrors of Civil War first-hand

The recent news that plans are in the works to save the Spirit of Peoria riverboat for the Peoria side of the river once the Par-A-Dice begins docking in East Peoria, is good news for all of us.

I've always believed that many of our local citizens would prefer an old-fashioned excursion on the Illinois River, and maybe a lunch or dinner, to a roll of the dice. Now we can have the best of both worlds, and with a little creativity, various activities on the Spirit could bring added traffic and revenue to our riverfront.

What was Levee Park, then Eckwood Park, and now The Boat Works, has always been one of the more romantic aspects of our river heritage. We became so accustomed to the Julia Belle Swain and the Spirit of Peoria, it would be a shame if plans for a Peoria boat should be scuttled simply because you can't play a slot machine on it.

This all bodes well for not only saving the Spirit, but its floating support vessels, the Katie Hooper and Belle Reynolds, as well. Under Jim Jumer's operation, the Hooper had been a restaurant while the Reynolds housed the Peoria Historical Society's riverfront museum.

It's interesting to note that Jumer had this latter boat renamed the Belle Reynolds in honor of a woman who lived in Peoria (when not with her husband on Civil War battlefields) between 1860 and 1864. It's most appropriate, too, since this Peorian was a true hero in that war between the states.

Arabella "Belle" L. Macomber was born in Shelburne Falls, Mass. on October 20, 1840. Among the Macomber family's friends was Harriet Beecher Stowe, the author of the book, "Uncle Tom's Cabin." Shelburne Falls was also a station on the Underground Railroad and Belle's sympathies were strongly abolitionist.

When she was 14 years old, Belle's family moved to Iowa and a few years later, Belle taught in the first school to be established in Cass County, Iowa. She later married William S. Reynolds on April 19, 1860, and they moved to Peoria where Mr. Reynolds became a clerk in a store at 97 Main St.

While they were in church on their first anniversary, a messenger brought the delayed news of an attack on Fort Sumter.

William immediately enlisted in the 17th Illinois Regiment with the rank of lieutenant. Belle was determined to join him (as many women did during that war), so she joined him at his camp at Bird's Point, Missouri, and remained with him until his enlistment expired in 1864. She cared for the wounded in many of the regiment's battles.

Belle was there when the Union Army won skirmishes at Frederickstown, Mo., taking possession of Cape Girardeau. She also shared in the horror of the battle of Shilo at Pittsburgh Landing, Tennessee, where Grant's plan for a quick Union victory in the West was thwarted by the Confederates.

She was cooking pancakes for her husband's breakfast on April 17, 1862, when she and a lady companion heard musket sounds in the distance.

Later, she related: "We were startled by cannon balls howling over our heads. Knowing my husband must go, I kept my place before the fire, that he might have his breakfast before leaving; but there was no time for eating, and shells were flying faster, and musketry coming nearer, compelling me involuntarily to dodge as the missiles shrieked through the air, I still fried my cakes."

Tents were torn to shreds and they could see Confederate soldiers coming over the hill. A wagon master told them to run for their lives. They grabbed their baskets and bonnets and fled camp, she said.

The thunder of artillery was deafening and the air seemed filled with leaden hail. Union soldiers were half-crazed with panic, all rushing toward the boats for safety, she remembered.

"The rebels now occupied all the camps of the Federal army, and the alternative to perish beneath the waves of the Tennessee (River), or surrender to the exultant foe was before them," she said. "Never had the fate of an army been more desperate, or its run more inevitable... Many attempted to crowd upon the hospital boats; others swam to the opposite shore."

A Union captain handed Belle a revolver at the height of the melee and ordered her to shoot any but the wounded. Just then, Union gunboats arrived and started firing on the Confederates, so she didn't have to use the gun.

Belle later wrote: "At night I lived over the horrors of the field hospital and the amputating table. If I but closed my eyes, I saw such horrible sights that I would spring from my bed; and not until fairly awakened could I be convinced of my remoteness from the sickening scene. Those groans were in my ears; I saw again the quivering limbs, the spouting arteries and the pinched and ghastly faces of the sufferers."

Belle stayed another week before accompanying some of the wounded back home to Peoria, and also receive a much needed rest herself.

Major Belle Reynolds (Photo courtesy of Peoria Public Library)

Among the passengers on the boat back was Illinois Governor Yates. Upon hearing of Belles' work in the hospitals and at Shilo, he immediately commissioned her to the rank of major, which was higher than her first lieutenant husband.

Although the position may have been only semiofficial, after spending a short time resting in Peoria, Belle Reynolds returned to join her husband during the siege at Vicksburg, which became a decisive northern victory in the war.

(Some of the information for this column was taken from the book, "The Women and the Crisis," by A. Young, and from a 1987 Journal Star article by Pam Adams.)

Benny drew thousands to BU's new field house

For several years now I've admired a photo in the hallway at the Red Carpet Car Wash on Jefferson Street that shows Jack Benny and a couple of his radio characters in a replica of his old Maxwell automobile. It was obviously taken in Peoria but I could never find when it occurred until the other day in a conversation with Bob Jamieson.

Jamieson remembered it was on "Straw Hat Day," Monday, May 22, 1950. And well he should, because he personally planned the event to bring Benny and an all-star cast of 40 entertainers to Peoria to put on the first big show (other than basketball) in the recently dedicated Robertson Memorial Field House.

Bob's now retired, but at the time he was assistant to Bradley University president Dave Owen. (Bob later became dean of Bradley's School of Business.)

The new field house was planned to seat 8,300 for this stage show-type performance - considerably more than its normal capacity - and the new "Home of the Bradley Braves" was the largest arena in town at the time.

The university wanted to show off its new pride and joy to the public, and not only as a basketball gymnasium. The administrators were searching for something special for the students and public alike, and at the same time, promote their new facility.

Jamieson came up with the idea to bring a top-notch troupe of entertainers to the hilltop, and who could fill the bill in 1950 better than Jack Benny, whose radio show was at the top of the charts, and who was currently touring the country.

By the way, Bob's father, Alex "Scotty" Jamieson, was custodian of the new field house and continued in that capacity until he dropped over in the field house with an aneurism in 1957 and died at the hospital a short time later. Scotty was much loved by the students and public alike.

Bob Jamieson put together a gala affair, hoping for a packed house of around 8,000. Making money on the event was secondary to promoting the new building. Tickets were sold at $5.00 and $3.00. Students could also sit on the basketball floor for $1.00. Part of the proceeds would benefit the Bradley Library Fund.

In covering the day's events, the *Peoria Journal* stated, "America's funniest 'tightwad' arrived at Peoria airport this afternoon with a plane-load of gold - a million dollars worth of 40 entertainers - including Rochester and Phil Harris. (Mary Livingstone, Jack's real-life wife and character on the radio show, didn't make the trip.)

"Radio's legendary Midas, Jack Benny, and the troupe will present a mammoth show at 8:45 tonight at Bradley field house after a whirl of activity in the city.

"...Recognizing Benny's thrift and his probable need for headwear, the city honored him with "Straw Hat and Thrift Day."

Benny, his valet on his show, Eddie "Rochester" Anderson, orchestra leader Phil Harris and movie actress Vivian Blaine were all part of Benny's touring show. Accompanied by Peoria Mayor Joe Malone, the group led a parade of cars from the airport to Western Avenue, up Western to Main, then down Main past the field house to a grandstand on N. Jefferson, across from the courthouse square.

At the Mitchell-Cassell auto dealership on upper Main Street, they transferred to a 1917 Maxwell (Benny's trademark) and chugged on to Courthouse Square, where more than 5,000 people were waiting.

Mayor Malone gave straw hats to Eddie Anderson and Phil Harris, and then, turning to Benny, he said: "Now here's yours, Mr. Beany," referring to Benny's balding pate. This brought a flurry of toupee gags, along with references of tight-fisted bosses, Maxwells and money vaults.

Milton Budd was master of ceremonies, and Benny took the time to com-

During the parade welcoming Jack Benny to Peoria in 1950, he picks up a 1917 Maxwell at the Mitchell-Cassell agency on Main Street. L to R: Jack Benny, Eddie "Rochester" Anderson, Peoria Mayor Joe Malone and Phil Harris.

(A Lee Roten photo courtesy of Roger Seghetti, Red Carpet Car Wash)

Robert A. "Bob" Jamieson (center) welcomes Jack Benny and Vivian Blaine to Peoria in 1950.

(Courtesy of Bob Jamieson)

mend WMBD-Radio's Chuck Barnhart for the fine job he did of preparing the show.

Given the choice of $5.00 or a key to the city, Benny, after serious consideration, chose the key, remarking, "After all, fellows, I can pass this straw hat around if things get too bad."

Benny recalled earlier performances at Peoria's old Hippodrome as a boy violinist in pre-World War I days, and he played in other Peoria theaters several times before vaudeville died.

But the big performance was the one that night that more than 8,000 people paid to see. And Benny knew how to please a Peoria audience. He caused a near-riot when he bounded out on stage in a Bradley basketball jacket.

Vivian Blaine sang three songs and entered into some funny dialogue with Benny about his sex appeal, or lack of it.

Phil Harris sparked the audience every time he came on stage. He also announced that this particular day marked his 14th anniversary on the Benny radio program. He convulsed the audience with his habit of directing the orchestra on one leg, and also sang his specialty numbers, "The Preacher and the Bear," "Darktown Poker Club," and "Is It True What They Say About Dixie?"

Rochester did a "phone" bit from backstage before walking on, to the delight of the audience. In his bit, he stated, "I'm the only man in the world who can cash his paycheck on a streetcar." Rochester also sang a couple songs and treated the crowd to some expert dancing.

The rest of the show was made up of vaudeville-type acts, including a quartet of adagio performers and an outstanding juggling act. Benny closed out the evening by leading his "Benny Band of Beverly Hillbillies" in outlandish music and costumes.

Well, Bob Jamieson's gala affair certainly did what it was intended to do... put Bradley's new Robertson Memorial Field House on the map as, not only the home of the Bradley Braves, but also as Peoria's largest entertainment center in 1950.

...and it seems like only yesterday!

Eagle's scoreboards a revolutionary idea

Last week's Yester Days column, about the early days of Bradley's Robertson Memorial Field House, brought to mind a man I worked with at the theaters for many years, and an invention of his. His name was Merle Eagle.

Many Peorians remember Merle as the manager of the Palace Theater, but he also managed other Publix Great States Theaters, as well.

He first came to Peoria to manage the Rialto Theater, which Great States had purchased back in the 1930s. Later, Eagle managed the Madison Theater, and then, in 1936, when the Palace was remodeled and Dusty Rhodes designed a new huge canopy for it, Merle became its permanent manager.

Eagle was at the Palace through those great "Bank Night" days, when all four Great States Theaters - the Madison, Palace, Rialto and Apollo - were connected by special phone lines to simultaneously hold Peoria's biggest lottery. Merle was the master of ceremonies for it for many years.

I can still hear Eagle calling over the microphone: "This is Merle Eagle at the Palace Theater calling the Madison... come in Madison." Then the Madison's manager, Bill Harding, would answer: "This is the Madison... back to you Palace."

This would be repeated for the Rialto and Apollo, and once all theaters were on the line, the winning name would be drawn from a huge drum. If that person had purchased a ticket stub at any of the four theaters that night (they didn't have to see the show), and reported to the stage within around three minutes, he or she would be the big winner.

As I recall, the pot always started at $500, and $100 was added each week there was no winner. It wasn't uncommon for the pot to swell to more than $1,000 and that was a tremendous amount of money in those post-depression days. It seemed that half of Peoria would participate in the lottery, either by sitting in one of the four theaters, or by purchasing a ticket and standing with the overflow of people outside.

I started at the Madison in 1941, and by 1943 became its manager. Eagle went into the service and I wasn't far behind. After the war, we both returned to our respective theaters. But in the early 1950s, television came to Peoria, which had a tremendous impact on the theater business. I recall many conversations with Merle about the future in the theater business (or the lack of it) and we both had a great desire to leave.

I finally did take a position at WEEK-TV but Eagle was several years older, and he stayed at the theater, perhaps because of his age.

Regardless, along the way he came up with a great idea: a new, revolutionary basketball scoreboard. I suspect that he had visions of forming a company to build his scoreboards, which might have been his way of leaving a depressed theater business.

His scoreboard was made of two electrically controlled panels, one for the home team and one for the visitors. They could be seen from either the bleacher side or theater-seat side of the field house. It listed the names of twelve players for each team and would light up the names of the five players on each team that were playing at any given time.

But it did much more than that.

Someone sitting at the control panel could change the scoreboard's tally of the number of field goals, free throws, total points and personal fouls for each player as the game progressed. This became a running record for each player during the game, much like the boxscores listed in the next day's newspaper. It was truly a revolutionary idea.

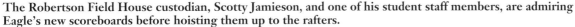

Merle Eagle, former theater manager and inventor of revolutionary basketball scoreboards for Bradley's field house.

The Robertson Field House custodian, Scotty Jamieson, and one of his student staff members, are admiring Eagle's new scoreboards before hoisting them up to the rafters.

Eagle designed and built the boards backstage at the Palace Theater, along with his stagehand, Earl Miller. They worked many months back there, building and perfecting his brainchild.

Eagle sold then-Bradley president Dave Owen on the idea of installing the boards at the new field house.

Merle told me that once his boards were in use, he was sure he'd have no problem selling them to the Missouri Valley Conference schools, and then maybe even the NCAA would sanction them. But it never happened.

The boards were quite expensive to build. To cover construction costs, Eagle sold the J. D. Roszell Dairy exclusive advertising space on each board for five years.

Flossie and I have had season tickets to Bradley games ever since they've played at the Civic Center, and as I go to the games now, I can't help but think how far ahead of his time Merle Eagle really was.

With all the new micro-chip technology today, it seems it should be possible to design a four-sided scoreboard that lists the same individual player statistics you get when you stay home and listen to the game on the radio or watch it on TV.

I, for one, can't wait to get to the car after the game and tune into Dave Snell and Joe Stowell on WMBD-Radio to hear all the stats. More times than not, I have no idea how many points were scored by each player or how they scored them, until after the game or by reading it in the the next day's sports section.

Which makes me wonder: Why hasn't someone come up with a new version of Eagle's brainchild? It would certainly add interest to the game, and might sell more tickets, too.

Anyway... it seems like only yesterday that Merle Eagle was building his revolutionary scoreboards backstage at the Palace Theater!

Promotional jar brings back memories

Readers send me so many interesting things.

Over the years I've received everything from a theater chair from the Rialto Theater, to window cards and posters advertising stage shows and movies, to a piece of wood from the stage of the Palace Theater. People also send tapes and records of radio programs, big bands, pit bands and organs, and I enjoy them all.

But the other day I received what is probably the most unique gift of all.

Jan Charlton of Chillicothe sent me a plain glass jar about five inches high. The jar itself wasn't unique, but what was imprinted on its tin lid was. It was an advertisement for a radio program printed in red and blue, which read, "Listen to... 'The Great Gildersleeve' Radio's Laugh King - Wednesday evenings - NBC - 8:30 p.m. Eastern Time - 8:30 p.m. Pacific Time (Repeat Broadcast)." It also showed a caricature of the face of Harold Peary, who originated the Gildersleeve role.

There was no label on the jar to indicate what brand or product it originally contained. But a quick search through some of my old radio reference books soon solved the mystery. It was undoubtebly a product of Kraft Foods, since that company sponsored this excellent comedy show for 13 years.

Jan Charlton's jar must date back to 1946, because that was the year the show moved from its original Sunday night slot on NBC to Wednesday nights. Kraft obviously didn't want the public to forget about the new time slot, so they advertised it on their products in every grocery store in the country.

The Peoria connection to this show, of course, is that the Throckmorton P. Gildersleeve character got its start on our own Jim and Marian Jordan's program, "Fibber McGee and Molly." And I've often wondered if the Jordans might not have had Peoria's Throckmorton Drug Store at the corner of Main and Monroe in mind, when they gave Gildersleeve his unusual first name. Say, I wonder if his middle initial "P" stands for Peoria?

Harold Peary created the role on the "Fibber McGee" show in 1937, and by 1939, Gildersleeve had become a regular character. He became so popular that by August 31, 1941, he had his own NBC show on Sunday nights, and this became the first spin-off show in broadcast history.

Peary (real name was Harrold Jose Pereira de Faria) was the son of a Portuguese immigrant and had nine years of radio experience before "Fibber McGee and Molly."

He made his radio debut with the Oakland Tribune Juveniles on January 21, 1923, on KZM and later signed a long-term contract with NBC in San Francisco. In 1928, he was on a show called "The Spanish Serenader."

Peary was very good at dialect voices and came to Chicago in 1935, which was then the hub of national radio programs.

When he joined the Jordans' show, he developed the Gildersleeve character, a blundering windbag with a soft heart. He became a perfect foil to Fibber McGee, and "Gildy" became the McGee's next door neighbor.

Two of his trademarks were his "dirty laugh" and his most famous line on the show, "You're a haaaarrd man, McGee!" He was the only one on the program who could match Fibber in the hot-air department.

Throckmorton P. Gildersleeve became "The Great Gildersleeve" in the summer of 1941, when the 42-year-old Harold Peary had his character board a train at the mythical town of Wistful Vista for a business trip to a another mythical town named Summerfield. He told his employees at the Gildersleeve Girdle Works that he'd probably be gone for about three days. The truth was, he would never return.

He became water commissioner in Summerfield and set about raising his nephew Leroy (Walter Tetley) and his niece Marjorie (originally played by Lurene Tuttle). Gildersleeve was still the same old windbag on his new show, but he also became the town's most eligible bachelor and (at least in his own mind) quite a lady's man.

Gildy's long-running feud with Fibber McGee was transferred to crusty old Judge Horace Hooker (played by Earle Ross), on the new program. Two other great characters were Mr. Peavey (Richard LeGrand), the henpecked druggist with a nasal twang, who's famous line was "Well, now, I wouldn't say that," and Birdie Lee Coggins (Lillian Randolph), Gildersleeve's cook. (She was obviously copied from McGee's maid, Beulah.) Shirley Mitchell played the conniving widow, Leila Ransom, and Bea Benaderet played Eve Goodwin, another of Gildy's several lady friends.

Arthur Q. Bryan played Floyd Munson, the barber (he later joined "Fibber McGee" as Doc Gamble) and Gale Gordon (Mayor La Trivia on the "McGee" show) played Rumson Bullard, Gildy's rich but obnoxious neighbor. By the way, Peoria's own Ken Carpenter was the show's announcer during the mid-1940s.

After the show aired for nearly ten years, Harold Peary tired of doing the role and eventually quit. Without Peary's unique Gildersleeve voice, the program

Willard Waterman (center) with Marylee Robb and Walter Tetley, took over the Gildersleeve character when Harold Peary bowed out.
(An NBC photo)

Harold Peary, who originated the role of Throckmorton P. Gildersleeve on the "Fibber McGee and Molly" radio program.
(An NBC photo)

should have ended, but a funny thing happened.

A radio actor named Willard Waterman, who had a deep voice similar to Peary's, was hired to do the Gildersleeve role. His voice inflections were so like those of Harold Peary, the radio audience couldn't tell the difference. The similarity was startling.

Peary quit the show on June 14, 1950, and Waterman took over the role on September 6, after the summer hiatus. "The Great Gildersleeve" continued on in its half-hour format until 1954, when it became a 15-minute show. Then, in 1955, it returned as a 30-minute program and ran on Thursday nights until 1958.

It was one of the last great comedy shows to air on radio.

...and it seems like only yesterday!

Amusement park was big attraction in Peoria Heights

Peoria Heights is 95 years old this year, which means that in five short years it will be celebrating its 100th anniversary.

Back in 1973, when the village celebrated its Diamond Jubilee - its 75th anniversary - this progressive village formed a commemorative booklet committee that produced a book that has become a wonderful legacy of its people, places and events of days gone by.

A couple of stories that catch my eye every time I glance through it are about Al Fresco Park, a famous amusement park that once graced the shores of the Illinois River. It was about 4 1/2 miles northeast of downtown Peoria on Illinois Route 29, commonly known as Galena Road.

Al Fresco Amusement Park was built in 1904 by a Chicago capitalist named Vernon Seaver, with backing from the old Central City Streetcar Co. (For years, a streetcar line ran all the way up to the park.)

The park was designed after a famous Chicago park named "White City." It had a huge ferris wheel that measured 65 feet from the axle to the ground, and each seat held eight people. Its giant aerial swing also had seats seating eight.

Its figure-eight roller coaster was built by the Standard Coaster Co., and several of the Woodruff brothers helped build it. Fred Woodruff operated the coaster and also had his living quarters under it.

The park also featured a merry-go-round (with brass ring), a tunnel of love and a house of mirrors. You could ride through the North Pole building, which was bedecked with icycles and effective northern light displays inside, and there was also a "Temple of Palmistry," where you could have your palm read for a nickle.

The "Japanese Garden" was a two-story beer garden that overlooked the river. The establishment was said to have been operated by a relative of the emperor of Japan. Silent movies, including those by Charley Chaplin, were shown from the second floor, and music, sometimes from just a piano or a couple fiddles, could be danced to at five cents a dance.

Later Cary Robards Orchestra played there for many years. Each night usually featured a free band concert. The 100-piece Banderosa Band, the House of David Band, and the Kiltie Band were some who performed there.

Many prominent people entertained at Al Fresco, including world heavyweight boxing champions John L. Sullivan and James J. Corbett; the great escape artist, Harry Houdini; two of the top cowboy movie stars, Tom Mix and William S. Hart; high-wire acts included the Great Calvert, and Hill the Great; and a high diver, Master Tommy, who dove 75 feet into four feet of water.

There also was an act called the "Slide for Life" in which a wire was attached to the top of the circle swing ride and stretched to a spot in the river. A man doused with kerosene was set afire; to extinguish the blaze, he slid into the river.

In an act called "Rollo the Limit," a man went down a 75-foot incline on roller skates, turned a back somersault and landed on a platform.

One of the most unusual acts back then was that of the three Cherry Sisters. They sang so badly the audience threw things at them. Sometimes, they performed behind a screen.

Buffalo Bill brought his Wild West Show here several times, and he also stored his equipment there for the winter.

A tribe of Sioux Indians camped at Al Fresco in their tepees for the season. Big

Left — The theater in Al Fresco Park featuring "2 Big Shows in One" and "10 Big Scenes."
From the Grassel file, Peoria Public Library)

Right — Part of the big "figure eight" roller coaster, just to the right of the entrance to Al Fresco Park. It was razed in the mid-1920's.
(From the Grassel file, Peoria Public Library)

excursion boats docked at Al Fresco's boat dock, including the steamer York, the David Swain, Fred Swain, Vern Swain, Julia Belle Swain, Percy Swain, and the Columbia.

Unfortunately one of the Columbia's excursions to Al Fresco turned out to be (and still is) the most tragic catastrophe in the history of inland waterway navigation in the United States.

On July 5, 1918, the South Side Social Club of Pekin planned an evening excursion on the Columbia from Pekin and Kingston Mines to Al Fresco Park; 496 people were reported to be on the trip. Near midnight, on the return trip, after an enjoyable evening at Al Fresco, the boat had just passed Peoria when it struck a submerged tree stump in the river's narrows on the Peoria side, just across from Wesley City.

Although the boat only partially sank, 87 people lost their lives in the tragic catastrophe.

Al Fresco's boat dock also rented rowboats, in which fellows could take their girls for a ride on the river. Its swimming beach sported a high diving tower and at one time had as many as 15 lifeguards.

Balloon ascentions were often made on holidays at Al Fresco. The park's season ran from Decoration Day to Labor Day, and admission was ten cents. As many as 10,000 people attended daily.

Fred C. Feyler leased the park in 1929, the year of the great depression, and the bathing beach was a popular spot until 1944, although the concessions were no longer in use.

During World War II, Feyler made an announcement that men in uniform would be admitted free. Hundreds of soldiers from Camp Ellis descended upon Al Fresco.

But since many of the local men had been drafted into the service, Feyler eventually was forced to close the park.

The land of Al Fresco Park was owned by Thomas Webb, a prominent Peoria diamond jeweler, who leased the land to the park's developer. At his death, he bequeathed the land to St. Francis Hospital.

Peoria remembers its many streetcars

The mention of streetcar service to Al Fresco Park in last Monday's column reminds me of some of the early history of Peoria's electric streetcars, as described in Paul Stringham's wonderful book, "76 Years of Peoria Street Cars."

Peoria's very first streetcar began its run in the early morning hours of January 15, 1870, when the Central City Horse Railway hitched a horse to car #1 and it left the South Street car barn. Car #2 followed a short time later, and both were loaded with people, while others followed on foot.

Our early streetcars were pulled by horses and/or mules until September 1889, when the Central Railway ran its first electric cars on North Adams Street, between the Union Depot and Central Park.

According to Stringham's chronology, there were no fewer than 21 different corporate names for various rail lines serving Peoria and surrounding villages between 1867 (when Central City Horse Railway first organized) until 1964. The list includes firms when they either organized, incorporated, changed names, or consolidated, and they all eventually consolidated into one.

Central City wasn't the only "act" in town for long. The Peoria Horse Railway followed in 1871, and the Fort Clark Horse Railway began in 1873. Over the years, several systems covering various parts of the area received franchises, either from Peoria or the other villages, and for a time, transfers were not honored from one company to another. When you changed company cars, you payed an additional fare.

Some later companies were the East Bluff Peoria Horse Railway; the Riverside Railway (which later became the Lake Side Electric Railway); the Richwoods Street Railway; and the Glen Oak & Prospect Heights line (which became the Peoria & Prospect Heights Railway).

It was September 23, 1889, when electric streetcars began here, and on November 26 of that year, the Riverside Railway Co. was organized. On January 21, 1890, Peoria County gave the new company a franchise to build a road, to be powered by motor or animal, up Galena Road (now N. Adams Street) from the Avery Planter Works to the Water Works, but no work was done.

On April 2, 1890, the Lakeside Electric Railway organized and acquired the Riverside franchise. After some delays due to problems with the Averyville Village Board, the first car ran on the line the following September. The fare, including a transfer to the Central Railway streetcars, was 7 cents. Horse cars were first run in Averyville but electric cars began regular service on February 7, 1891. This company consolidated with the Central Railway in 1895.

It wasn't until nine years later that the Central Railway would build an extension line north of the Water Works. Al Fresco Amusement Park opened in July 1904, about 3/4-mile north of the Water Works, and there were several beaches in the area, including Virginia Beach and Kelly Beach.

The company thought that, with all this recreational activity, there would be a heavy demand for service during the summer months. There were also enough permanent residents to make year around service on a limited scale seem profitable.

The route lay between Averyville and Peoria Heights. Averyville granted a franchise from the north end of the Adams Street line at Lorentz Avenue, on June 30, 1904, but Peoria Heights was reluctant to do so unless the company agreed to frequent year-around service. So, the company decided to build only to the northern limits of Averyville, about a half-mile north of Lorentz.

Grading started August 22. Galena Road was very narrow and squeezed between the Rock Island Railroad and the steep bluff. Workers had to dig away huge amounts of earth to provide two lanes of team traffic and track.

The Peoria Heights Village Board finally gave in and granted a franchise from the Averyville limits to Virginia Beach (now the Ivy Club) on September 1, 1904. The first streetcars ran over the line on May 6, 1905. The following day (a Sunday) two trains, consisting of a motor car and two trailers, shuttled more than 10,000 people back and forth.

At the time, passengers had to transfer to and from Adams Street cars at Lorentz Avenue. It wasn't until May 1909 that the Adams Street line would run all the way to Virginia Beach without transferring passengers. That was when a new loop of track was installed at the line's end. The loop ran around a tavern across from Virginia Beach.

Paul Stringham recalls that his father was a motorman on this line. He remembers his dad telling stories of watching

An electric streetcar pulling five former horse cars as trailers in the 800 block N. Adams, enroute to a St. Joseph's School picnic at Central Park on June 25, 1890. **(From Paul Stringham's book, "76 Years of Peoria Street Cars")**

Halley's Comet in the evenings on this run along the river in 1910.

When it first opened, Al Fresco Amusement Park wasn't as large as it later became. In Novemeber 1905 (which was after its first two seasons), the park acquired an additional five acres.

I wasn't around when Al Fresco was an amusement park, but I do recall Al Fresco Beach, which it later became. I also recall Kelly Beach in the 1930s. Our family thought that Kelly's was the cleanest beach along the river back then.

... and it seems like only yesterday!

County's first murder an interesting affair

I've written about many murders in Peoria's past, especially about the wide-open days when the Shelton Gang held reign.

Peoria County's very first murder, though, occurred shortly after the county was formed in 1825, and it had a number of interesting elements to it. The long passage of time has clouded over some of the facts but it doesn't make the incident any less significant.

The exact date of the murder is no longer available, but we do know it happened in the summer of 1825, shortly after Peoria County was established.

The county had just been approved by the Illinois General Assembly on January 13 of that year, and the accused murderer had to be imprisoned in a log hut that served as the first county jail, while waiting for Peoria County's first court to convene. At the time, the village of Peoria consisted of about 20 houses.

The accused was a Potawatomi Indian named Nomaque. He had engaged in a quarrel with a man named Pierre Landre, a "coureur de bois" (French hunter and trader) from the French settlements to the north. During the fray, Landre was fatally shot.

It was indicated that the two men had been drinking together and that Nomaque became so drunk he was unable to flee. He was subsequently thrown in jail, where he stayed until November 14, the day the county's first court was organized. On that same day, Nomaque was indicted, along with four other prisoners.

Two days later, he went to trial before Judge John York Sawyer.

John Turney was the prosecuting attorney and William S. Hamilton - the son of the first U.S. Treasury secretary, Alexander Hamilton, and also the man who first surveyed the site of Peoria - was counsel for the defense. Peoria County's first sheriff, Samuel Fulton - the brother of two Peoria founders, Josiah and Seth Fulton - also performed his new duties as sheriff.

It's generally thought that Hamilton agreed to defend Nomaque in a desire to see that the Indian received a fair trial, because public sentiment was greatly against him. After he was seized, he was manhandled by the whites and was forced to run the gauntlet. The Indian was also severely beaten in the process.

There is some conjecture as to why Hamilton was in Peoria at the time. Did he come here for the sole purpose of surveying the town, or was there another reason?

It's been reported that a penciled note in the margin of an old circuit court record states that the young lawyer/surveyor was pursuing Aaron Burr, the man who had killed his father in a duel. It goes on to say that, in the interim of this trial, he went down river to St. Louis, where he found Burr, accosted him in the street, and publically challenged him to a duel but was refused.

Although Nomaque's trial was brief, it did seem to be rather lively. Two fines for contempt of court were levied against Hamilton, and another one against a justice of the peace named John L. Bogardus.

Hamilton attempted to get Nomaque off on the grounds of a treaty between the whites and Indians which stated that Indians should be judged before their own tribal court. He was overruled. He was also prevented from introducing an almanac, which he hoped would discredit the identification of some state witnesses.

On November 19, three days after the trial began, the jury returned a verdict of guilty and prescribed the death penalty. The case was appealed to the Supreme Court and in December 1825, the judgement was reversed and remanded.

The next court session wasn't until October 1826 and, at this time, a second attempt was made to try Nomaque. Counsel for the defendant claimed this proceeding out of order on the grounds it would constitute double jeopardy. After much argument, the court bundled up the whole case and sent it back to the Supreme Court for clarification.

A decision wouldn't come down again until sometime in 1827, which meant that Nomaque would have to stay in jail until then. So, a short time later, Nomaque disappeared. Peoria County had little tax revenue in those early days and was hard pressed to feed prisoners, so there was little said about his vanishing.

There are three versions of how he disappeared. One was that he made good his escape with the assistance of Indians from his own tribe. Another was that the county set him free with orders to leave Peoria under the threat of a retrial.

But the most probable version was that a group of citizens decided that the county was spending too much money on his keep, so they took the law into their own hands by setting Nomaque free. It's

said that, after he started to run, they tried to shoot him for escaping but by this time they were so full of liquor, they couldn't hit the broad side of a barn, much less a fleet-footed Indian, so Nomaque escaped into the dark.

Whatever the case, Nomaque surely didn't die then, because some Peorians later recognized his body following one of the battles of the Blackhawk War.

In May 1827, the grand jury returned an indictment against Sheriff Fulton for misconduct for permitting his prisoner to escape.

The charges were dropped, however, when it became apparent the court was at fault for failing to issue the necessary papers authorizing Sheriff Fulton to hold the prisoner for the pending trial in the first place.

Well, as I've said before, there have been many unsolved murders in Peoria's checkered past, but none more unique than its very first one!

WILLIAM STEPHEN HAMILTON, the surveyor who laid out Peoria's first streets, and also the defense attorney for Peoria County's first murder trial, in 1825. **(Photo courtesy of the Peoria Public Library)**

WEEK-TV: Spending 40 years on the air

It seems like only yesterday, but it really was 40 years ago that WEEK-TV, then Channel 43, went on the air, bringing local television to Central Illinois for the very first time. The station's signal first hit the region's airwaves on February 1, 1953.

In addition to Bob Arthur's newscasts, Bill Houlihan's weather and Chick Hearn's sports, the NBC affiliate could also pick and choose prime time programs from all the networks, because it was the area's only TV outlet.

In those "black and white" days, the station had no video connection with the networks, so their programs were shipped in for delayed broadcasting. This was also long before videotape was developed. Programs were transferred to film via a process called kinescope.

For the sake of nostalgia, lets take a closer look at that first week's prime-time programs:

Sunday, February 1, 1953 "Stagecoach" was the 1939 movie that propelled John Wayne to stardom. Directed by John Ford, it also starred Claire Trevor, Thomas Mitchell (who won an Oscar for his role as the drunken doctor), Andy Divine, George Bancroft, John Carradine, Donald Meek and Tim Holt.

"The Adventures of Ellery Queen." At this time Lee Bowman played Ellery Queen and Florenz Ames took the part of his father, Inspector Queen.

"The Pretender," a 1947 movie starring Albert Dekker and Catherine Craig.

Monday, February 2: "What's My Name?" (also known as the "Paul Winchell-Jerry Mahoney Show"). Ventriloquist Winchell and dummy, Mahoney, starred in this variety series. It ran on NBC from 1950 to 1954.

"I Love Lucy" This classic sitcom aired from 1951 to 1961 on CBS.

"Robert Montgomery Presents," followed by "Douglas Fairbanks Presents" (this was Doug Fairbanks Jr.). Both were dramatic anthology programs with these stars introducing each telecast of their respective show. They would frequently appear in the shows as well.

Tuesday, February 3: "Texaco Star Theater" starred Milton Berle, who became known as "Mr. Television." It's said his wacky performances sold more TV sets than any advertising campaign. People bought early TV sets just to see this crazy comedian, because everyone was talking about him.

"Life is Worth Living" hosted by Bishop Fulton J. Sheen. This weekly half-hour religious talk show featuring a charming well-spoken Catholic Bishop (formerly from Peoria), who offered sermons in the form of anecdotes and little lessons in morality. He spelled out his main points by drawing and writing on a blackboard. Many of his talks revolved around the evils of world communism. His show became so popular that he once beat Milton Berle in the ratings.

"Two for the Money" with Herb Shriner as master of ceremonies. This was a quiz show, not unlike "You Bet Your Life," and was designed as a showcase for Shriner's homespun humor.

"Club Embassy" was a 15-minute variety show that originally starred Bob and Ray. But by 1953, it featured singer Mindy Carson and the emphasis changed from comedy to music. Miss Carson was backed by the Embassy Quartet and dancer Danny Hoctor.

Wednesday, February 4: The musical variety show, "Kraft Music Hall," and an action-adventure series, "Dangerous Assignment."

Thursday, February 5: "You Bet Your Life," starring Groucho Marx fol-

BOB ARTHUR, WEEK-TV's first news director, checks out the lighting on the news set at what was, then, Channel 43.

MILTON BERLE became "Mr. Television" on NBC's Texaco Star Theater back in the early 1950s.

lowed by the western adventure series, "Cisco Kid."

"Dragnet," starring Jack Webb as Joe Friday, but at this time, his sidekick was Officer Frank Smith, played by Ben Alexander.

"My Little Margie" a sitcom starring Gale Storm, with Charles Farrell as her father.

Friday, February 6: "The Dennis Day Show." Day played himself, a singer whose mother felt he was underpaid on the Jack Benny radio program.

"March of Time" copied after the movie featurettes and an earlier radio program.

"Big Story," a long-running documentary-drama series on NBC, was based on actual case histories of reporters who solved crimes. The narrator in 1953 was Bob Sloane.

"Old American Barn Dance," a Dumont network series of country music, featured various country stars including Pee Wee King, Tennessee Ernie Ford and others.

Saturday, February 7: "Big Top," a full-hour CBS-TV show of live circus acts. The ringmaster was Jack Sterling (formerly known as Jack Sexton of WMBD-radio), with Ed McMahon (of "Tonight Show" fame) and Chris Keegan as circus clowns.

"My Hero," a sitcom starring Robert Cummings with Julie Bishop and John Litel.

"Your Show of Shows," a 90-minute major comedy variety show starring Sid Caesar, Imogene Coca and Carl Reiner.

"Wrestling," a popular form of professional wrestling that appeared at one time or other on all four networks. One of its stars was Gorgeous George.

"Your Hit Parade" was the TV version of radio's popular "Lucky Strike Hit Parade." In 1953, it starred Snooky Lanson, Dorothy Collins, June Valli, Russell Arms and Gisele MacKenzie, with Raymond Scott's Orchestra.

Well, that's what prime time was like just 40 years ago, when WEEK-TV, Channel 43, first brought television to Central Illinois.

Flanagan House home to Peoria's history

Peoria is fortunate to have, not one, but two mid-19th century homes that have been preserved for all of us to enjoy. The Peoria Historical Society assumed both properties in the 1960s.

One is Flanagan House (circa 1840), at 942 N. E. Glen Oak, and the other is the Pettengill-Morron House (built in 1868), at 1212 West Moss Avenue, which I'll discuss in next week's column. A visit to either will immediately transport you back into the Peoria of 100 to 150 years ago.

John C. Flanagan built Flanagan House, at what was then 912 Bluff Street, sometime after he purchased the land in 1836. The wealthy lawyer from Philadelphia moved here with his widowed mother, two sisters and a brother. After Flanagan died on June 4, 1891, his relatives continued living in the house until 1901 or 1902.

His niece, Louise Williamson, then sold it to Joseph F. Vincent and Joseph F. Faber. A year later, Vincent sold his interest to Faber, who eventually sold the house to Benjamin C. Koch in 1917. Koch lived in the Flanagan House a year before selling it to Fred and Emily Faber,

the son and daughter-in-law of the previous owner, Joseph Faber.

In 1919, the Fabers sold to Lena B. Gray, who lived there until 1923, when she sold it to the Dr. Frank G. Morrill family. The doctor and his wife, Mabel Nortrup Morrill had a son, Scott. This family retained possession until 1962, when the Peoria Historical Society bought the house.

Flanagan House was placed on the National Register of Historic Sites in 1975, and now serves as the headquarters and museum for the Peoria Historical Society and also the chapter house for the Peoria Chapter of the Daughters of the American Revolution.

Its original state was typical of the late Federal-style house. The first- and second-story rooms are symmetrically organized around a central hall. The staircase is the main focus inside and is the first thing a person sees when entering the front entrance, which is on the river side. (The rear of the house actually faces Glen Oak Avenue.)

Originally, there was a low wing on the north side, which was later replaced by a similar wing with a higher roof. The

original porches were smaller than the present ones, and were predominated by columns, instead of the iron work that was added later. The large, evenly spaced windows with heavy lintels are also typical of the Federal-style house.

Many changes were made by various owners, ranging from the installation of electricity, to the addition of larger front and back porches. The iron work was made in the United States and may have been installed as early as the 1850s. The front and back dormer windows, as well as woodwork underneath the roof, were also added later.

Inside, most of the original doors, baseboards and door, window and ceiling molding, remain intact. The original floor still lies under the modern hard-wood floor throughout most of the house.

The original fireplaces remain in two of the upstairs bedrooms and in the parlors downstairs. These parlors were originally separated by a diaphragm wall, which no longer exists. Upstairs, the two south bedrooms were first separated by a single wall, which was later torn out and replaced by closets. Closets were just coming into vogue when the house was built, and the Flanagan's probably used large moveble wardrobes.

All the original windows were divided by small panes of glass, but they were later replaced by single window glass. At least two upstairs bedrooms and the central hall were originally covered by wallpaper, traces of which can still be found.

The dedication of Flanagan House as the Peoria Historical Society's headquarters building on June 9, 1963 by its then president, State Senator Hudson Sours. The young man in the background is Keith L. Barr, the Society's former executive director.

(Photo courtesy of Keith Barr)

Most of the materials used to build Flanagan House were either made on the spot or nearby. Its bricks were fired on the grounds and the milled lumber came from Chicago.

In 1961, the *Journal Star* sponsored a contest to determine the oldest residence in the city, and the Flanagan House won. The Morrill family offered it to the Peoria Historical Society for the sum of $15,000 and the money was raised by a local fund drive, the entire amount of which came from private sources.

Mabel Nortrup Morrill, the wife of Dr. Frank Morrill, was once considered "Peoria's First Lady of the Theatre." She, along with Julia Proctor White, was one of the founders of Peoria Players, when it first began giving plays on the second floor stage of the Women's Club, at 301 N. E. Madison. When Peoria Players opened its own theater (a converted firehouse) at 209 Jackson, "Berkeley Square," under Mrs. Morrill's direction, was its first attraction in April 1933.

Mrs. Morrill's education included Northwestern University, followed by her study of direction at schools in Chicago, London, Paris, Dresden, Geneva and Vienna. And for two seasons she was affiliated with George Bernard Shaw at Malvern, England, and the Shakespeare Memorial Theater at Stratford-On-Avon, England.

At one time Mrs. Morrill also headed her own small theater and studio (which later burned) on the spacious grounds of Flanagan House. It was used for experimental plays and private teaching.

The house was opened to tours in 1963. Tours of the Flanagan House are available weekdays from 10 a.m. to 4 p.m. Admission is $3 for adults and $1 for children 15 and under. Large groups can arrange special tours by calling 674-1921.

Sources: The Peoria Historical Society and "The Way It Was" by Alice Oakley, Penny Press.

Pettengill-Morron House has place in local history

Peoria's two museum homes maintained by the Peoria Historical Society are Flanagan House at 942 N.E. Glen Oak Avenue (which we described last week), and Pettengill-Morron House at 1212 W. Moss Avenue.

The name of this second home comes from the first and last private owners of the property. It became a gift to the Peoria Historical Society in 1967.

Moses Pettengill built the 11-room, Second Empire-style home in 1868. He lived there until his death in 1883, and his family continued to do so until 1892.

Pettengill was born in New Hampshire and taught school for seven years before becoming a merchant. In 1833, he came to Peoria by horseback (and various other means along the way) with a man named Sweat. Here, he bought a lot at the corner of Washington and Main streets from Alva Moffatt, before returning east to his family.

On June 1, 1834, he and his wife, Lucy, came back to Peoria, accompanied by Jacob Gale, who later became a judge. The two men opened a hardware store and stove business. A year later Gale left the business, and A. P. Bartlett became Pettengill's associate. Pettengill was probably Peoria's first merchant of any great size.

He built a three-story brick commercial building on the west side of the 200 block of Main Street, while his first residence was a log cabin in the same block.

A very religious man, he was later known as Deacon Pettengill. He and his wife helped establish the Main Street Presbyterian Church in 1834, and as that group changed, he became one of the key organizers of what became the First Congregational Church. He also later operated the Pettengill Female Seminary, at the corner of Perry and Jackson streets.

Pettengill's second home was built in 1844 on the site of what later became the Jefferson Hotel at Jefferson and Liberty streets (now a part of the Civic Center complex). The Pettengill's were interested in the anti-slavery movement, and this home was believed to have been a part of the Underground Railroad.

In 1862, Pettengill built a home out in what was then the country, 424 Moss Avenue. His wife, Lucy, died in 1864 and the following year the house and most of the furnishings burned. Moses rebuilt his home in 1868 (which is the current house), and he and his second wife, widow Hannah Brent Tyner, and her son, Blanchard, whom he adopted, occupied the new residence. Pettengill died in 1883; Hannah died the following year.

Samuel Clark bought the house in 1892, and it was subsequently owned by William Jack (1901-03) and Dr. Charles Thomas (1903-41). It was rented from 1941 until 1945, when it was bought by John Boyd Stone of the First National Bank. He and his family resided there from 1945 to 1953. (His daughter, actress Cynthia Stone, was married to movie star Jack Lemmon there). Much of the renovation of the home was done by Mr. and Mrs. Stone.

Miss Jean Morron acquired the property from the Stones in 1953, when her ancestral home at 305 N.E. Jefferson was slated for demolition to make way for Interstate Highway 74. She not only moved her household furnishings but also the fine ornamental iron fence, the once highly polished brass rails from the front porch, the silver nameplate on the front door, the gas lighting fixtures (which had been converted to electricity), and a marble fireplace mantel piece from her bedroom.

Miss Morron, who never married, occupied the house until her death in 1966. Most everything stands as she left it: the furniture, china, silver, crystal, paint-

**The Pettengill-Morron House, built in 1868.
(Photo courtesy of the Peoria Historical Society)**

ings, and ornamental rugs, much of which was handed down from her ancestors.

Attorney William Rutherford and his brother, Dr. Robert Rutherford, were named in her will as executors. Because of Miss Morron's closeness to the Forest Park Foundation, much of her estate passed to that organization, which donated her home and its contents to the Peoria Historical Society in 1967. The house was placed on the National Register of Historic Sites in 1976.

Jean Morron was a descendant of the Cooper-Reynolds-Morron family. Her mother, a Reynolds, married Reverend John Herschel Morron, who served the First Presbyterian Church here, from 1865 to 1870. The parallels of the Reynolds and Pettengill families are striking.

Miss Morron's grandfather, John Reynolds, came to Peoria a short time after Moses Pettingill, and their backgrounds were very similar. They were both interested in education and church, and both were merchants. Reynolds came from the east with two cousins, Abraham McKinney and Hugh Williamson. They first went to Chicago, but thought the land to be too marshy there, so they moved down to Peoria in 1835.

Reynolds returned to Pennsylvania, where his wife's family had lived for 100 years, and returned by wagon with her and their three children, in 1836. He bought property on the lower side of Adams Street, from Main to Fulton, which, coincidentally, was just around the corner from Pettengill's business. Like Pettengill, he also opened a hardware business, but in conjunction with dry goods, not stoves. His partner was P.R.K. Brotherson. Reynolds later formed a packing company bearing his name.

John Reynolds built a Greek Revival-style house at 305 NE Jefferson, and the family lived there for generations, until Jean Morron bought the Pettengill house from John Boyd Stone in 1953.

The Pettengill-Morron Victorian mansion is open to the public Tuesday through Saturday from 10 a.m. to 4 p.m. Tour Admission is $3 for adults, and $1 for age 15 and under.

So, if you'd like to take a walk back into the Peoria of the mid-1800s, all you need do is visit one or both of Peoria's two fine historical homes, Pettengill-Morron House and Flanagan House.

Source: The Peoria Historical Society's "Pettengill-Morron House Guide Book."

Air of mystery lingers around early murder

Some of Peoria's early murders were important because of their historical significance (such as the one I recently described as Peoria County's first murder trial in 1825). Others were important because of the mystery or unusual circumstances that surrounded them. This is one of the latter.

Otis and Gertrude (Slagle) Botts seemed to be an ideal couple when they married in 1904. He was a handsome young man who was popular with the women and his wife was also very attractive. Happiness seemed to be theirs but within the year, a shadow of tragedy fell across their path.

On Monday, January 5, 1905, a chambermaid in a rooming house on Monson Street became disgruntled when she couldn't enter the room of Mr. and Mrs. Botts to do her daily chores.

Failing to arouse anyone by knocking, she peaked through the keyhole. Unable to see anything, she then climbed up and peered through the transom above the door.

The chambermaid screamed when she saw Gertrude Botts' lifeless body lying huddled on the bed. She called the landlord and two other roomers who witnessed her gruesome find.

The four broke into the room to verify that the young woman was indeed dead, and the police and a physician were soon at the scene.

Suicide was momentarily considered until a blue silk ribbon was found tightly bound around her neck. A man's handkerchief had also been stuffed in her mouth. Bruises on her face suggested a bitter struggle.

But vital clues as to the identity of the murderer were found under the fingernails on her right hand: pieces of skin and flesh and small drops of dried blood. Police knew the killer could be identified by long scratches, probably across the left side of his face.

A search was begun to find her 21-year-old husband, Charles Otis Botts.

A few hours later he was found hiding in the home of a black friend whom he knew rarely went into town and wasn't likely to immediately hear of the murder.

And, sure enough, when the police apprehended him, Botts' face was marked with scratches.

The handkerchief was identified as one Botts had in his pocket the morning of the murder. The couple was also known to have quarreled and it had been said that Botts had made threats against his wife.

Botts secured a lawyer and went to trial, but the evidence was so strong against him, he received a speedy sentence to be hanged.

Now, all of this might have been checked off as just another domestic tragedy, but on the day of the murder, Otis Botts had told a friend: "I have loved only one girl, and she is dead. I cannot love Gertie."

A check of the coroner's files showed Otis to also have been a suspect in the death of another girl, Birdie Hoffman, in April 1900.

Miss Hoffman was from a highly respected family and considered one of the most popular young women in the city. She had also been "keeping company" with Botts. He had taken her for a buggy ride the night of her death and her body was found along a lonely road near the Prospect Heights Hotel. A pistol Botts had purchased was found near the body.

Botts maintained he had given the gun to Miss Hoffman as a present, that they had quarreled and that she had jumped from the buggy and fled.

The police had been unable to break his story. A medical examination also disclosed a possible motive for suicide, which was the verdict returned by the coroner's jury.

Botts finally paid with his life for murdering his wife, Gertrude, but the ghost of Birdie Hoffman may have come back to seek vengeance because of the ironic way he died at his hanging. A gruesome and little-known detail of his execution came to light later.

It was said that, when the Peoria County scaffold was being prepared, the rope used to hang Botts had not been properly measured and turned out to be several inches too long. As Botts fell through the trap door of the gallows, this allowed his body to drop to the floor.

Since his neck was not broken in the fall, an iron-nerved deputy sheriff reached over and pulled upward on the rope until his feet cleared the floor. He maintained his grip until a physician finally pronounced him dead.

Some folks felt that the hand of fate had conspired to bring death to Otis Botts slowly, the same way his wife had died - by strangulation! Source: An article by Howard Kinney of the Journal Transcript in January 1931, reviewing a history of Peoria murders.

CHARLES OTIS BOTTS, hanged in 1905 for murdering his 19-year-old wife.
(*Journal Star* photo, courtesy of the Peoria Public Library)

GILDERSLEEVE MYSTERY. In my February 15 column, I speculated (which is always dangerous) That Jim and Marian Jordan (Fibber McGee and Molly) may have named their Gildersleeve character, "Throckmorton P." because of their Peoria connection. (Throckmorton was the name of a downtown Peoria drug store and the middle initial P. may have represented Peoria, or so I thought.)

But I received a letter from Frank Thomas of radio station WCBU/FM90 that blew my theory sky-high.

Frank plays old radio programs every Sunday evening from 7 to 10:30 p.m. starting off with "Do You Remember These?" Frank once interviewed Harold Peary, the actor who originated the Gildersleeve role. Peary told him that the character started out as just "Gildersleeve."

As the part was fleshed out, the show's directors decided Gildersleeve needed a first name.

Peary was living in Chicago on a street named Throckmorton Place at the time, so he suggested the name "Throckmorton." The middle initial "P" represented his own name, "Peary."

Thanks, Frank, for clearing up this little mystery.

Anyway... it all seems like only yesterday!

Memories of band era's Bob Crosby

One of the great fringe benefits of managing TV stations back in my day was having the opportunity to go to the networks' annual meetings, which were usually held in Hollywood. That's a misnomer, really, because all three networks held their conventions at the Century Plaza hotel in Century City, a community neighboring Hollywood. The Plaza was actually built on the old back lot of Twentieth Century Fox studios.

But during those visits to both NBC and CBS affairs, Flossie and I met many of the stars of motion pictures and TV. Most were very nice, while a few (who shall remain nameless) were real stinkers.

You couldn't help but like James Stewart and his wife, Gloria (Flossie met them; unfortunately, I didn't), Dick Clark and Bob Newhart and their wives, and Jack Lemmon, just to name a few.

But one at the top of our list was a man who died March 9: Bob Crosby. We had the good fortune to meet Bob and dance to his outstanding Bob Cats on two different occasions.

While playing one night at Universal Studios, his wife, June, sat next to the bandstand, just enjoying and listening to her husband and his band the entire night, right along with the rest of us.

A couple years later, we were on a set at MGM Studios, and Bob Crosby and the Bob Cats were again providing the music. During one of the band's breaks Crosby walked over to our table and joined us, as though he'd known us all his life. Asking if we had any requests for the band, I indicated I'd love to hear "The Big Noise from Winnetka." He laughed, "That's not a special request. We have to play that or they won't let us out of here."

George Robert "Bob" Crosby was born August 23, 1913, in Spokane, Washington, the youngest of seven children in a poor Irish family. Another of the kids was his famous older brother, Bing.

According to biographer Joseph F. Laredo, Bob Crosby spent a year at Gonzaga University before landing his first job as a vocalist, with the Anson Weeks Orchestra. He was picking cucumbers back home in Opportunity, Washington, when he received a telegram about the job. Bob recalled saying: "Anything beats picking cucumbers. I'm gone."

He was vocalist for that band in 1933-34, and then went with the Dorsey Brothers Orchestra in 1934-35.

Before joining the Weeks band, he went to Hollywood and asked brother, Bing, for some singing lessons, but for some reason he never got them.

Years later, after the Bob Cats went broke on the road, Bob wired Bing, asking for money. None came, but an agent called with a booking offer for Bob. Later, he found out that Bing had arranged for the job offer.

The great Ben Pollack Band dissolved in 1934, and saxman Gil Rodin organized the nucleus of it into a new group. With him were Yank Lawson on trumpet, Matty Matlock on clarinet, Eddie Miller on tenor sax, Nappy Lamare on guitar, Ray Bauduc on drums, Gil Bowers on piano and Dean Kincaide playing tenor sax and arranging. Rodin hired Bob Crosby to front the band in 1935, and the group also signed with Decca that year.

Arrangements by Kincaide, Matlock and bassist Bobby Haggart gave the band a distinctive, Dixieland sound. Leonard Feather's Encyclopedia of Jazz lists it as "one of the 10 best big bands of all time."

"Summertime" became their theme song, and other noted jazz men joined the group, including Billy Butterfield, trumpet; Muggsy Spanier, trumpet; Irving Fazola, clarinet; and Buddy Morrow on trombone. Doris Day sang with the band, briefly, in 1940.

A young Bob Crosby at the start of his bandleading career in the middle 1930's.

Bob Crosby leading his Bob Cats on an outdoor movie set in Hollywood in 1984. (Photo by Bill Adams)

It couldn't have been easy being the kid brother to a star the stature of Bing Crosby, and it wasn't. When the Dorsey Brothers formed their band, Bob was hired as its vocalist, but Tommy Dorsey wasn't thrilled about it. He first greeted Bob by saying, "You little bastard! We got the best band in the land, we need the best Crosby, and you ain't it!" And every time Bob walked past Tommy, Dorsey would say, "We got the wrong Crosby."

But after Bob joined the Bob Cats, he always said he had no problem competing against his older brother. He said, "Bing was a better singer and I had a better band."

He also had a humorous approach to his brother's fame. A West Coast columnist, Don Freeman, quoted him with this tongue-in-cheek comment: "Actually, it was just a matter of luck that I didn't become Bing. One night my father lined up all the children - five boys and two girls - in the big house in Spokane. My father said, 'Who Wants to be Bing?' Nobody thought much of the idea.

"But then Harry Lillis Crosby, born 10 years before me and always a dutiful son, stepped forward. 'I'll be Bing,' he says. So he became Bing Crosby.

"It was just a matter of timing. I wanted to be Bing, too. But I was only a baby and I couldn't talk." Although Bob never played an instrument (although the union forced him to play the drums in the beginning) he became the catalyst of the Bob Cats. When he was on the bandstand, he brought out the best in the players. They always played their best for him. It was obvious they loved Bob, and he loved them, too.

...and it seems like only yesterday when everyone loved Bob Crosby and the Bob Cats!

(Special thanks to Frank Troth of Peoria for providing background material on Bob Crosby)

A bowling feat for the record books - unofficially

Back in 1906, a Peorian named Clarence Wesley Brayshaw became famous in the world of bowling when he became the first person ever to bowl back-to-back perfect 300 games.

But before you start reaching for your American Bowling Congress record books, let me hasten to add you won't find it recorded there. The reason: the four alleys in the Empire, where he performed this phenomenal feat, were not certified by the ABC, even though they met that organization's requirements.

The bowling federation's records show a man named Frank Carauana of Buffalo, New York, to be the first to perform the feat in sanctioned play, on March 5, 1924... 18 years after Brayshaw's accomplishment.

But why weren't the alleys certified?

Mainly because George Young, the manager of the Empire, and Walter Payne, manager of the alleys, didn't want their lanes tied up with league bowling. They wanted them for open play bowling. They felt that other bowling establishments like Peter's, Bauer's, the Faust, the Star, the Alps, and Schindler & Miller provided the town with ample alleys for league play.

Charles Catlin of Peoria had bowled a perfect game on the new lanes in December 1904, when five of Chicago's best teams came and bowled against five of Peoria's best, to dedicate the new Empire lanes that year. This was two years before Brayshaw's performance.

The better city bowlers had urged the management to certify the lanes but were refused.

Finally the city's best bowlers, wanting to bowl on the newest alleys in town, decided to form a league and bowl at the Empire anyway. Young and Payne finally granted their wish and the new league was called the Peoria League.

For years, it was said that there was something wrong with the Empire alleys... that they were too short and not wide enough. But Ott Thieme, who was then secretary of the Peoria Bowling Association and was to become Peoria's first American Bowling Congress executive director, later put all that heresay to rest.

He stated he had measured the Empire alleys and found them to be the correct length and width. In his official report to the ABC national secretary, Samuuel Karpf in Dayton, he reported Brayshaw's games were rolled under ABC rules and that the equipment met that group's requirements.

Then why wasn't Brayshaw's feat recognized as a world record? Because the alleys had not been certified.

George Doty had been a longtime Peoria bowler at the time of Brayshaw's two perfect games. He went to Chicago to see if these successive 300 games set a world record. Chicagoans were astounded at the news and the next day Doty took a train to Dayton, Ohio, headquarters of the ABC secretary.

The secretary, Samuel Karpf, told Doty that Brayshaw's feat was "an unofficial world's record" and that he had already received such acknowledgement all over the land in press reports.

Karpf said: "The record will always be unofficial as the alleys were not certified, although the games were rolled under ABC rules and requirements and I have the report of Peoria secretary Ott Thieme in detail that he measured the alleys, weighed the pins and reported all equipment to have met ABC specifications.

"History will always record that Clarence Brayshaw was the first man to roll two successive 300 games under perfect ABC rules and conditions, but his record will never be official."

Well, certified or not, Brayshaw's effort was a major accomplishment 87 years ago, but it was only a part of his record performance that night.

He did it while bowling 15 games in a team, doubles and singles tournament where he averaged 230 for five games in the team event, 229 in the five doubles event games, the last game of which was his first 300, and he averaged 241 in his five singles games, the first of which was his second consecutive perfect game.

His last game of the night was a 193, the only game under 200 during the 15 game marathon performance.

Howard Miller, who later became the sports editor of the *Decatur Review*, was a boy of 15 at the time and was on hand that night to witness the great event. His aunt, Mrs. J. B. Dodge, operated the Del Prado hotel, located above the Empire alleys, and he had dropped in at the alleys before going up to bed. (This hotel catered to theatrical people who came to perform in Peoria's nearby legitimate theaters and vaudeville houses.)

Clarence Brayshaw was just 23 years old when he rolled his back-to-back perfect 300 games. He was one of three sons of Abraham Brayshaw, who worked for their father in his Mexican Amole Soap Company in Peoria.

Abraham was born in Yorkshire, England in 1838, and founded his shaving soap company here in 1884. He was so proud of his son's bowling record that he advertised the feat nationwide by putting

Clarence Brayshaw worked for his father in his Mexican Amole Soap Co. of Peoria, makers of a men's shaving soap.
(Photo from the book, "Men of Illinois," Peoria Public Library)

a celluloid card, telling of the event, in each order of Amole Shaving Soap.

The designer of the ad, however, apparently missed two of his consecutive strikes because the ad stated that the young Clarence Brayshaw had rolled "TWO 300 GAMES AND 26 STRIKES IN SUCCESSION." The *Peoria Journal* files record 28 straight strikes.

(Source: A 1955 article by the, then, Peoria Journal sports writer, LeRoy Chase.)

NEXT WEEK: The *Peoria Evening Journal's* actual coverage of the 1906 event.

Reliving Clarence Brayshaw's historic bowling feat

Second of two parts

Last week's story of Peoria's Clarence Brayshaw, the first man in bowling history to bowl two successive 300 games, seemed to me to be one of the most fascinating feats in the annals of local sports. It was even more interesting since they were rolled on alleys (they call them lanes today) at the old Empire saloon in the 100 block South Jefferson Street in 1906.

The *Peoria Evening Journal* described the historic event the next day, so let's go back to that evening of January 25, 1906... and you are there through the eyes of a *Journal* reporter!

"The Terre Haute Giants team of the Peoria League and a club of Bradford, Il. stars approached the alleys amidst much hand-clapping and cheering. (Terre Haute was a regional beer that sponsored the Peoria team.)

"They were meeting in a team, doubles, and singles tournament for $500 in prize money. All tourney competition in each event was for five games. (This type of tourney was later changed to three games in each event.)

"The Empire was dimly-lit and tobacco smoke hung heavy in the small building. More than 100 persons had assembled for this tournament, which had been advertised in the newspapers and on window sign cards for the 'state championship' outside Chicago.

"The Peoria Socials Football Rooting Club, led by a youngster, Vic Michels (later to become Peoria county states attorney, Peoria mayor and a successful lawyer), gave cheers for each Peoria bowler as he approached the foul line to roll his first ball in the team event. The Socials cheerleaders wore uniform derbies, cravats, turtle-neck sweaters and tight-fitting trousers.

"Spectators were lined down two of the alleys. The alleys had been covered with canvas and chairs two rows deep were placed on each alley.

"In the background the bar was doing a big business and the tinkle of the money drawer could be heard from time to time.

"The Peorians beat Bradford in the five team games, 5046 to 4402, averaging 1009 per game. Brayshaw paced the Peorians with a 230 average, getting 1149 for games of 204-265-234-210-236. Louis Payne had 1070 (214 average), Eddie Hall 892, Hubert Andres 1068 (213 average) and John Doering 867.

"The doubles competition began at 10 p.m. Brayshaw continued to amaze the onlookers with games of 205-222-201-214. (Then his amazing feat began.)

"It was the last game of the doubles. Brayshaw had whipped seven straight strikes. Cheering and hand-clapping began.

"He struck in the eighth and three more made it 11. He was going for a perfect game. The twelfth ball sailed into the 1-3 pocket and cleared the alley of pins.

"Bedlam broke loose. Fifty men tried to reach him at once, to shake his hand.

"Brayshaw totaled 1142 for his five doubles games and averaged 229. He and Hall defeated E. Hallock and Nick Peterson, 2125 to 1809.

"Following the 300 game at midnight it was with great difficulty that singles play got underway at 12:30 a.m.

"Brayshaw poured in strike after strike to start the first game of the singles with another 300. All the while the Empire shook to the rafters as the cheering, clapping and whistling mounted in intensity.

"When he shot his second 300, Brayshaw was borne aloft on the shoulders of admirers and carried around the Empire for five minutes. When set upon the floor he was mobbed by seemingly everyone who was trying to shake his hand.

"Strong men were weeping, laughing and talking incoherently.

"Here was drama, history being made and the gallery knew it.

"Brayshaw struck in the first and second frames of his second singles game to run his string of strikes to 28 straight, counting his last two in the fourth game of the doubles.

"It had to happen. He left up the No. 10 pin on his next ball and the strike orgy had ended.

"Brayshaw went on to shoot subsequent singles scores of 223-245-244-193. (The tourney ended at 2:30 a.m., and the 193 last game of the singles was Brayshaw's only game under 200 in the 15 he rolled.)

"For his singles Brayshaw totaled 1205 for the five games and a 241 average. He opposed J. H. Hall of Bradford, who totaled 930.

"The Empire never closed that night and many people were celebrating and discussing Brayshaw's feat at 6 o'clock (a.m.) when workmen stopped in for a drink, tobacco and notions learned of it first-hand." (His average for all 15 games was 233.)

Left: Clarence Brayshaw as he appeared at age 23, when he bowled his two perfect 300 games. Right: As he appeared at age 72 on a visit to the *Journal* sports department. (*Journal Star* file photos)

"...When Brayshaw rolled 223 following his second successive 300 game, it gave him a total of 823 for three games, considered another world's record.

"In his 15 games of tournament play, Brayshaw had no errors. He encountered five splits and made one.

"Two members of prominent Peoria families were there that night; Dan Thede and Charley Gipps. Each won big wagers. Gipps gave Brayshaw $100 and Thede bought him a suit of taylor-made clothes."

Clarence Brayshaw was just 23 years old when he performed his remarkable feat.

Bishop's robbery made front-page headlines

Most of you no doubt remember Bishop's Cafeteria's last Peoria location before it finally closed its doors at the corner of Washington and Main streets. And, I'll wager a good many readers recall when it moved into the old Lekas' Sugar Bowl location across from the Palace Theater on Main Street.

But I wonder how many remember where it was in 1940, when it was the scene of a spectacular robbery by a lone gunman in the middle of a busy day?

At that time, Bishop's was doing business at 111 N. Jefferson St., where the First Financial Bank is now located.

The startling robbery occurred shortly after 11 a.m. on Tuesday, September 3, 1940. A lone bandit pulled a gun on the cashier, grabbed a canvas money bag containing $1,400, and ran out the back of the cafeteria while customers looked on in horror. It made the front page headline in the *Peoria Evening Star* that day.

The cashier, Miss Louise Bottenberg, was about to leave by the front entrance to take the money to the Central National Bank, at the corner of South Adams and Main streets, when a man entered and said, "This is a stick-up." He grabbed the money bag and she held onto his arm as he pulled her to the back of the cafeteria. She refused to let go, and he hit her over the head with his gun.

Bishop's manager, H. Clay Gardner, saw what was happening and lunged toward the bandit, but was greeted with two shots. Finally, managing to break the woman's grasp, the gunman ran through the kitchen and into the back alley.

While all this was going on, Mrs. Dean V. Stewart was sitting in her car in the 100 block of North Madison Avenue. She was parked behind an empty car that had its motor running when she noticed a man emerging from between two buildings. The man jumped into the car and, in his haste, backed into her car before speeding up North Madison Avenue, narrowly missing several pedestrians.

Miss Bottenberg and Mr. Gardner described the hold-up man as about five feet, six inches, weighing around 140 pounds. He wore a gray suit and shell-rimmed glasses.

It seemed odd that both shots, fired at close range, missed hitting the manager, who said he didn't have time to get excited. "The first thing I knew, I made a lunge at him and the man fired twice."

It was believed the gunman may have fired blanks, because Gardner wasn't hit and, after a thorough search of the restaurant, no bullet holes were found.

Detectives John McAllister and Dario Lolli investigated the robbery and said both the cashier and the manager were positive the bandit had eaten breakfast in Bishop's that morning.

Miss Bottenberg said she at first thought the robber was kidding, but "I soon changed my mind."

It wasn't until a month later that a break in the case came - in a most unusual way. The clue came from the bandit's brother-in-law in Rock Island, in connection with a robbery in that city on October 3, 1940, a month to the day of the Peoria escapade.

Clarence Swanson of that city broke under questioning by Rock Island officials and confessed that his brother-in-law, Orley O. Mason of Quincy, was the one who robbed the Huesing Bottling Co. in Rock Island, of $1,100.

Swanson must have told authorities where Mason was hiding because three Rock Island officers drove to Peoria and accompanied Peoria officers to the New National Hotel in the 200 block of North Jefferson Street (just a block away from Bishop's) and placed Mason under arrest. He was staying there with his 20-year-old wife and their 22-month-old baby.

Mason was taken to the Peoria police station and viewed by Bishop's employees in police superintendent Leo F. Kamin's office. Bishop's manager, Gardner, and cashier, Bottenberg, positively identified Mason as the lone Bishop's bandit. Two other employees, James Mann and Mrs. Evelyn Mann also identified Mason.

At first, Mason denied the charge, saying he was not in Peoria at the time, but he later admitted being in town when the holdup took place. After three hours of questioning, Mason signed a confession admitting to four armed robberies between August 31 and November of that year.

In Rock Island, the robberies included a drug store, netting $52; an ice cream store, which netted $5.30; and a liquor store, where he rifled the cash register of $47.45.

So, it sounds as though Orley O. Mason was nothing more than a "petty cash" thief until he came to Peoria and "hit the jackpot" at Bishop's Cafeteria for the, then, staggering amount of $1,400.

What seems so curious to me is; Why would he be holed up a month later, with his family, in a hotel just a block away from his most sensational robbery?

Anyway, whether he used blanks or real bullets, his bold action made front page headlines back in 1940, at a time that

...seems like only yesterday!

Orley O. Mason, the lone gunman who held up Bishop's Cafeteria on Sept. 3, 1940.
(A *Peoria Star* photo courtesy of Peoria Public Library)

Bishop's cashier, Louise Bottenberg and manager, H. Clay Gardner shortly after the holdup occurred.
(A *Peoria Star* photo courtesy of Peoria Public Library)

"Lum and Abner" brought special charm to radio

Back in 1929, after Peoria's Charles Correll and his partner, Freeman Gosden, made it big as "Amos and Andy" for Pepsodent Toothpaste on NBC Radio's Red Network, a lot of imitators had similar ideas to become blackface comics.

Two young men from Arkansas were a part of that rush to put an act together, and they auditioned at a local radio station, only to find that the building was full of "Amos and Andy" twosomes with the same idea.

Their real names were Chester Lauck and Norris Goff, and it didn't take them long to decide the competition was too strong to make it in blackface, so they changed their dialects to two old country boys from the fictitious town of Pine Ridge, Arkansas, and became famous as "Lum and Abner."

Although Lauck was four years older than Goff, they knew one another in grade school in their hometown of Mena, Arkansas. Later on, during the summers, Goff worked in his dad's grocery store (similar to the later radio Jot 'Em Down Store) and Lauck worked in his father's lumber yard. They'd meet after work and experiment with different radio voices.

After graduating from college, they had both returned to Mena and married their childhood girlfriends. They found steady work and might have continued the small-town life had it not been for a performance at a benefit in 1930, which led to another radio audition.

They were first heard over station KTHS in Hot Springs, Arkansas, in April 1931. This 15-minute comedy had a continuing plot, not unlike the popular soap operas in those days. Lauck became Lum Edwards (which he pronounced as "Eddards" on the air) and Goff became Abner Peabody, proprietors of a fictitious establishment named the Jot 'Em Down Store.

Despite their "old man" radio voices, both men were in their 20s when they started the program.

After their initial success on the local station, they moved to Chicago. In 1931, they became a summer replacement on the NBC radio network for a variety show called "Gene and Glenn." Their first sponsor was Quaker Oats. In 1935, Horlick's Malted Milk became the sponsor of the 15-minute program, five nights a week.

Abner was the whining, checker-playing partner of Lum, who was overly careful about money. Both were easy prey to con men, especially Squire Skimp (played by Goff), the local loan shark. Goff also played Dick Huddleston, the owner of a rival store and the town's postmaster. (In real life the men had a friend named Dick Huddleston.)

In addition to Lum, Lauck also portrayed the village idiot, Cedric Weehunt, and Grandpappy Spears, who was always challenging Abner to a game of checkers. Since just these two men did all the voices in the early shows, female characters were mentioned but never heard. They were either just discussed or maybe talked to on the phone.

Some of the "silent" females were Lysbeth, Abner's wife; Sister Simpson, who ran a boarding house and had her "cap set" for Lum; and various heart-throbs of Lum's such as Evalina and Miss Fredricks, the school teacher. (The show's theme song was named "Evalina," and was composed and played on the organ by Sybil Chism Bock, the wife of a network publicity man.)

Other actors were later added, including Andy Devine, Zasu Pitts, Cliff Arquette and Clarence Hartzell. Hartzell played Ben Withers, a character that was close to his characterization of Uncle

Fletcher on the "Vic and Sade" soap opera.

But in the early days, Lauck and Goff not only did all the voices, but also did all the writing while ad-libbing through much of the show.

To celebrate the program's fifth anniversary in April 1936, by act of congress, the small town of Waters, Arkansas, changed its name to Pine Ridge.

In 1938, the program moved to CBS. It was sponsored by Postum and ran just three times a week. Then, in 1940, the partners dropped out of radio and made movies for a year.

In 1941, "Lum and Abner" went to ABC, where it was sponsored by Alka Seltzer and ran four times a week. Then, in the fall of 1948, it became a Sunday half-hour prime-time sitcom on CBS for Frigidaire. The following year Ford Motor Co. sponsored the show when it moved to Wednesday nights.

In the early 50s "Lum and Abner" made its final run as a 15-minute show, once again on ABC. Its last broadcast aired on May 15, 1953.

The expanded half-hour format added other actors, writers, elaborate sound effects and the music of Opie Cates' orchestra but, to me, it was never as interesting as the original 15-minute format, where these two talented performers took all the parts and wrote the show themselves. It had a charm that could never be duplicated.

LUM AND ABNER - Chester Lauck (left) was "Lum" and Norris Goff was "Abner," the proprietors of the Jot 'Em Down Store in Pine Ridge, Arkansas. They were on old radio from 1931 to 1953.
(an NBC photo)

I can still hear the old party line phone ringing to open the show, which was followed by this dialogue:

Lum: "I Granny's, Abner, I believe that's our ring." Abner: "I Doggies, Lum, I believe you're right."

Lum: "I'll see...Hello, Jot 'Em Down Store... this is Lum and Abner."

(Organ theme up)

... and it seems like only yesterday!

(Some of the material came from the book, "Tune in Yesterday" by John Dunning.)

Correction: Thanks for the memories

Last October I wrote about Bradley's old Sigma Phi fraternity.

By most counts it was reasonably accurate, using data anywhere from 43 to 81 years old. But shortly after the column appeared, I received a call from Gill Siepert, a history professor at Illinois Central College, who questioned my comments about the authorship of the "Sigma Phi Sweetheart Song." I had credited the song's writing to Tom Greer, Auren Muir and Max Bass, but Mr. Siepert said he was sure his father, Albert F. Siepert Jr., who later became a NASA executive, wrote the song.

Well, last month I received a letter from Al Siepert, who now lives in Tucson, Arizona.

He not only acknowledged authorship, but sent me a copy of the song, which shows credit after the title "by Al Siepert, arranged by Harold Osborne of the Harry 'Tiny' Hill Orch." The Osborne mentioned, of course, was our late friend, Ozzie Osborne.

I'm more than happy to set the record straight. In fact, Al's letter was so interesting, I thought you might like to read some of what he had to say:

"Actually, the song was composed much earlier (than the World War II years) in the fall of 1932, when Tom (Greer) and Max (Bass) and I were Sigma Phi freshman pledges. Muir was a classmate but had no connection with the venture...

"'The Sweetheart Song', oddly enough, evolved as a Hell Week chore. It was an acceptable alternative task to some absurd prank that the senior active members thought I should perform... Several years earlier, Tommy Greer and I had whacked together some catchy lyrics for a tune I had written about a girlfriend we had both dated (and lost!). It took very little time for us together to make up the lyrics for 'Dream Girl of Sigma Phi.'...

"Our favorite dance spot was the Inglaterra Ballroom... where the Friday Student Night at 50 cents-a-head drew many Bradley students. There I had gotten to know Mr. Harry Newsom, an officer of the Jefferson Bank, who, as the bank's representative, had taken over the management of the Inglaterra... I happened to be at the 'Ing' (in 1935) the night a new and unknown band from Decatur appeared. Its leader was an ex-drummer of truly impressive physical size, Harry 'Tiny' Hill. His new band was an immediate success, so I booked it for our Christmas dance...

"Tiny" Hill wanted to make a hit with our college crowd. He offered to orchestrate our Sigma Phi theme song as a surprise at our Christmas dance... Hill did it with a unique background rhythm he had devised recently using drum brushes and a stick rubbed on a hollow gourd. This 'double-shuffle' beat, along with 'Tiny's' hoarse baritone vocals, soon became established as distinctive Hill hallmarks.

"I was graduated in 1936 but Tiny Hill and I kept in touch, even after I started work in the federal service in Washington.

"In the spring of 1937, Harry phoned me that he had been offered a great chance to open at the Melody Mill Ballroom in Chicago with a regular air time on the WGN radio station. In those pre-war days before TV, a live radio broadcast series from WGN could be the 'golden door' into the big time. WGN's most famous outlets were the Aragon and Trianon Ballrooms and the Blackhawk Restaurant, but the Melody Mill and, as I recall, the Drake Hotel, were close behind.

"However, Harry Hill had run into an unexpected obstacle. With the *Chicago Tribune* as WGN's newspaper owner, the station told him it could not air his band unless Hill had copyright control of the necessary theme song!

Unfortunately, he had been using the well-known song, 'Can't We Be Friends?,' whose composer and publisher were uncooperative. So he asked me whether he could copyright Osborne's arrangement of the Sig Phi song (without fraternity lyrics) in his and my name. I agreed. It was officially registered as 'Dream Girl' - and Hill got his chance at the Melody Mill and WGN. The song became his theme for many years, and was recorded on Mercury Records.

"Perhaps the band's highpoint came later on the nation-wide 'Lucky Strike Hit Parade' when it headed one of the summer series.

"The collaboration of Tom Greer, Max Bass and Al Siepert covered the Stunt Show Follies for three years, 1933, 1934 and 1935, all of which were winners. Sigma Phi had established a previous reputation as the year-after-year winner of this campus inter-fraternity competition...

"Max Bass, a gifted journalist and editor of the *Bradley Tech* weekly, was our script and gag line writer. He had a marvelous sense of hillarious absurdity. Tom Greer choreographed our all-male follies 'dance steps,' and as a versatile comedian, always acted one of the lead roles. I played the piano by ear and was the follies director.

Al Siepert, Jr., the author of "The Sigma Phi Sweetheart Song,"as he appeared in Bradley's 1937 yearbook, Polyscope.

Ozzie Osborne (right, with guitar), who arranged the "Sweetheart" song while with Tiny Hill's orchestra. Here, he's later playing with WMBD-Radio's musical staff, Dick Coffeen (bass), Mary Jane Doebler LeMaster (vocalist), and Wayne West (piano and vocalist).

"Finally, your article mentions that 'the 1935 stunt show was so good that it played the Palace...' That weekend appearance involved the prize-winning Lambda Phi (sorority) and Sigma Phi (fraternity) stunts...

"It happened that the Class of 1936 (our senior class) had lost a lot of money on its Junior Prom held the previous spring. It seemed a good idea to recover the loss with a professional appearance at the Palace Theater, then Peoria's stage and vaudeville house. The Palace bookers were delighted to cooperate. None of our cast received any personal payment, so the theater management evidently could overlook any Equity Union restrictions on such amateurism. At any rate, as the hoofers on Broadway liked to say... 'It was great fun when we played the Palace!'"

Many thanks, Al, for the correction of the song's authorship, and the pleasant walk back down one of Peoria's wonderful memory lanes once again

...it truly does seem like only yesterday!

Pioneers of culture got started in 1886

The other day I received a call from Meredith Houghton, who walks by the Peoria Women's Club to work each day. She couldn't help noticing that the building's corner stone is dated 1893, which would make that historic edifice at the corner of Fayette and Madison 100 years old this year.

But the club itself is even older than that.

It was formed seven years earlier, on January 20, 1886, and consisted of 27 members headed by its first president, Mrs. Clara Parsons Bourland. The club was really the outgrowth of an even earlier women's organization.

On June 12, 1878, the Peoria Ladies' Art Society, consisting of five original members was organized. Mrs. Bourland was also its first elected president. Miss Alice M. Dodge was secretary; the other members were Mrs. Mary McClure, Mrs. Mary Whiteside Emery, and Miss Jennie S. Stone.

The art society's constitution stated that its objectives were "to promote art culture, and to develop a taste for the decoration and adornment of home." This was in a day when most people looked askance at any women's activities outside the confines of the home fires.

The first meetings were held in the private office of Mrs. Mary Whiteside Emery in the Transcript building. (The reason for Mrs. Emery's office is not stated). In September of that year, the society accepted the offer of a room in the offices of Bourland and Bailey. Meetings were held once a week, and after one year, the membership had grown to 18. Each month one of the members prepared a resumé of topics studied, which was published in the *Saturday Evening Call* newspaper.

But the club wanted to do more than promote art. It had a desire to teach as well, and the following year nine members received instruction in china painting under Miss Sadie Lindsay of Galion, Ohio. They later also hired a Mr. Sammons as instructor of classes to teach women (and men) in drawing, oil painting and watercolor during one of the summer months. In September 1881, a young lady taught classes in the Society rooms throughout the school year.

By now the club held rooms in the Spurck Building at the corner of Main and Madison streets. The following October, an "Exchange for Women's Work" was opened, and Mrs. G. W. Rouse was its first manager. Its purpose was to encourage workers in the art crafts by providing a means of selling their products.

One of the Art Society's outstanding events was a great loan exhibition held in the spring of 1879. A 64-page catalog listed 1,032 objects of art loaned for exhibition, and 79 works of art made by Peorians. The loaned art included oil paintings, engravings, watercolors, statuary, laces, fans and combs, furniture and wood-carving, pottery and porcelain, glass, books and coins, textile fabrics and embroideries, a Japanese department, mosaics, jewels and miniatures, curiosities and miscellaneous articles.

In 1882, Mrs. Bourland left to spend three years in Europe. That September the club decided to move to new quarters on the second floor of the Brown's Block building at 508 Main Street, where they only had to climb one flight of stairs instead of two. But a majority of members thought they had made a mistake in moving because there was less space in the new location, so they returned to the Spurck Building.

In September 1882, a school was opened with a Professor Van Lear as teacher but after a month Miss Nellie Wilson became the teacher in charcoal and crayon.

The school was placed under the management of Miss Alice M. Dodge, the

Mrs. Clara Parsons Bourland, founder of both, the Peoria Ladies' Art Society and the Peoria Women's Club.
(Photo courtesy of the Peoria Public Library)

The Brown Block building (center), in the 500 block of Main Street, where the Peoria Ladies' Art Society temporarily moved in 1882. This 1918 photo shows it about two years before the Madison Theater was built around it.
(Photo courtesy of the Peoria Public Library)

society's secretary; Miss Mary V. Bestor; and Mrs. Minnie B. Stewart. In 1884, they announced they had hired Professor A. Chatain of the Art Institute of Chicago and a pupil of the famous French artist, Gerome. His first salary of $60 per month was later raised to $100. Tuition was $6.00 for 12 lessons in a month or $9.00 for 24 lessons a month.

This school opened in September 1884, and the following May the secretary of the Central Illinois Art Union, Mrs. E. D. Hardin of Peoria, reported that the school was in "a flourishing condition." The average number of pupils had been 33

per month during the seven months, and four young people who lacked the means had received free lessons.

At first the outlook for the school was encouraging, but after a few months it changed. The second year was its last and Professor Chatain left Peoria. In June 1885, the treasury showed a balance of only $3.63.

Peoria artist, Headley Waycott, stated that the reason for the school's failure was that most women went to classes because they were interested in making some pictures to hang in their homes. Once they

had made a sufficient number, they were no longer interested in attending. It was also said that the professor didn't get along well with his students.

But Peoria's pioneers of culture were not disheartened by the school's failure. The Peoria Ladies' Art Society ceased to exist, but on January 20, 1886, the Peoria Women's Club was formed and Mrs. Clara Parsons Bourland, who had been the Art Society's president, was also elected as the new club's president.

NEXT WEEK: The Peoria Women's Club and its 100-year-old building.

Club's building was city cultural center from start

Second of Two Parts

The Peoria Women's Club was formed January 20, 1886, the outgrowth of a previous club known as the Peoria Ladies' Art Society, which began in 1878.

This "new" club began with 27 members and Clara Parsons Bourland as its president. Mrs. Ida B. Knowles was first vice president; Jane Wheeler, second vice president; Alice M. Dodge, recording secretary; and Abbie T. Blair, treasurer. Mrs. Bourland also had been president of the previous Art Society, as mentioned last week.

The Peoria Women's Club was chartered in 1891, and less than a year later, work was started on a community recital hall and club house at the corner of Fayette and Madison.

Work was completed at a cost of $45,000 in 1893, which makes it 100 years old this year. It was formally dedicated the following year. Its architects were Jenney and Mundie, and its builders were John L. Flinn and Frank Hasbrouck. Money for the project was raised by issuing stock at $10 per share, and selling it to friends and neighbors.

The building immediately became a cultural center for Peoria. Its auditorium was one of the city's popular social centers and, over the years, many celebrities came to speak there, including Julia Marlowe, Max Heinrich, Herbert Witherspoon, Catherine Fisk, Julia Ward Howe, Edna Ferber, Max Eastman and others.

In 1894, Mrs. Bourland saw the need for statewide cooperation of women. She called representatives of 11 leading state clubs to Chicago, where they founded the Illinois Federation of Women's clubs.

One of the Peoria club's earlier activities was establishing a protective agency to secure legal rights for women and children. It also was instrumental in having travelers' aid provided at railroad stations and securing care for blind children. Also due to its efforts, the State Hospital for the Insane was located in Bartonville.

The club was instrumental in securing a truant officer for Peoria schools, placing a woman on the library board, engaging a trained librarian, and placing golf courses and tennis courts in municipal parks.

The Peoria Women's Club became the mother club of most of the major organizations in our town's social and cultural life: The Amateur Musical Club, Peoria Players, the Peoria Symphony Orchestra, art associations and various civic groups, and many of them began their activities in this building.

Mrs. Bourland remained as president for 25 years, until 1911, when Julia Proctor White became its second president.

The magnificent clock in the foyer of the building was the gift of Howard Knowles for his wife, Ida B. Knowles, a charter member and the club's original first vice president.

The beautiful mantel in the drawing room was a gift of William H. Murtagh for his wife, Carolin, an honorary and life-long member of the club. Also in that room is a painting by the Swiss artist, Frank Peyraud, the man who painted the murals in the old Peoria Public Library.

The large, impressive oil painting above the antique love seat was presented to the club by Sarah Proctor Howe (the mother of Julia Proctor White, the club's second president) in 1894. It was painted by Miss Ellen K. Baker in Paris, France and called "The Rose Fete." The portrait of the club's founder, Mrs. Clara Parsons Bourland, also is Miss Baker's work. The watercolor of yellow roses is by a Peorian, Miss Nona White.

Three more of Miss White's floral watercolors are in the dining room, along with an oil of a river scene from Grandview Drive by Peoria artist Headley Waycott and a small woodland scene by Mrs. Louise Fritz. The marble-top chest in that room was a gift from Mr. & Mrs. Frederick M. Bourland.

The mantel in the dining room is centered in an alcove of woodwork. Its tile facing is original, along with the very unusual black iron fixtures.

The first floor also consists of the entry foyer, central foyer and president's office. Handsome old iron ornamental gates decorate the club's entrance doors.

The second-floor auditorium has not been used since 1970, when a fire caused damage primarily on the left front under the stage, and to the dressing room at that side. Its theater chairs seat 453.

Also upstairs is the Baldwin room, which was decorated originally by former newspaper columnist Miss Sydney Baldwin in memory of her mother.

The Peoria Women's Club building is now an historic landmark, and is on the National Register of the Northside Peoria Historical District.

Today the club's officers are Mrs. Darlene Hunt, president; Mrs. Marian Yeager, first vice president; Mrs. Corabelle Chuse, second vice president; Mrs. Margaret Johnson, recording secretary; Mrs. Jane Guthrie, treasurer; and Mrs. Louise Northrop, assistant treasurer.

An early view of the Peoria Women's Club building at the corner of Fayette St. and Madison Ave. (Photo courtesy of Peoria Public Library)

Mrs. Hunt is the 34th president of the club since its inception in 1886. After Mrs. Bourland, most presidents served only two years until Mrs. Ruth Swardenski, who was president from 1978-1986. She added to the club's art collection and stimulated much outside interest.

Its current membership numbers 150 and the club holds luncheon meetings each Monday from September to May. The Peoria Women's Club is still an educational group, with the same basic format as in the past.

Hunting down the story of attorney's disappearance

Without a doubt, the most elusive story to come to me is one about a prominent Peoria attorney who disappeared many years ago. His name was Walter W. Donley Jr. and he has never been heard from since.

It was about a year and a half ago that retired Associate Circuit Judge William H. Young told me about the case and suggested it would make an interesting column. Little did I know then, just how elusive and mysterious a story it would be.

I began by searching the library files for a date of the disappearance, which would allow me to find it in the newspaper archives. Without a date, finding a story is sometimes like finding a needle in a haystack, and my on-again, off-again searching stretched out to well over a year. For a long while I could find nothing on the man. Then I found out why. I was looking for him under a different spelling of the name.

I talked to many local people, including retired certified public accountant Charles Ginoli, who later handled the Donley estate. Before Ginoli and his wife, Betty were married, Betty was a babysitter for Donley's daughter, Dianne, and Cynthia Stone, the daughter of Boyd Stone of the First National Bank.

I also talked to several lawyers who remembered the case, but none could give me a year when the disappearance may have occurred. From their various recollections, it could have happened before, during, or even after World War II.

One day, at the suggestion of Bob Pomeroy, I contacted Lela Post, secretary of the Peoria Bar Association. She suggested that I contact retired Circuit Judge Robert Hunt, who is somewhat of a history buff.

Judge Hunt couldn't help me with the date, but made the interesting suggestion that I check the archives at the Peoria County Clerk's office to find a date when Mr. Donley might have been declared legally dead. By tracing back seven years from that date (the length of time required by law for someone missing to be declared legally dead), I might be able to find my elusive story.

I eagerly took his advice and immediately found the probated will of a man named Donley in 1947. I was sure I had my man, until I discovered that this Donley was Walter's brother, John, who had died in St. Francis Hospital of natural causes.

My heart sank when I realized I'd found the wrong Donley. Dejectedly, I read his probated will. Suddenly, the date I was seeking jumped off the page.

During the reading of John's will, his sister, Hope C. Wardwell, was asked if any of the family's siblings were deceased. She answered that one might be, because their brother, Walter W. Donley Jr., disappeared from Peoria on or about June 1, 1943, and his whereabouts were unknown.

Bingo! Now I had the elusive date and could follow up on the newspaper accounts.

Sure enough, a quick search of newspaper micro-films brought the story to light on the front pages of the local papers. On Tuesday, June 8, 1943, one week after Walter Donley Jr.'s disappearance, the police released word that the Peoria attorney, Walter W. Donley Jr., had been missing since the previous Tuesday.

Now things began coming to me instead of eluding me.

After a talk I gave at Independence Village, where I told of my search for this story, a lady came up to me and said she not only knew of Donley but she had been the best friend of his wife, Marjorie, back then.

She also remembered their daughter, Dianne, who later married Robert O'Neil, and that they had three children. She was sure Dianne's son, John, still lived in Peoria. A couple quick phone calls and I was talking to John D. O'Neil, who was, indeed, Walter Donley's grandson.

John knew very little about his grandfather's mysterious disappearance, but he'd like to know more. He put me in contact with his mother, Dianne, who had since remarried, and was now living in Florida.

My phone conversation with Dianne, along with newspaper accounts of the case, allowed me to piece together at least part of the story.

For example, I knew that at the time of his disappearance, Donley had been subpoenaed to appear as a witness in a federal grand theft case against another man.

But I still lacked most of the information regarding the indictments involved and the several attempts to bring the case to trial.

In desperation, I called Robert J. Kauffman, this district's U. S. magistrate judge, and told him my problem. Much to my pleasant surprise, he put his staff to work to find the files on a case that was now 50 years old.

In a few days, Judge Kauffman called to say they had found the proper case numbers, but the files were now in the federal court archives in Chicago. He contacted Chicago and requested copies

Walter Donley left his law offices in suite 1144 of the Jefferson Building (now River Valley Plaza) with two men on June 1, 1943. He has never been heard from again.
(Photo courtesy of the Peoria Public Library)

of the case papers and any other information connected with it.

After several weeks and a few complications, the judge received the requested information. Most important to me, he'd been sent a copy of the April 1942 statement to the federal grand jury from then - U. S. Attorney Howard L. Doyle.

It was a case against one Lawrence Drewer.

Drewer and another man, Clyde Milton Cornett (who had since pleaded

guilty), were charged with transporting stolen money from St. Louis to Peoria, in the amount of $15,000.

NEXT MONDAY: The mysterious disappearance of the prominent Peoria lawyer Walter W. Donley Jr. ...on the same day he had been served with a subpoena to appear as a witness in the case. He left his office in the Jefferson Building with two men, never to be heard from again.

Attorney may have left office against his will

Second of Two Parts

Last Monday, I told of the difficulty in finding a story regarding the mysterious disappearance of a prominent Peoria attorney back in 1943.

On Tuesday, June 1, of that year, Walter W. Donley Jr. disappeared - it was the very same day he received a subpoena to appear in federal court. He was the key witness in a case against two men accused of transporting $15,000 in stolen money from St. Louis to Peoria.

Donley previously had been the Peoria city attorney and acting corporation counsel from 1929 to 1931.

On June 8, exactly one week after his disappearance, the police released the information that he was missing, which made front page news.

Donley was last seen about 4:45 p.m. June 1, when he left his law offices in Suite 1144 of the Jefferson Building (now River Valley Plaza). He had just called his residence and informed his daughter, Dianne, that he would be home at once. He lived at 300 W. Armstrong with his wife, Marjorie, and their daughter, who was a freshman at Peoria High School at the time.

But apparently he didn't just walk out of his office. His secretary told the family he left with two men. The following events indicate he may have left with them against his will.

Donley's abandoned car was found parked in the 100 block of South Bourland and, according to an eye witness, it had been there since about 5 p.m., which would have been just 15 minutes after he left his office. The witness saw two men get out of the car and walk toward Main Street, talking loudly to one another. They turned the corner and continued to walk toward University.

One of the men was said to have been carrying a briefcase and wearing a blue shirt. Mrs. Donley said her husband wasn't wearing a blue shirt or carrying a briefcase that day, and the witness couldn't identify the other man as Donley.

With Donley's disappearance, the FBI entered into the investigation.

The U. S. District Court case was against two defendants, Lawrence Drewer and Clyde Milton Cornett, and the U. S. attorney's statement to the grand jury gives the following scenario:

On January 30, 1942, Cornett, alias J. Adams, together with one William Ruemker, stole approximately $65,000 from the safe of the Cummings Manufacturing Co. in St. Louis. On February 3, Cornett held a conversation with Lawrence Drewer, alias Wilford Drewer, alias C. Snarr, at 5800 Collinsville Road in East St. Louis.

On February 12, Drewer and Cornett drove to Peoria, where they held a conversation with Louis Koren and another one with Walter Donley. (They had apparently asked Donley to be their attorney).

The two registered as guests that same day at the Mayer Hotel and held a meeting with Donley in their hotel room.

The statement goes on to say that the following day they gave Donley $15,000, and he deposited the money in the First National Bank. He later drew four certified checks against the aggregate amount of $15,000. (He apparently didn't know it was stolen and cooperated with authorities in their investigation.)

Later, on October 23, 1942, Clyde Milton Cornett entered a guilty plea and was committed for a term of three years in the Missouri state prison at Jefferson City, Missouri.

Lawrence Drewer entered a plea of not guilty, and the federal court trial against him was called for 2 p.m. on June 21, 1943.

In addition to Donley, the following people were subpoenaed to appear:

Three St. Louis police officers, John Sinclair, James M. Ogden and Robert Egan; Mrs. Minnie Cummings and Charles Bormann, both of St. Louis (and

Left — Walter W. Donley, Jr., a prominent Peoria attorney, former city attorney and acting city corporate counsel, disappeared on June 1, 1943 and has never been heard from since.
(Photo courtesy of the Peoria Public Library)

Right — The Mayer Hotel, at the corner of NE Adams and Hamilton Boulevard, where the two men, accused of transporting $15,000 in stolen money, were staying under assumed names.
(Photo courtesy of the Peoria Public Library)

probably connected with the firm that was robbed); the manager of Illinois Bell, (who was ordered to bring records showing the people to whom phone numbers 27672, 27029, 6502 and 43481 were listed); the desk clerk of the Mayer Hotel (ordered to bring the hotel guest register of February 12 & 13, showing the registration of C. Snarr and J. Adams in room 544 and record of telephone calls made from the room); J. Boyd Stone, vice president of the First National Bank; and George M. McKibben, cashier of the First National Bank (ordered to bring records relating to cashiers checks 92994, 92995, 92996 and 92997, each dated February 13 and payable to Walter W. Donley).

A writ of habeas corpus ad testificandum was issued to the warden of the Missouri prison and the U. S. Marshall, to release and transport Clyde Milton Cornett to Peoria to testify at the trial.

But on June 21, Walter Donley failed to appear, and the court ordered the bailiff to call out his name three times in the open court, as well as in the lobby. When he did not respond to the call, Judge J. Leroy Adair commanded the U. S. marshall to apprehend him, and the trial was delayed until Thursday, June 24. When Donley still was not found, Adair ordered a continuance of the trial until September.

But the fact is, Walter W. Donley Jr., the key witness - and maybe the only person who could connect the defendants with the stolen money - never was found.

Six months later, on December 8, 1943, the other man involved in the robbery of the Cummings Co. of St. Louis was machine-gunned in southern Illinois, and died immediately.

And three years after Donley disappeared, Lawrence Drewer, the defendant - and also the chief suspect in Donley's disappearance - was shotgunned to death on a St. Louis street.

With this, the investigation into the disappearance of Walter W. Donley Jr. also died, as did the case against Lawrence Drewer.

...and it seems like only yesterday!

Whiskey fed 1935 Hiram Walker blaze

On July 22, 1935, Peoria suffered what may be considered its most spectacular disaster. It was the devastating explosion and fire at Hiram Walker & Sons, the world's largest distillery.

Although I wasn't on the scene, I remember as a 10-year-old child hearing family stories about it. My mother's sister, Lola Zimmerman, worked on the bottling line.

It was about 10 that night when the south wall of the recently completed rack house No. 3 collapsed, causing a huge explosion and fire. The fire fed by 81,000 barrels of whiskey, soon spread to the combination shipping, cooperage and cistern building, and the rectifying and bottling plant.

Firefighters from Peoria, Bartonville, Peoria Heights and Pekin, along with hundreds of volunteers and employees, battled the blaze for more than six hours. For a time, the flames threatened the entire plant.

Because of the burning alcohol, mountainous flames leaped hundreds of feet in the air. The fiery glare illuminated the sky and could be seen for miles.

Probably the largest throng of spectators ever assembled in Peoria came to watch the blaze. It was estimated that the crowd numbered around 75,000, and traffic was blocked in every direction.

It's said that hundreds were attracted by the flow of whiskey and came equipped with tin cups and dippers, sipping while they watched. All the side streets leading from Adams Street were packed with humanity, while the huge yards at the foot of Lisk Street presented a solid mass of flame-lighted faces. Many more folks lined the bluff area, where they had a great view of the inferno.

Amazingly, only one person lost his life in the $2,500,000 catastrophe, although another dozen firefighters were injured.

John Barden, a 32-year-old construction laborer who lived in East Peoria, was the only victim. He was one of a group of about 12 construction workers in the area when the wall collapsed around them.

Searchers later found one of his work gloves and a section of the ladder on which he had been working. He was married, and the father of three children.

Barden's crew was called back to work at 6 that night to shore up a building wall of the rack house. Harry Houghton, who was working with Barden, said, "It all happened so quickly, I can't see why more of us were not trapped with Barden in there."

Workmen at the site said the catastrophe started with the collapse of the south wall of the recently completed rack house. The building was built on "made" land, filled in when the course of the Illinois River was altered. The weight of 81,000 barrels of whiskey may have caused a shift in the structure's supports.

Frank Dorenberger was hurled about 20 feet down an excavation embankment but was unhurt. Carl Fisher and Roy Dean were standing near the entrance to the administration building, about 200 feet from the rack house, when they were knocked down by the blast.

In addition to the thousands of barrels of whiskey, another hazard came from the row of alcohol-laden cars standing on the CB&Q railroad tracks adjacent to the plant. Also, piles of lumber were stacked in the yard. They were being used in the construction of this new rack house and rack houses No. 4 and 5, which were to be built next.

Fire Chief Ben Butler and his assistants, Patrick Malone and Carl Prohmer, successfully directed more than 100 firemen, in addition to many Hiram Walker employees, in fighting the blaze. Chief Butler said that a sudden shift in the wind was their greatest ally.

"When we started to fight the fire, there was a breeze from the south and it looked bad. Then the wind shifted, blowing the flames away from the other buildings and that gave us our chance to bring the fire under control."

William E. Hull, vice president and general manager of the Peoria distillery, said the next day: "Although approximately one-third of our stock on hand was destroyed, there will be no interference with the regular business of the company..."

He indicated production would be stepped up from 1,700 to 2,000 barrels a day and said 221,000 barrels of whiskey still were on hand and women were on duty, as usual, in the bottling house, which adjoined the smoking ruins.

Hull also said: "Seven million gallons of whiskey contained in rack houses Nos. 1 and 2 were undamaged, the fire being confined to only one warehouse. Hiram Walker & Sons have 13,500,000 gallons of matured whiskey in their warehouses at Walkerville, Ontario, as well as consider-

The 1935 fire at Hiram Walker's distillery shortly after the explosion that destroyed a rack house and 81,000 barrels of whiskey.
(*Peoria Star* photo, courtesy of the Peoria Public Library)

able stocks in warehouses in various parts of the United States.

"...practically all of the whiskey in rack house No. 3. was less than three months old."

July 22, 1935, must have been quite a night for those spectators who came from miles around to watch the spectacular fire, especially those with tin cups and dippers.

But it must also have been an interesting night for the fish down-river, too, because thousands of gallons of whiskey flowed directly into the Illinois that night. I wonder which had the bigger hangovers the next day, the fire watchers or the fish?

...and it seems like only yesterday!

Sally Rand kept show going until she was 74

It must have been in the late 1940s or early '50s when the Royal American Shows would come to the East Peoria fairgrounds.

I was still managing the Madison Theater. And on this particular morning, I was performing one of my least enjoyable duties - checking in a truck load of candy - when a woman came in looking for the manager.

She was quite small. I judged her to be around 50 years old, and she looked an absolute mess. She was in a filthy work shirt and dungarees, and her dirty blond hair wouldn't have made a good bird's nest. At first glance I suspected she was a street person, looking for a handout.

"Hello," she said, "I'm Sally Rand."

I thought to myself, "Sure, and I'm the King of Siam." But, fortunately, I held my tongue because, as it turned out, she really was Sally Rand.

Now, in case you've forgotten (or just don't know), Sally Rand was the sensation of the 1933-34 Chicago World's Fair when she presented her fan and balloon dances. She became the fair's hottest attraction.

I shook her grubby hand while Miss Rand apologized for her appearance,
hastily explaining that she'd been up all night after fighting a fire that wiped out part of the East Peoria carnival and all of her sideshow. She said her entire show - curtain, sets, costumes, everything - was lost in the fire.

She went on to say that she needed material to fashion a new set and costumes because she was determined to put on a show that night. It's the best example of the term, "The show must go on!" I've ever encountered.

I told her that our local theaters stored all old sets and material in the closed Orpheum Theater, just across Madison Street, and she was welcome to use anything she could find there.

I let her in the old theater and she rummaged around in the dust and cobwebs until she came across several old theatrical trunks. Then her eyes lit up. She said, "If you'll let me use this stuff, I'll bring it back to you all cleaned and pressed."

That very same night, Sally Rand was back in business with her all-girl revue sideshow, with makeshift set and costumes made from those trunks of material in the old Orpheum Theater. (And she was a woman of her word. Before her show left
town she brought it all back, cleaned and pressed.)

Back in 1933, Sally Rand became famous by artfully and strategically twirling two seven-foot ostrich feather fans around her nude body, as she danced to the strains of DeBussy's "Claire de Lune" and Chopin's "Waltz in C Sharp Minor." It all sounds quite subdued now, but back then it was very provocative, and she became the biggest attraction at the Chicago World's Fair.

Then in 1934, when the fair was continued for a second year, Miss Rand changed her act by introducing what would become her equally famed bubble dance. She used huge bubbles (balloons) that she manipulated in front of and around her, in much the same manner as the fans.

In 1935, the year after the World's Fair, Miss Rand took her show on the road, and one of her appearances was here at Peoria's Palace Theater, where she was billed as "Sally Rand and Her Review."

Sally Rand was a stage name. She said it was chosen for her by none other than Hollywood's eminent producer/director, Cecil B. De Mille. He "borrowed" the last name from the Rand McNally map company.

Helen Gould Beck (her real name) was born January 2, 1904, in Elkton, Missouri. Her father was a retired Army colonel. Her mother taught school and was also a correspondent for several Kansas City and Missouri newspapers.

As a teenager, her first stage job was as a chorus girl in a Kansas City nightclub. It was there that she caught the eye of Goodman Ace, then the drama critic of the *Kansas City Journal*. (Ace and his wife, Jane, later became famous for an old radio show called "The Easy Aces.")

Ace's newspaper comments were seen by Gus Edwards, who produced a juvenile vaudeville company named "School Days." Miss Rand joined the unit and studied dancing, voice and drama. For a brief time, she had a career in silent films. She had also appeared in summer stock with Humphrey Bogart and, by the later 1920s, was an acrobat with the Ringling Brothers circus. But her forte was vaudeville, and she formed her own troupe.

She created her fan dance after seeing some moth-eaten feathers in a costume shop shortly after arriving in Chicago in the early '30s.

"Those ostrich feathers gave me an idea," she said. "I remember my days as a youngster in Missouri, when I watched the ducks and geese and the herons flying south, their wings graceful against the sky. I had wanted to fly like a heron and I then thought of a dance that would incorporate their movements."

She bought the ostrich feathers on credit and changed her dance act in a Chicago nightclub as the opening of the World's Fair approached.

Miss Rand applied for a job dancing at the fair's "Streets of Paris" concession

A 1971 photo of Sally Rand at age 67, with the fans that made her famous.
(Photo courtesy of the *Peoria Journal Star*)

and came up with the idea of appearing at the concessions preview as Lady Godiva. She got the job the next day.

Sally Rand, whose face and figure belied her age, continued to perform her dance - which, she said, changed "not a whit, not a step, not a feather" - until 1978, when she was hospitalized with congestive heart failure... at the age of 74!

She died a year later in Glendora, California. She had been married three times and had an adopted son, Sean.

Sally Rand and the Chicago World's Fair

... it seems like only yesterday!

Jokes late addition to Benny act

Earlier this year I told of the Peoria visit of Jack Benny back in 1950, when he and part of his radio cast put on the first big show (other than basketball) at Bradley University's brand new Robertson Memorial Field House. It brought back fond memories of Benny's popularity during the "golden era" of old radio.

But Jack Benny was no stranger to Peoria even then. For many years he played on the vaudeville circuit, and my old boss, Len Worley, the Publix Great States Theaters' Peoria city manager, was a good friend of his.

Benny and Worley were great walkers, and Len used to love to tell about the times when Jack Benny played at one of his theaters. He and Jack would walk for miles around our town.

Jack Benny - whose real name was Benny Kubelsky - was born in Chicago and raised in Waukegan. His father was a Polish immigrant who became a Chicago peddler and later owned a haberdashery store in Waukegan.

When Benny was very young, his father bought him a $50 violin. By the time he was eight years old, he had performed at Waukegan's Barrison Theater. He later became an usher and violinist there.

The teenager became enamored with vaudeville and left high school in his sophomore year to try his luck on the stage. He joined the Barrison Theater pianist, Cora Salisbury, in an act called "From Grand Opera to Ragtime," touring with small shows around the midwest.

After a couple of years Miss Salisbury retired, and Benny joined pianist Lyman Woods, playing the Orpheum circuit.

For several years, Benny didn't even speak in the act much less tell jokes.

He joined the Navy during World War I and while stationed at Great Lakes Naval Training Station, he agreed to play a violin solo for a benefit show. His first "lone act" bombed so, in desperation, he began talking... and the audience laughed.

This was the first time young Kubelsky realized he could be funny. So when he returned to vaudeville after the war, he worked out a comedy routine and the violin became just a prop.

Kubelsky changed his name to Ben K. Benny until 1921, when it became confused with orchestra leader Ben Bernie (remember "The ol' maestro, Ben Bernie, and all the lads"?) That's when he changed it to Jack Benny.

This new, funny Jack Benny soon made it on the big time vaudeville circuit and played every actor's dream theater, New York's Palace.

While touring California in 1926 he met Sadie Marks who sold hosiery in the May Company's Los Angeles store. They were married the next year in Waukegan and she joined his act.

By the early 1930s, Benny was making $1,400 a week. He was appearing on Broadway in Earl Carroll's "Vanities" in 1932 when a New York newspaper columnist, Ed Sullivan, invited him to be on his CBS radio talk show. On March 29, 1932, Jack's first radio words were: "Ladies and gentlemen, this is Jack Benny talking. There will now be a slight pause while you say, 'Who cares?'"

While listening to the early radio shows of Amos and Andy and others, Jack decided that radio was the coming thing. So he quit his high paying stage job to co-star on an NBC variety show sponsored by Canada Dry. With him were Ethel Shutta and her husband, bandleader George Olsen. It premiered on May 2, 1932, and Jack Benny became a radio hit.

He later moved over to CBS on Thursday nights, but the following year he was signed by Chevrolet and moved back to NBC at 10 p.m. eastern time (9 p.m. central).

In 1934, the show was picked up by Jell-O and moved to the 7 p.m. eastern time period on NBC. Jack Benny and Jell-O became synonymous for many

A 1936 publicity photo of Jack Benny and his wife, Sadie, who became Mary Livingstone on radio's "The Jack Benny Program."   (An NBC photo)

Left, Portland Hoffa (Fred Allen's wife) restraining Jack Benny while Mary Livingstone, right, (Jack Benny's wife) holds back Fred Allen in a mock-up of their radio "feud."   (An NBC photo)

years, until Lucky Strike cigarettes bought the show.

When the "Mary Livingstone" character was written into an early show, Jack auditioned several actresses for the part before he finally decided to let his wife do the bit. Sadie Benny did the "Mary" part so well, it was written into the show and her identity as Jack's real-life wife was soon forgotten by the audience. Sadie's brother, Hilliard Marks, also became Jack's longtime producer-director.

Many other radio characters were performed by some great talent over the years. People such as singers Kenny Baker and Dennis Day; orchestra leader Phil Harris; Eddie Anderson as "Rochester," Mel Blanc, "the man of a thousand voice characterizations," and announcer Don Wilson.

Although Jack Benny became one of the super star comedians of the entertainment business, in real life he was not what you would call a funny man. He was a great audience for other comedians, though, especially his old friend George Burns.

Jack's timing was his greatest gift - that and the wonderful ability to know what was funny.

His need for writers was almost legendary. His first writer was Harry Conn, who wrote nearly all the shows until 1936, when Ed Berloin and Bill Morrow joined the staff.

For years, he and his good friend Fred Allen maintained a running feud on their individual radio programs, and would often appear as "enemy" guests on each other's shows.

One night, when Jack appeared on Fred's show, Allen hit him with several stinging one-liners. Finally Jack used one of his long pauses (which became his trademark), then answered with this rebuff, "You wouldn't have said that if my writers were here!"

...and it seems like only yesterday!

BU student murdered in the '40s

On the night of December 3, 1947, a 20-year-old Navy veteran and Bradley University sophomore disappeared. The popular fraternity member had failed to keep a date with a girlfriend that evening and later was murdered.

The victim, Flavel Dean Fueger, was the son of Mr. & Mrs. Flavel L. Fueger; his father was the proprietor of Fueger's Jewelry store at 439 Main Street.

Shortly before Fueger was to meet his date at a downtown location, he drove his shiny new Pontiac sedan from the Bradley campus. Sometime later, he died when three bullets were fired at him. It's believed the attack occurred at a lonely spot behind the Peoria State Hospital in Bartonville.

Fueger resided with his parents on Stratford Drive but they were out of town at the time. When his unexplained absence extended into several days, his relatives and friends became concerned.

The entire city detective bureau went to work on the case. His fraternity brothers and even the Boy Scouts covered a great area of the West Bluff in organized searches, but to no avail.

Nearly two weeks went by before the first break came in the case.

A Bradley friend of Fueger's was taking his father to work at the Peoria Stockyards when he spotted the missing youth's Pontiac parked on South Street, near SW Washington.

City detective Fred Montgomery found a cap of the type usually worn by motorcyclists in the car. It was identified as belonging to the wife of a young man named Herman F. Weber. Under questioning, Mrs. Weber let it slip that her husband and a man named Fred Wright of Bartonville were buddies.

The police then picked up and questioned the soft-spoken Wright. When they brought up some shady automobile deals between Wright and Weber, Wright's tongue began to loosen.

He said that a short time before, Weber had borrowed money from him, saying he was "getting out of town." Wright also mentioned that Weber had arranged to meet him in a town near Houston, Texas, "if things got too hot here in Peoria."

Knowing that Weber was traveling in a stolen Buick, FBI agents picked him up three days later after a car chase on the outskirts of Houston. Shortly after his arrest, Weber made the first of a long series of "confessions," which did more to confuse the case than solve it.

Weber first said he entered Fueger's car when the victim stopped for a traffic light on a downtown Peoria corner, the night of December 3. He said he forced Fueger to drive over the Cedar Street Bridge toward East Peoria. He claimed that on the bridge, he ordered Fueger out of the car, shot him in the head and dumped his body in the Illinois River.

But on the way back to Peoria from Texas with Montgomery and chief deputy sheriff William Littell, he changed his story, saying the shooting occurred near Peoria State Hospital. He now named Wright as his companion, and that the body was disposed of in the Thompson drainage ditch in Fulton County, near Lewistown. A search of the area was futile.

Wright was held as an accessory to Fueger's murder and also on an auto theft charge of the Buick Weber used to make his getaway. While in custody, Wright supplied an important piece of information: he said Weber told him Fueger's body was in a drainage ditch below the Sepo Bridge, near Illinois Route 78.

About 11 a.m. December 15 (12 days after Fueger disappeared), Montgomery and a group of Fueger's fraternity brothers went to the designated spot. There, in the partially ice-coated water, lay the victim's body.

On January 31, 1948, Herman F. Weber was indicted by the Peoria County

Left — FLAVEL DEAN FUEGER, the 20-year-old son of a prominent Peoria jeweler was murdered in December, 1947.
(*Journal Star* photo file)

Right — The 24-year-old Herman Frederick Weber (right) was held in Houston, Texas in connection with the disappearance of Flavel Dean Fueger. He's pictured here with U. S. Deputy Marshall V. B. Richard.
(AP wire photo from the *Journal Star* files)

grand jury on three counts: murder, robbery and rape. The jury failed to indict Wright, but states attorney Roy P. Hull ordered him held on the auto theft charge. He was subsequently placed on probation.

The rape charge against Weber was based on an allegation by the wife of a Peoria nightclub operator.

She stated that Weber had hidden in her car in the afternoon of the same day that Fueger disappeared. She said her car was parked near what was then the downtown post office.

She stated that when she got back into her auto, Weber, who was hiding in her car, had taken a .25-caliber pistol from the glove compartment and forced her to drive out in the country, where the alleged assault occurred.

Her revolver was the same one found by the FBI when they searched Weber's stolen car in Texas. Ballistic reports also indicated that the three bullets that killed Fueger were fired from this gun.

Now Weber began adding to his "confessions." He said he had lied about Fred Wright being in on the murder. He later named a mysterious "Jack Crowley" as his companion on the night of the killing.

NEXT WEEK: Herman F. Weber's jury trial and subsequent electrocution at Joilet's new Stateville Prison.

143

Murder of jeweler's son leads to death sentence

Second of Two Parts

Last Monday I told about the murder of Flavel Dean Fueger, the 20-year-old son of a prominent Peoria jewelry store proprietor, in December 1947.

Herman F. Weber, age 24, accused of the murder, skipped town and was apprehended in Texas after a car chase on the outskirts of Houston.

Weber's friend, Fred Wright, who the police had questioned about some shady automobile deals between the two, tipped them off as to Weber's whereabouts. The two were suspected to be car thieves.

Weber was indicted by a Peoria County grand jury on murder, robbery and rape charges.

The rape charge was based on an allegation by the wife of a Peoria nightclub operator. She stated Weber had hidden in her car the afternoon of the same day Fueger disappeared and, with a .25-caliber pistol he took from her car's glove compartment, forced her to drive into the country, where he assaulted her.

This same gun was found in Weber's stolen car in Texas, and FBI ballistic reports indicated that Fueger was killed with this gun.

Weber changed his confession several times. At first he said Wright was with him when Fueger was murdered, but later he introduced a mysterious "Jack Crowley" as his companion the night of the murder.

Weber's trial began February 2, 1948, with Fred Wright as a principal witness. Weber was called to testify in his own defense by his attorneys, John Dougherty and Fred Stiers.

Repudiating all five of his previous confessions, he insisted that a man named Jack Crowley loaded Fueger's body into a stolen Buick and disposed of it in the drainage ditch where it was later found. He testified he had failed to tell the truth at first because Crowley had threatened to kill his wife, Norma, if he did.

Dr. C. W. Maganet, the coroner's physician, testified that, in his opinion, Fueger's body had not been in the water more than a few days before it was found. Fueger had been missing about two weeks, leaving nine or ten days for which Weber could not account.

City detective Fred Montgomery said he had made an exhaustive search for the "John (Jack) Crowley" named by Weber but was unable to find any trace of such a person.

Assistant state's attorney Charles McNemar accused Weber of being a "colossal liar," but Weber's attorneys firmly contended it would not have been possible for their client to have committed the crime under the related circumstances.

After deliberating only 2 1/2 hours, the jury found Weber guilty on February 7, 1948, and recommended the death penalty. On February 18, Weber entered the "death house" at Illinois' new Stateville Prison at Joliet, where he remained in solitary confinement for 19 months.

During that time, Weber was granted five stays of execution, and twice Illinois governors granted him reprieves. Throughout the day before his execution he waited, hoping for another reprieve that didn't come.

After exhausting every other avenue, Weber sent a personal letter to Illinois governor Adlai Stevenson, asking for an 11th-hour stay on the grounds of alleged technical errors during his trial. The following afternoon (Weber's last one), Stevenson sent word to Joliet Warden Ragen that there was "no substantial basis for a further reprieve."

Weber was calm and even jovial at times, and his first outside visitor was his

Herman F. Weber (left), convicted killer of Flavel Fueger, is flanked by (center) Lt. Don Bedwell and (right) Warden Joseph E. Ragen. Picture was taken February 19, 1948.
(A *Journal Star* file photo)

wife, Norma. After a two-hour visit, she left for Peoria.

When William Littell, Peoria county's chief deputy sheriff, entered the death house about 4 p.m., Weber and the Rev. Gervaise Brinkman were playing cards. Father Brinkman, a young prison chaplain, who recently had converted Weber to the Catholic faith, spent most of the day with Weber, who declined to see any newspaper reporters. Weber also told the warden he had no desire to see anyone else.

Weber was still maintaining his innocence, declaring that "Jack Crowley" actually killed Fueger. At 5 p.m. he ate his last meal, with Father Brinkman as his dinner guest.

At six minutes after 1 a.m. September 16, 1949, Herman F. Weber was led by the priest the 50 feet from his cell to the execution chamber. His last words to the warden, five guards and chaplain were, "Thanks for everything." At 1:09 a.m. he was pronounced dead.

It was the first execution ever held in the new Stateville Prison, but it was not the first one in this particular electric chair.

As strange as it may seem, this same chair had been used in the old prison 14 years earlier, and that time the condemned man was also from the Peoria area: his name was Gerald Thompson.

Thompson was convicted of murdering 19-year-old Mildred Hallmark in Springdale Cemetery on the night of June 16, 1935.

...it seems like only yesterday!

Father of aviation was Peoria resident for several years

As nearly everyone knows, the Wright brothers invented the first motor-driven airplane back in 1903. But did you know a former Peorian assisted them in their experiments, and it was his early glider designs that made it all possible?

This former Peorian was Octave Chanute. He was later named "the father of aviation," and Chanute Air Force Base at Rantoul, Illinois, established in 1917 to train World War I flyers, was named in his honor.

Chanute not only was a resident here for several years, but also married a Peorian and is buried here.

Octave Chanute was born February 18, 1832, in Paris, France, the son of a history professor. He came to America at a very young age. Having a natural aptitude for engineering, he got a job with the Hudson River Railroad in its engineering department. The wages were meager, but he gained much in experience.

From 1849 to 1869 he was a consultant for several railroads and, as early as 1853, was named chief engineer for the Chicago and Alton Railroad.

The Peoria Directory of 1856 lists Chanute as a resident of the historic Peoria House hotel. The following year, on March 12, 1857, he married Miss Annie James of Peoria. (According to "Oakford's Peoria Story," she was the daughter of Charles P. and Eliza Cooke James, but later newspaper accounts list her father as Peoria Circuit Judge Louis W. James.)

The James residence was at about the site where the G.A.R. Hall is now, on Hamilton near N E Madison Street.

Following their marriage, Octave and Anna Chanute lived on the north side of Hamilton, above Perry Street. Their next residence was on the south side of Hamilton, one door above Jefferson Street. The Chanutes had two daughters (who later lived in Los Angeles).

Octave Chanute was the designer of the first railroad bridge to cross the Illinois River at Peoria. It was built for the Peoria and Oquawka Railroad, which later became the Toledo, Peoria and Western. The bridge was completed in 1857.

Also in 1857, Chanute was credited with laying out the town of Fairbury, Illinois in Livingston County with Caleb L. Patton, the former owner of the town's land. In return for Chanute's influence with the stockholders of the Peoria and Oquawka Railroad to get Fairbury a railroad station on the line, Patton gave him half of the town's lots.

Chanute's work as a civil engineer made it necessary for him to live in various cities around the Midwest, so the Chanutes moved from Peoria around 1864. But four years later he made the recommendations and preparatory plans for the Peoria Water Works, to be built at the foot of Steam Ferry Road in Peoria's north end. This is now Grant Street.

Chanute became an accomplished designer of bridges. He designed the Santa Fe Railroad bridge at Silbey, Missouri, the first important bridge over the Missouri River, and he designed the first bridge across the Mississippi River at Fort Madison, Iowa.

He also layed out the huge stockyards at Kansas City and Chicago.

It wasn't until Octave Chanute was 60 years old that he turned his attention to aeronautic engineering.

A German, Otto Lilienthal, and his brother, Gustov, began making glider experiments in 1867, but the first significant glider work was carried out by a French sailor named Captain Le Bris in the 1870's. Then, in 1891, Otto Lilienthal built his first man-carrying glider.

An Englishman, Percy Pilcher, added a design to Lilienthal's glider, but both Lilienthal and Pilcher were killed in their experiments.

In 1896, the 64-year-old Chanute began making gliding flights in America. He built a five-deck glider, followed by a triplane and, finally, by a biplane. This became the famous Chanute biplane, with wings held together by vertical posts and diagonal wires. This method was often used by later biplane designers.

Chanute discarded Lilienthal's method of controlling the glider by moving his body, which hung beneath the glider. Instead, he substituted a rudder and articulated wings, which could be swerved fore and aft to provide both longitudinal and lateral control, although the pilot's body still hung beneath the glider.

This glider weighed only 23 pounds but was so stable he made 2,000 flights without a single accident. Chanute became famous for his experiments with different types of glider planes which he and his assistant, A. M. Herring, conducted from 1896 to 1897 in Dune Park, on the north

Octave Chanute, "the father of aviation," was once a Peorian. He married a Peorian, and is buried in Springdale Cemetery.

shore of Lake Michigan. He was consulted by the Wright brothers in the designing of their various gliders even before they made their first airplane.

Octave Chanute remained in Chicago the rest of his life. He died there on November 23, 1910, at the age of 78. His body was brought to Peoria, where he was buried in Springdale Cemetery with his wife, Annie James Chanute. She had died in 1902.

How Carl Triebel cleaned up Peoria

Carl O. Triebel became Peoria's "reform" mayor in 1945.

E. N. Woodruff had been mayor for 12 terms (although not consecutively) and was a liberal. He strongly advocated a wide-open town. Most people considered him to be an honest man, personally, but Woodruff really believed that the majority of Peorians wanted the town the way he ran it.

Both Triebel and Woodruff came from old Peoria families but with two completely different philosophies.

Triebel became known as the "reform" mayor, but claimed he never was a reformer. He believed the people elected him because they were fed up with deteriorating city services such as poor garbage collection, potholes in the streets, etc., as well as the previous administration's underworld pets. Triebel insisted that he had no mandate to revoke the traditional "wide-open-town" policy.

But before he was mayor a month, Triebel learned that the underworld and the politicians were greedy, and there is no such thing as a "little vice."

In 1945, Peoria gambling was controlled by the notorious Carl Shelton, ruler of the Shelton Gang. Their feud with Charlie Birger during Prohibition turned Williamson County in southern Illinois into an outright war with the use of tanks, airplanes, homemade bombs and machine guns.

Carl and his two brothers, "Big" Earl and Bernie Shelton, had won the fight and Carl was later invited to Peoria to become bodyguard for local gambling kingpin, Clyde Garrison.

The Shelto's moved from St. Louis to Peoria and Carl soon took the place of the man he came to protect. It was said that "you couldn't spit in Peoria without asking Carl Shelton."

Shelton controlled most of the slot machines, punchboards and gambling houses, and Triebel indicated that many of Peoria's 20 aldermen were getting $200 to $500 a month from the slot machines that were in virtually every tavern, drug store or card shop in town. Some of this money was also paid directly into the city treasury.

Prostitution ran openly in two districts, one at each end of Peoria's downtown; around Jefferson and Walnut and on North Washington Street. A madam named Pam Dustman ran most of it, and the police were protecting the houses and the streetwalkers.

Triebel claimed that a few days before he took office, a representative from the Sheltons named Ferdie McGrane paid him a call. Triebel's account of the conversation went like this.

McGrane: "I've come about the slot machines."

Triebel: "What about them?"

McGrane: "We'll handle them for you."

Triebel: "You'll what?"

McGrane: "We'll take care of em. How much do you want out of em?"

Triebel: "Nothing."

McGrane: "All right; then we'll pay something into your campaign fund."

Triebel: "That won't be necessary."

McGrane: "No? Why?"

Triebel: "Because there aren't going to be any slot machines."

Triebel said Ferdie's mouth fell open about a foot.

McGrane left and about five minutes later, the phone rang. It was Carl Shelton. He asked to come over and Triebel told him to come ahead.

Triebel described Carl Shelton as "a big, breezy chap, sort of a western businessman type." Here's Triebel's description of that conversation.

Shelton: "I hear you couldn't get together with McGrane."

Triebel: "That's right."

Shelton: "Did you mean what you said?"

Triebel nodded his head.

Shelton studied him for a minute, then smiled and said, "Well, I guess that'll give me more time to farm."

Shelton owned a big farm near Fairfield, Illinois, and Triebel had an interest in a couple farms so, according to Triebel, they talked about farming for the next half hour. Then they shook hands and Shelton left.

Triebel said that that was the last time he saw the terrible Mr. Shelton.

Later, when Triebel was having trouble with some local hoodlums, Carl Shelton sent word to him that he'd take care of the situation if he wanted him to.

Triebel said, "Fortunately I was able to handle it myself, but it was comforting to know that Carl Shelton was not hostile toward me because I had pulled down his playhouse. Later, I learned that he liked and respected me for my position..."

Carl Shelton did retire to his farm, but on October 23, 1947, he was killed from ambush while driving his Jeep near his farm. Then on July 26, 1948, his brother, Bernie, was slain here in Peoria, while leaving his Parkway Tavern on Farmington Road. An older brother, Roy, was killed while riding a tractor on his southern Illinois farm in 1950.

Carl O. Triebel became Peoria's "reform" mayor in 1945. He was also owner and operator of Ideal Troy Cleaners and Laundry.

Carl Shelton, the boss of the Shelton Gang that controlled gambling in Peoria until 1945.

His other brother, "Big" Earl Shelton, also went back to Fairfield, where several attempts were made on his life, but he survived.

Triebel's comment about Earl was, "...he claims that he has retired from business. Maybe, but even so I'll bet he has trouble getting life insurance."

...and it seems like only yesterday!

(The above quotes are from an article titled "The Vice That Was Peoria," as told to Alson J. Smith, in an unnamed magazine clipping in the Peoria Public Library)

Memories flooding in with news

All the flooding around the Midwest these days brings back memories of those in Peoria's past.

But this 1993 flood is different in at least one respect: Past floods were brought about mainly from meltoff in the spring, when northern snows and April and May rains brought about the havoc. I don't recall a major one in mid-summer.

The Peoria-area flood, from which all later ones were judged, occurred in June 1844, when the river here rose to a, then, record 26.9 feet. In 1922, the river crested at 24.8; several other floods followed in the 1920s and '30s.

But in 1943, the river here reached a whopping 28.8 feet, nearly two feet above the flood of 1844.

Peoria's river stage as I write this column is at 20.2 feet, thankfully, well below the record.

But the flood most vivid in my memory was the one in the spring of 1933, because my family and I were living right in the middle of it.

My parents had leased a lot from Zealy M. Holmes in a development on the river, just north of Mossville, named Holmes Center. My dad and my uncle, Ed Williams, built the house, and we lived there for five years before my mother threw up her hands and demanded to move back to the city.

Holmes Center and the house are still there, across the road and a little south of Caterpillar's entrance off Illinois Route 29. It's now owned by friends of ours, Rich and Mildred Frasco.

But that house came as close to being taken by the Illinois River as any that have since survived.

It had been raining heavily for several days in May 1933, and the river already was swollen from the runoff of melting snow north of here. Heavy winds lashed huge waves against the embankment, causing the rising water to chew away huge hunks of our river frontage.

At the time the house was built, we had a nice big yard stretching from the home down to the beach. But when the river finally had its fill of our precious soil, only about six or seven feet was left in front of our cottage.

I was only eight years old but I vividly recall filling sandbags along with my parents and the other men and women who fought day and night to save our frontage.

One night as the river edged closer and closer to our door, we stayed up all night for fear that our house would be washed off its foundation and sink into the heavy current. Thankfully, the wind-driven river finally crested at Peoria at 25.4 feet, just 1.7 feet below the 1844 flood.

As it turned out, we weren't as bad off as others. The river completely isolated cottages between Al Fresco Park and the Ivy Club, and also at Walnut Grove, just south of Rome. Strong winds there pushed water over the seawall and cars moved slowly, if at all, through a foot or more of water.

Water also inundated Waterworks Park, nearly reaching the pumping station. The Upper Free Bridge (near where McCluggage Bridge is now) was closed for nearly a month while covered with nearly six feet of water.

Woodruff Field also was flooded, causing the cancellation of games between the Peoria Tractors and Quincy Warriors.

It was a frightening experience, and I can certainly sympathize with all those unfortunate people along the Mississippi and other Midwest rivers today.

But the 1943 flood probably did the most damage of all, threatening much of our commercial area. Caterpillar's East Peoria plant was closed down May 22. Workers were sent home at staggered times to avoid traffic conjestion on the few open streets and roads, while a sound truck warned of dangerous areas to be avoided.

Cat president Louis B. Neumiller ordered all second- and third-shift workers to report for duty to aid in the fight against floodwaters. All Caterpillar's doorways were sandbagged.

The LeTourneau Co. in Averyville was also saved by a wall of sandbags.

The Illinois reserve militia was mobilized here by Governor Dwight Green to help sandbag the levees.

Commercial Solvents Co. was closed and Altorfer Bros. Co. in East Peoria put 500 men to work on sandbagging. The P&PU Railroad in East Peoria was no longer able to run, and the Rock Island trains stopped at the foot of Fayette Street instead of running through the water to the downtown depot, which was completely surrounded.

The Trivoli-Landcaster Road, south of Trivoli, was closed due to a damaged bridge and water backing up from the mouth of Kickapoo Creek threatened outlying portions of Bartonville's business district.

The Rock Island Depot (now River Station Restaurant) was surrounded by the flood waters of 1943.
(Photo from the Grassell file of the Peoria Public Library)

Sightseers entering East Peoria hampered the flood fight, and the Peoria Police Department closed Cedar Street Bridge to all who didn't have urgent business on the other side.

1933 and 1943. Two major floods that, to me, at least

... seems like only yesterday!

Rouse's Hall bright spot for half a century

Peoria's first known entertainment halls came into being around 1850. But probably the most prominent hall of them all opened on May 18, 1857. This was Rouse's Hall on Main Street near Jefferson, and it was one of Peoria's bright spots for nearly half a century.

On September 15, 1902, according to one document in the Peoria Public Library, the hall became a vaudeville house and was renamed the Main Street Theater for several more years.

The structure finally was razed around 1919 to make way for what is now one of Peoria's most revered landmarks.

The new building that replaced it was first named the Peoria Life Insurance Building. When that company failed in the early 1930s, it was purchased by the Alliance Life Insurance Co. of Chicago. The First National Bank purchased it in 1949, and that bank called it home until the bank recently was purchased by the Commerce Bank.

Dr. Rudolphus Rouse, a prominent Peoria physician, erected his hall next to his residence on that corner, with the hall's entrance at 404 Main St.

Dr. Rouse was born in Renssaeller County, N. Y., on July 20, 1793, and as a young man attended the University of Pennsylvania Medical School, where he graduated with honors. He served as a surgeon in the War of 1812 and, after practicing for a time in New York, came to Peoria with his family about 1832.

He became the first president of the board of the new Town of Peoria in 1835, and also served as president of the Illinois State Medical Society.

Rouse died on April 30, 1873, and was survived by his wife and seven children. His funeral was held May 2 at the Baptist Church at Madison and Fayette streets, and he was buried in a vault in Springdale Cemetery.

His Rouse's Hall became the town's most popular place of entertainment, and innumerable uses were made of it. It was made brilliant with dances, festivals, graduations, public speakers and all kinds of shows, including legitimate theater and opera. A Peoria girl who became a famous international opera star, Emma Abbott, was once popular here.

So, let's take a trip back in time and read some newspaper accounts of the shows, performers and personalities who appeared at Rouse's Hall, beginning with its very first program. These quotes are from a "Peoriana" column that ran in the *Peoria Daily Record* between 1925 and the early 1950s:

■ May 18, 1857: "Rouse's Hall...was opened with many ceremonies and celebrities today by Dr. Rudolphus Rouse, the builder, who engaged a high-class show for the opening night.

"The first production was 'Charles II or The Merry Monarch,' starring Mr. and Mrs. Henry Howard, Broadway and Gaiety favorites; Madame Carlotta Pozzoni, of the Academy of Music, a popular singer in New York, Philadelphia and Baltimore; and M. N. Gilbert, orchestra leader."

■ January 22, 1862: "Charles F. Brown, humorist of note, although only 25 years old, kept the audience laughing at Rouse's Hall with his discourse on 'The Babes in the Wood.' (Later he was to become famous under the pen name, Artemus Ward.)"

■ February 1, 1862: "General Tom Thumb, the midget, made his first appearance in Peoria, playing in the two-a-day vaudeville at Rouse's Hall. He sang a few comic songs and cracked a few jokes and was well received. Before the performance, he put on a smart publicity build-up by driving through the streets in a midget-sized coach, drawn by four small ponies and attended by an undersized coachman in livery..."

■ October 3, 1866: "A delegation of Southern Loyalists touring the North in search of sympathy and financial aid for the war-torn South stopped in town tonight and several members explained their mission at a meeting at Rouse's Hall. They spoke bitterly against President Andrew Johnson and his stern control of the defeated Confederacy."

■ March 21, 1868: "Tonight's big attraction was a concert given at Rouse's Hall by Frank Lombard and his troupe from Chicago. Emma Abbott from Peoria, one of the players, pleased the audience with her soprano rendition of 'Within a Mile of Edinboro.' She was billed as 'The Queen of Song.'"

■ September 20, 1872: "The play, 'Drummer Boy of Shilo,' closed its nineteenth presentation (at Rouse's Hall). The play was a patriotic military allegory based on the Civil War happenings and undoubtedly set an all-time record for consecutive showings in Peoria."

■ July 30, 1875: "Tony Pastor, the Bowery favorite, and his troupe of Variety Vaudeville artists, were playing at Rouse's Hall."

■ November 15, 1875: "Col. R. G. Ingersoll delivered a two and one-half

Rouse's Hall at 404 Main Street, was built in 1857, up against Dr. Rouse's residence (built about 1837) at the corner of Main and Jefferson.
(Photo courtesy of Peoria Public Library)

hour lecture at Rouse's Hall on 'What I saw and what I didn't see in England and Ireland.' The collection was for the benefit of the National Blues Military Unit."

The following "Peoriana" piece suggests that the hall's change in name and policy to the Main Street (vaudeville) Theater in 1902, was in conjunction with the advent of moving pictures.

■ September 10, 1902: "An Edison kinetoscope (motion picture machine) of the latest model is to be installed in the Main Street Theater. It will require special stage effects and an operating house. It will add a thousand feet of motion picture each evening to seven acts of vaudeville."

Armstrong family left its mark on Peoria's streets

Have you ever wondered how some of our Peoria streets were named? One Peoria pioneer, John Armstrong, played a major role in naming four of them, although one of those has since been renamed.

Armstrong was a native of New Jersey but he spent many years in Cincinnati, Ohio when it was just a small village. He eventually became a cashier in the Pratt and Lambert Bank there.

John Armstrong married Susan H. Willis of Cincinnati, at the same time and place Miss Willis' aunt, Susan Conner, married the noted horticulturist, Nicholas Longworth, who amassed a fortune estimated at between 10 and 15-million dollars.

The Armstrong family came to Peoria around 1836, although not together. John and his older sons came by land, walking much of the way but he sent his wife, daughters and younger sons by boat, down the Ohio River to the Mississippi, then up the Illinois River to Peoria.

The family knew Bishop Philander Chase while living in Ohio, and one of the first people they visited after arriving in Peoria was that same Bishop Chase at his Jubilee College.

Shortly after John arrived here he bought a large tract of land in the middle bluff, which was then considered "out in the country." This land extended from Chambers Avenue (now Columbia Terrace) to Dry Run Creek, and from Elizabeth Street (now Sheridan Road) to Knoxville Avenue. He donated the street we now know as W. Armstrong Avenue to the city and it was named for him. Mr. Armstrong had named the original Chambers Avenue for Governor Chambers of Kentucky, who married Armstrong's sister.

Armstrong built a house on the northwest corner of Knoxville and Armstrong and planted a large orchard on his property. Some years later, the residence was destroyed by fire. Then Jacob Guyer built a large home there, which eventually became the Guyer Home for Aged People.

John and Susan Armstrong had 13 children: Anne, James, Martha, Hannah, John Jr., Sarah, Alexander, Carneal, Longworth, Lewis, David, William and Susan.

Their first son, James, became an early Peoria businessman. The first Peoria directory lists him as an "operator of a steam saw mill - at Rose Hill, just below town."

James joined the J. R. Forsyth party that left Peoria for the California gold fields on April 15, 1849, in the second oxen-drawn train of five covered wagons.

They apparently had little luck searching for gold and James returned to Peoria and became a soap manufacturer. He married Sarah Bigelow, daughter of Lewis Bigelow, Peoria's second practicing attorney. John Armstrong named Bigelow street for his daughter-in-law's family.

James and Sarah had six children, the last of whom was a daughter named Linn. John Armstrong named Linn Street after his granddaughter. (After James' death in 1869, his widow, Sarah Bigelow Armstrong, became closely associated with the Peoria Public Library).

Two of the Armstrong's sons, John Jr. and Lewis, operated one of Peoria's early brickyards. John Jr. married Agnes Smith and they had three children: Martha, Jane and James C. (Jane became the grandmother of Richard Whiting, the popular songwriter).

The third Armstrong son, Alexander (possibly with one or more of his brothers), also headed west for the gold fields, but he contracted lung fever and returned

The old Armstrong residence at 303 W. Armstrong Ave. was built by Alexander Armstrong in 1857.
(Photo from the Oakford File, Peoria Public Library)

to Peoria. He married Margaret Leech and they had two daughters: Mary and Agnes. Alexander built a house at 303 West Armstrong, which was also destroyed by fire.

Then in 1857, he built another house at the same location, which still stands today in excellent condition and unchanged from its original appearance. This home was occupied by their daughter, Mary, until 1940. After she died, the property passed from the Armstrong family.

Several of John Armstrong's sons seem to have been bitten by the gold fever and went west. One who went but never returned was their fourth son, Carneal. He died in California and an interesting story has been handed down about it.

It seems that their father, John, was an ardent believer in spiritualism and had a vision of his son's death before he was notified of it.

John sent word to his other sons in California that Carneal's body was in water and he requested them to move it.

Following this word from their father, the sons discovered that a river, near where the body was buried, had changed its course and had indeed covered their brothers grave.

The eighth Armstrong son, William, married Mary Lang, a niece of another prominent early Peorian, Isaac Underhill. (Another Peoria street name). Mr. Underhill built an imposing residence that later became the first unit of St. Francis Hospital.

(Facts are from Oakford's, "The Peoria Story" in the Peoria Public Library.)

Madison conjures up memories of theater magnate

The Madison Theater, the last of Peoria's beautiful old downtown "picture palaces," was the brainchild of a local showman named Dee Robinson.

According to an old article in the *Peoria Star*, Robinson gave himself the unusual first name - for an equally unusual reason.

When he was born in Cleveland, Ohio, on July 18, 1872, his official name was listed simply as D. Robinson. He later added "ee" to the "D" so he would have a real first name.

He was a son of Mr. and Mrs. W. W. Robinson of Cleveland, and he received his early education there.

Robinson started out in show business at the age of 26, traveling with an amusement company. He was making $200 to $300 a week, but he became ill and soon tired of life on the road. He settled in Peoria, where his brothers and a sister were living.

After recovering from his illness, he took a $6-a-week job as a bookkeeper for the Herschel Manufacturing Co. Quite a comedown from his show business days.

On June 4, 1901, Robinson married Virginia Tripp of Peoria; they later lived at 116 N. Institute Place.

His brother, Will Robinson, was the city editor of the *Peoria Star* newspaper before he bought an interest in the Crescent Theater in the 300 block of Main Street. Will was killed in a fire that later destroyed the Crescent.

Dee Robinson's rise in the motion-picture business was nothing short of meteoric. His first theater venture came in 1906 as a partner with Vernon Seaver. They built the Princess Theater in the 200 block of South Adams Street. Seaver, a Chicago capitalist, had built Al Fresco Amusement Park on Galena Road two years earlier.

Robinson's theater chain rapidly increased with holdings in the Duchess Theater in the 300 block of South Adams (where the First of America Bank building is now) and the Hippodrome on South Jefferson (which later became the Rialto).

After his brother's death in the Crescent Theater fire, Dee Robinson built the Apollo Theater at that same location. He also bought the Empress Theater in the 400 block of Main (just below the alley from the later Palace Theater).

But his crowning achievement came October 16, 1920, when his magnificent Madison Theater opened across the street, at the corner of Main and Madison. He was now president of the Apollo Amusement Co., the Robinson Theater Co. and the Seaver Amusement Co.

Later, when the Theaters Operating Co. was formed to operate all of Peoria's downtown theaters, he became its vice president and executive manager for motion pictures.

Robinson would also become identified with the motion-picture business in Bloomington as a member and officer in the Irvin Amusement Co. That firm owned and operated the Irvin and Castle theaters there. He was also very active in the Motion Picture Owners Association of Illinois.

But Dee Robinson was not to enjoy his beautiful new Madison Theater for long.

While returning on a train from Chicago around 1922, he suffered an attack of ulcers of the stomach. He was treated and was believed to have fully recovered when another attack seized him in September 1923.

His doctors said his only hope was an operation. He went to Chicago at the end of November for the operation at Chicago's Presbyterian Hospital.

The operation seemed a success but, while recovering, he had a relapse. His brother, Sam, hurried to Chicago for a blood transfusion but it never occurred.

Dee Robinson died on the morning of December 17, 1923. He was survived by his wife, Virginia; his brother, Sam; and a sister, Mary Robinson. (Incidentally, Miss Robinson was my eighth grade teacher at Irving School in the late 1930s.)

Services were conducted at the Universalist Church by Dr. B. G. Carpenter. Rev. Carpenter was the father of Ken Carpenter, who later gained fame as an NBC radio announcer on Bing Crosby's program and many others.

Dee Robinson was a much respected and loved man, and especially with the children who attended his theaters. Although he never had any children of his own, he was fond of them and was immensely popular with the youngsters who came to see his shows.

Out of his love for them, he began giving Peoria kids a Christmas present each year: a free show at his theaters.

As he lay near death, one of his last instructions was that the children of his beloved Peoria should not be forgotten during the Christmas season. And after he died, the local theater managers continued the annual tradition of free Christmas shows for the kids in the memory of Dee Robinson.

I can attest to the fact that the tradition was carried on for many years. During my later association with the

Dee Robinson, the man who had the vision to build the Madison Theater. (A *Peoria Star* Photo, courtesy of Peoria Public Library)

Madison during the 1940s and '50s, it was owned by Publix Great States Theaters, along with the Palace, Rialto and Apollo. And every year we still put on a free Christmas show for the kids. As a matter of fact, we improved on it.

Each Saturday morning before Christmas we ran not one, but two free shows. Youngsters could go to any one of the four theaters to see the first show, then change theaters and see a second show, all absolutely free. We would fill all three theaters twice.

All this was done for them by a man they never even knew...Dee Robinson

...and it seems like only yesterday!

The September 6, 13 and 20, 1993 columns were repeats of columns that originally ran in the *Journal Star* on May 28, 1990, April 8, 1991 and September 2, 1991 and appear in the book of *Yester Days - Volume II*.

"Proctor bums" stage a homecoming

You'd think that a 50th anniversary high school reunion would be enough for some folks. But that's not the case for many of those who attended the Manual High School's Class of '42 reunion in June 1992.

Just before that get-together, a group of locals joined some out-of-towners for a dinner before the big night. Among those attending were Shirley (Taylor) McGrath and her husband, John, along with Larry and Barbara (Hedrick) Tudor. The Tudors had come all the way from Tekopa, California, for the reunion.

As nostalgia began dominating the conversation around the dinner table, the talk eventually turned back to those wonderful 1930s and '40s at Proctor Recreation Center, where many of these folks, who were born and raised in the "South End," spent many happy hours involved in a variety of activities.

Larry Tudor suggested to Shirley McGrath that it would be great to have a reunion of "Proctor Bums" sometime. Shirley didn't consider herself a "bum" but said she might take on the project if she received enough local help to put it together. Larry pledged then and there that he and Barbara would certainly return for it and felt others would do the same.

Shirley first contacted Glen Hagen, Joe Palmer and Larry Lulay, who agreed to help; soon others joined the crusade, including Walt Eisele and Lou Grant, who promised to spread the word. Announcements appeared in the *Journal Star* and the *Observer*.

The committee became very active, but since this sort of thing had never been attempted before, they had no idea whether it would be a hit or a flop.

On Thursday, September 9, a near phenomenon happened at the Elks Club: more than 200 people showed up for an afternoon of Proctor Center nostalgia and a buffet dinner.

When Flossie and I walked in around 1:30 p.m., two rooms were already packed with "Proctor Kids," many of whom hadn't seen one another since their Proctor days.

Larry Lulay had enticed Peoria based comedian Royce Elliott to come and entertain and, yes, Larry and Barbara Tudor did return from California. This time, Shirley McGrath's brother and sister-in-law, Morey and Shirley Taylor, who live in Placentia, California, also returned.

Proctor Recreation Center at 309 S. Allen (now DuSable) Street, and surrounded by Kettelle, Martin and Warren streets, was established in 1913, an outgrowth of an endowment fund created by John C. Proctor, a prominent Peoria businessman and philanthropist. Proctor also founded Cottage Hospital, which was later named Proctor Hospital in his honor, and the John C. Proctor Endowment Home.

When Proctor Center first opened, it was described as having its fieldhouse directly in front of Lee School, but within a total school population of at least 4,000 youngsters. Most of these children's families lived in homes built close together on small lots, and in those early days, many were without plumbing and/or hot water.

Organized games were encouraged and play was supervised by a man and a woman director. The open space included a small children's playground 130 x 150 feet, with a shelter, sandbox, wading pool, swings, slides and space for kindergarten games.

A girl's playground of the same size included gymnasium apparatus, giant slide and swings, and space for various ball games and folk dancing.

The men's and boy's athletic field was 268 x 300 feet, with a running track, a straight 100-yard dash track, a baseball diamond and equipped tennis courts.

The fieldhouse itself was for the older people, as well as children. Its first big attraction was its baths for men, women, boys and girls. Its swimming pool measured 40 x 96 feet, with a nine-foot depth at the diving end.

The men and boys end of the fieldhouse included a bowling alley and billiard room. It was considered an evening club, to help keep boys off the streets at night, and to offer men a substitute for the saloon. It was called "The Poor Man's Club."

Above the baths and locker rooms were the assembly room, library and club rooms. The main room included a dance floor, a stage, and a dressing and cloak room. It was designed for social parties, lectures, vaudeville or dramatic shows, movies, club meetings and informal gatherings. Proctor also featured two large gymnasiums, one for girls and one for boys.

But one of the most interesting features at Proctor (which I didn't know before) was its bathing facilities. It was estimated that more than 500 people a day came to Proctor for baths and nothing else. One 83-year-old woman took the first real bath of her life there, while one man brought a wagonload of 12 children to Proctor for baths. When the center

The Proctor Recreation Center fieldhouse.
(Photo courtesy of Peoria Public Library)

first opened, its showers were such a luxury, children were found bathing two or three times a day. In 1915, a staggering 86,800 people came to bathe and swim at Proctor.

During this year's reunion, one name was mentioned probably more than any other: Neve Harms, who dedicated so many years as Proctor's recreation director... and we'll talk about him next week.

Harms' way kept boys off the street

Second of Two Parts

The name Neve Harms and the Proctor Recreation Center go hand-in-hand. Neve was the untiring athletic director at Proctor back in the 1930s and '40s.

Harms was a dedicated individual who firmly believed that keeping kids (especially boys) busy at sports and other activities was the best way to keep them off the streets and out of trouble. He became a role model to them and was probably responsible for saving more young men from going down the wrong path of life than anyone in his time... or maybe since.

Nevious Henry "Neve" Harms was born April 18, 1909, in Peoria. He was one of three sons and a daughter of Otto and Viola Adams Harms. He married Marion Scott on April 11, 1936; they had four sons.

During his school years he was one of Manual Training High School's most outstanding athletes. He was active in all four major sports and earned 12 varsity letters before graduating in 1930.

His first recreation work was as a playground leader at Bradley Park in the summer between high school and college. That fall he enrolled at Oregon State College but suffered an injury that kept him out of sports there, so he returned to Peoria and enrolled at Bradley Polytechnic Institute the following year.

He received a bachelor's degree in industrial arts at Bradley in 1935, and was placed in the Bradley Hall of Fame, having starred on the hilltop in football, baseball and basketball.

After graduation, Neve took the job of physical instructor at Proctor Center before joining the Navy. Barney Maticka was then the new Proctor director. The center had just reopened after financial problems forced it to close during the Depression.

While stationed at Great Lakes Naval Training Center, Harms suffered a near-fatal injury when he was struck by a car on the base. He received a fractured skull and back, and a double compound fracture of one leg.

After his naval discharge in September 1945, Neve returned to become director of Proctor Center. Then in July 1951, he was made acting superintendent of the Playground and Recreation Department, an independent agency of the city. It was absorbed by the Park District in January 1963, and Harms became assistant director and recreational supervisor of all the parks, under parks director, Rhodell Owens.

When Harms was later asked about highlights of his career, the first thing he mentioned was a teenage boys club at Proctor named The Comets. He had started the club in April 1938. It was organized to head off mischievous acts committed by boys in the neighborhood and to prevent them from getting into serious trouble.

The club organized various activities ranging from mud-slinging contests and "grease-ball" to boxing. The club's basketball team even went on the road, defeating teams in Decatur, St. Louis and Springfield. The Comets held plays and social events and sponsored programs to aid the needy.

Back when the city's playground and recreational department was taken over by the park district, politics apparently entered into the situation and Neve nearly lost his job.

He said: "For some reason or other, they didn't think I was qualified, and they separated me from the department." But he was quickly reinstated when it was found, as Neve put it, "I had more friends than I, and others, had anticipated."

After the recent Proctor reunion at the Elks Club, I reminisced with Joe Palmer about Neve Harms. Joe's family lived at the corner of Butler and Shelley

Neve Harms as superintendent of the Playground and Recreation Board in 1954.
(A _Journal_ Staff Photo, courtesy of Peoria Public Library)

Neve Harms and his Proctor basketball team in 1935.
(A _Journal_ Staff Photo, courtesy of Peoria Public Library)

streets, where they also operated The Palmer House, an Italian restaurant, just a block from Proctor.

My dad's family lived just a half-block down Shelley Street from the restaurant and, after the war, Flossie and I rented a house from my grandmother, just across Butler from The Palmer House.

Joe Palmer said he was a "Proctor Bum" from the time he could hobble around. He was also a member of The Comets teenage club, but he remembers there was also a Fox Club, which was for the younger kids. Joe also recalls a camera club Harms created for the kids.

Palmer remembers Neve Harms as a tough taskmaster. He said he had to be to keep those kids in line, but they loved and respected him for his strictness and dedication.

Joe recalled that Neve was a smoker. He said you could sometimes smell it in his office, but he never let anyone see him smoke. He apparently knew he had an image to protect, and didn't want to be responsible for any kids picking up the habit because of him.

Neve Harms became a legend over the years and, although he died at the young age of 58 in January 1968... he was still fondly remembered 25 years later at the recent Proctor Center reunion.

...and it seems like only yesterday!

Proctor left more than a fortune

Reminiscing about Proctor Center and Neve Harms the past two weeks, brings to mind the Peoria philanthropist whose generosity made that and many other projects possible: John C. Proctor.

John Cleveland Proctor was born on October 11, 1822, in Henniker, New Hampshire, the fourth son of John and Edna Dean Proctor. He received his "common school" education there, but as a young man he moved west to Mississippi. He remained there for one year before moving to Fulton County, Illinois, where he taught school for a short time.

He came to Peoria in 1843 to join his brothers, I. Francis and Ezekiel Allen Proctor, who had arrived here two years before. Upon arrival, John joined brother, Ezekiel Allen, in the business of manufacturing fanning mills. This business operated until 1858.

John never married, and made his home with Ezekiel's family, whose early residence was on lower Fayette Street. About 1853, Ezekiel built a brick home on the southwest corner of Seventh and Franklin Streets, and John resided there with them for more than 50 years.

In the early 1850s, John went into the lumber business with H. G. Anderson. The Anderson & Proctor Lumber Co. was located on Water Street, between Hamilton and Fayette.

Proctor later joined C. W. Tripp in two lumber yards, one dealing in pine lumber and the other in hardwood and wagon stock. The Proctor and Tripp Co. eventually became the John C. Proctor Lumber Co. at about the same time his brother Ezekiel and a half-brother, David C. Proctor, were also in the lumber business. (David later joined Richard Culter in the Culter & Proctor Stove Co., which I wrote about in March 1992).

John C. Proctor was one of the founders of the First National Bank of Peoria in 1863 and in 1875 he became its president, a position he held until he retired in 1906, the year before his death.

Over the years, Proctor accumulated substantial wealth and donated liberally to worthy causes. His financial support gave Cottage Hospital its beginning in 1883. It began out of a two-story residence at 415 Second Street and Proctor became its principal benefactor.

Cottage Hospital was incorporated in 1891. Proctor deeded the ground and a four-story brick structure was added to the initial frame building. Mr. Proctor also established the John C. Proctor Training School for Nurses.

In 1900, a more substantial building was erected on the corner where the hospital had its beginning, and the earlier brick building was remodeled. Proctor also donated by "deed of trust," several valuable properties, and the income from them helped fund Cottage Hospital.

In 1907, the year Mr. Proctor died, the hospital name was changed to the John C. Proctor Hospital in his honor. Proctor Hospital remained on Second Street until the current facility opened on North Knoxville in April 1959.

Shortly before his death, Proctor built the beautiful stone building at 1301 N. Glendale, at the foot of Spring Street hill, which was named the John C. Proctor Endowment Home. The property was the former site of Spring Hill Park.

The endowment home was built to house 200 people, and on August 27, 1906, it opened with 20 elderly men and women as its first occupants. Eight months later, Proctor himself became a resident of the home he had so generously founded.

Peoria philanthropist, John C. Proctor.
(Photo courtesy of Peoria Public Library)

Cottage Hospital at the corner of Second and Fisher streets, before the turn of the century.
(From the Grassel files/Peoria Public Library)

He died there at the age of 85 on June 22, 1907. The new J. C. Proctor Endowment Home on West Reservoir Boulevard opened on April 26, 1976, and the Spring Street home has since become St. Augustine Manor.

Under his will, Mr. Proctor created the John C. Proctor Endowment, and he named seven prominent Peoria business-men as its first trustees: William E. Stone, Charles Proctor, Frederick F. Blossom, Aaron S. Oakford, Oliver T. Bailey, Rudolphus R. Bourland and John S. Stevens.

The Proctor Recreation Center, established in 1913, was an outgrowth of the endowment fund, as mentioned in a recent column.

When Mr. Proctor came to Peoria, it was a struggling little community of around 3,000 people. When he died 64 years later, it had grown into a city of about 65,000.

John C. Proctor made a huge fortune during that time, but through his great generosity, he returned that and more, to the citizens of his beloved Peoria.

Lindbergh's luck nearly ran dry

A few weeks ago, Larry Byerly of Byerly Aviation, sent me copies of "For the Record," the official publication of the National Aeronautic Association.

In the magazines were two articles written by Charles A. Lindbergh about a couple harrowing experiences he had while flying the mail between St. Louis and Chicago, which included Peoria.

Lindbergh was the first person to fly the mail into Peoria, on April 15, 1926, and in a previous column I told of him parachuting from a mail plane after leaving Peoria the following September 16. But less than two months later, on November 3, he was forced to jump a second time.

The first article in the 1926 NAA publication was titled "Leap Fog at Night" by Charles A. Lindbergh. Here, in part, is what "Lucky Lindy" had to say about that first jump and crash:

"I took off from Lambert-St. Louis Field at 4:25 p.m., September 16, and after an uneventful trip arrived at Springfield, Ill., at 5:10 p.m., and Peoria, Ill. at 5:55 p.m.

"Off the Peoria Field at 6:10 p.m. There was a light ground haze, but the sky was practically clear but with scattered cumulus clouds.

"Darkness was encountered about 25 miles northeast of Peoria, and I took up a compass course, checking on the lights of the towns below until a low fog rolled in under me a few miles northeast of Marseilles and the Illinois River.

"The fog extended from the ground up to about 600 feet, and, as I was unable to fly under it, I turned back and attempted to drop a flare and land. The flare did not function and I again headed for Maywood (Chicago's air mail port), hoping to find a break in the fog over the field.

"I continued on a compass course of 50 degrees until 7:15 p.m., when I saw a dull glow on the top of the fog, indicating a town below... At no time, however, was I able to locate the exact position of the field...

"Several times I descended to the top of the fog, which was 800 to 900 feet high, according to my altimeter...

"After circling around for 35 minutes I headed west to be sure of clearing Lake Michigan, and in an attempt to pick up one of the lights on the Transcontinental.

"After flying west for 15 minutes and seeing no break I turned southwest hoping to strike the edge of the fog south of the Illinois River.

"My engine quit at 8:20 p.m., and I cut in the reserve. I was at that time only 1,500 feet high, and as the engine did not pick up as soon as I expected I shoved the flashlight in my belt and was about to release the parachute flare and jump when the engine finally took hold again...

"There were no openings in the fog and I decided to leave the ship as soon as the reserve tank was exhausted. I tried to get the mail pit open with the idea of throwing out the mail sacks, and then jumping, but was unable to open the front buckle.

"I knew that the risk of fire with no gasoline in the tanks was very slight and began to climb for altitude when I saw a light on the ground for several seconds. This was the first light I had seen for nearly two hours...

"Seven minutes gasoline remained in the gravity tank. Seeing the glow of a town through the fog I turned towards open country and nosed the plane up. At 5,000 feet the engine sputtered and died. I stepped up on the cowling and out over the right side of the cockpit, pulling the ripcord after about a 100-foot fall... I was falling head downward when the risers jerked me into an upright position and the 'chute opened...

The wreckage of Lindbergh's mail plane after he ran out of gas between Peoria and Chicago, and parachuted to safety. This photo was of his second crash.
(An International News Photo)

Young Lindbergh in the pilot's seat of "The Spirit of St. Louis" before his flight to Paris.
(Photo by Underwood & Underwood)

"I pulled the flashlight from my belt and was pointing it down towards the top of the fog when I heard the plane's engine pick up... I had neglected to cut the switches... Soon she came into sight, about a quarter mile away and headed in the general direction of my parachute... The plane was making a left spiral of about a mile diameter, and passed approximately 300 yards away from my 'chute, leaving me on the outside of the circle...

"When I settled into the fog I knew that the ground was within 1,000 feet... I crossed my legs to keep from straddling a branch or wire, guarded my face with my hands and waited.

"Presently I saw the outline of the ground and a moment later was down in a cornfield...

"In a few minutes I came to a stubble field and some wagon tracks which I followed to a farmyard a quarter mile away. The occupants of (a car) asked whether I had heard an airplane crash and it required some time to explain to them that I had been piloting the plane, and yet was searching for it myself. The farmer was sure... that the ship had just missed his house and crashed nearby...

"I had just put in the long distance calls (to St. Louis and Chicago) when the phone rang and we were notified that the plane had been found in a cornfield over 2 miles away.

"The plane was wound up in a ball-shaped mass. It had narrowly missed one farmhouse... The ship had landed on the left wing and wheel and skidded along the ground for 80 yards, going through one fence before coming to rest in the edge of a cornfield about 100 yards short of a barn. The mail pit was laid open and one sack of mail was on the ground. The mail however, was uninjured.

"The sheriff from Ottawa arrived, and we took the mail to Ottawa post office to be entrained at 3:30 a.m. for Chicago."

NEXT WEEK: Lindy bails out a second time.

Once was not enough for Lindy

Second of Two Parts

Last Monday I quoted Charles Lindbergh as he described his first of two parachute jumps while flying the mail between Peoria and Chicago on September 16, 1926.

As strange as it may seem, on November 3, 1926, - less than two months later - the not-so-lucky Lindy was forced to make a second jump, again between Peoria and Chicago. Lindbergh described the second jump as "even more thrilling than the first."

Stories describing the two jumps were recently reprinted in "For the Record," the official publication of the National Aeronautic Association.

Both stories were written by Lindbergh and were originally published in the NAA's magazine in 1926, which was then titled "Aeronautic Review."

Here are highlights of the second story, titled "He Does it Again":

"I took off from Lambert-St. Louis Field at 4:20 p.m., November 3, arrived at Springfield, Ill., at 5:15, and after a five-minute stop for mail took the air again and headed for Peoria.

"The ceiling at Springfield was about 500 feet, and the weather report from Peoria, which was telephoned to St. Louis earlier in the afternoon, gave the flying conditions as entirely passable.

"I encountered darkness about 25 miles north of Springfield. The ceiling had lowered to around 500 feet and a light snow was falling. At South Pekin the forward visibility of ground lights from a 150-foot altitude was less than one-half mile, and over Pekin the town lights were indistinct from 200 feet above. After passing Pekin, I flew at an altimeter reading of 600 feet for about five minutes, when the lightness of the haze below indicated that I was over Peoria. Twice I could see lights on the ground and descended to less than 200 feet before they disappeared from view. I tried to bank around one group of lights, but was unable to turn quickly enough to keep them in sight.

"After circling in the vicinity of Peoria for 30 minutes, I decided to try to find better weather conditions by flying northeast towards Chicago...

"Enough gasoline for about one hour and ten minutes flying time remained in the main tank and 20 minutes in the reserve...The only lights along our route at present are on the field at Peoria...

"I flew northeast at about 2,000 feet for 30 minutes... I pulled up to 600 feet, released the parachute flare, whipped the ship around to get into the wind and under the flare, which lit at once, but, instead of floating down slowly, dropped like a rock... My ship was in a steep bank, and for a few seconds after being blinded by the intense light I had trouble righting it...

"When about 10 minutes gas remained in the pressure tank and still I could not see the faintest outline of any object on the ground, I decided to leave the ship rather than attempt to land blindly. I turned back southwest towards less populated country and started climbing in an attempt to get over the clouds before jumping.

"The main tank went dry at 7:51, and the reserve at 8:10. The altimeter then registered approximately 14,000 feet... I rolled the stabilizer back, cut the switches, pulled the ship up into a stall and was about to go out over the right side of the cockpit when the right wing began to drop. In this position the plane could gather speed and spiral to the right, possibly striking my parachute after its first turn. I returned to the controls and, after righting the plane, dove over the left side of the cockpit while the airspeed registered about 70 miles per hour and the altimeter 13,000 feet.

"I pulled the rip cord immediately after clearing the stabilizer...

"The last I saw or heard of the D.H. (his deHavilland plane) was as it disappeared into the clouds just after my chute opened... It was snowing and very cold.

"...The snow had turned to rain and, although my chute was thoroughly soaked, its oscillation had greatly decreased... but the ground appeared so suddenly that I landed on top of a barbed wire fence without seeing it.

"The fence helped break my fall and the barbs did not penetrate the heavy flying suit... I rolled (the chute) up into its pack and started towards the nearest light. Soon I came to a road, which I followed about a mile to the town of Covell, Ill... The only information I could obtain (about where the plane had landed) was from one of a group of farmers in the general store, a Mr. Thompson, who stated that his neighbor had heard the plane crash, but could only guess at its general direction.

"I rode with Mr. Thompson to his farm... After searching for over an hour without result, I left instructions to place a guard over the mail in case it was found before I returned, and went to Chicago for another ship.

"On arriving over Covell the next morning I found the wreck, with a small crowd gathered around it... The nose and wheels had struck the ground at about the same time, and after sliding along for about 75 feet it had piled up in a pasture beside a hedge fence... The wings were badly splintered, but the tubular fuselage, though badly bent in places, had held its general form even in the mail pit.

Charles Lindbergh (left) and Phil Love, pose after flying the first air mail into Peoria on April 15, 1926. Love was Lindy's old friend from Army flying school, who assisted him in flying the mail between Chicago and St. Louis.
(Photo courtesy Peoria Public Library)

"There were three sacks of mail in the plane. One, a full bag, from St. Louis, had been split open and some of the mail was oil soaked, but legible. The other two were only partially full and were undamaged. I delivered the mail to Maywood by plane, to be dispatched on the next ships out."

Yes, Lindbergh had to bail out, not once but twice, while flying our mail. Fortunately, his luck improved the following year on his heroic trip to Paris.

How women helped feed the soldiers

It seems like only yesterday that women became a prominent part of our country's work force but, looking back, it really began - by necessity - 50 years ago, during World War II.

In 1943, the year before Flossie and I were married, she landed a "high paying" job at Pabst Brewery in Peoria Heights, in their shipping department. She had been working for $11.00 a week decorating windows at Kresge's dollar store downtown when one of her girlfriends went to work for Pabst. Flossie then also applied and nailed down a Pabst job that paid $32.50 a week Monday through Friday, or $42.50 if she worked on Saturday. That was a lot of money back in 1943.

Women, who were then considered the "weaker sex," also began doing what was considered "man's work," and were doing it well. Any number of local factories and industrial plants were hiring hundreds of women to fill their defense contracts with Uncle Sam.

Also by necessity, women were driving trucks and taxis, pumping gas, painting and wallpapering houses, as well as running tractors on the farms.

Before the war, Caterpillar employed women only for office work, but women were soon working in the factory, handling detail work in the engineering department, designing tools, working as chemists and testers in the metallurgical lab, filing burs by hand and machine, and operating all types of machine tools.

Back in those World War II days, many industries were converting to produce for the war effort, and a perfect example was Hiram Walker and Sons, operator of the world's largest distillery here.

Since it opened in 1934, after Prohibition, Walker's had carried the name of Peoria to every corner of the globe as a producer of liquor, but in February 1944, one of its main bottling departments was converted to the exclusive packaging of what became famous as K-rations. It was the concentrated emergency food that kept America's fighting men fed while operating under fast-changing conditions at the combat fronts.

Row upon row of women, many of whom used to work on the whiskey bottling line, were now working on two eight-hour shifts, six days a week, packing K-rations into containers for shipment overseas.

Many of these women had sons, husbands, sweethearts or brothers, fighting for their country and relying on K-ration production back here.

One middle-aged woman who paused for a moment as she watched the endless chain of packages flow by, summed up the feelings of many of the women working here on the homefront. She said, "For all I know, one of these very packages may go to my boy out in some foxhole. I have the feeling that I am actually doing something for him - and for all the thousands of other boys who are over there."

There were a lot of jokes making the rounds about K-rations back then. I thought it was something akin to beef jerky or hard tack. But what was being packaged at Hiram Walker's was described as the finest food money could buy (even if it didn't taste like it), and the most extreme care was used to see that it reached the men in excellent condition. The rations were packed in three separate cardboard containers weighing less than a pound each and stamped with the letters B, D or S, which identified them as breakfast, dinner or supper.

Breakfast consisted of: A package of biscuits (energy crackers), a can of ham and eggs (with canned cheese as an alternative), a package of soluble coffee, a fruit bar (which could be eaten cold or made into a jam by stewing slowly for three minutes), four lumps of sugar, a package of four cigarettes, and a piece of chewing gum.

Dinner included: A package of energy crackers, a can of cheese, an envelope of lemonade or orange powder (which could be made into a drink by mixing it in a canteen cup of cold or hot water), four lumps of sugar, a package of four cigarettes, a package of candy and a piece of chewing gum.

The supper menu included: Two packages of biscuits, a can of meat or cheese (which could be eaten hot or cold), an envelope of bouillon powder, a package of four cigarettes, a chocolate bar, (which could be eaten as is, or dissolved in water to make hot chocolate), a piece of chewing gum and, believe it ot not, a package of toilet paper.

The main objective of the assembly line was to carefully package the K-rations to keep them edible under any climatic conditions, even if they were dropped into salt water or exposed to poison gas.

After each package was sealed in cellophane, it was given a thorough coating of paraffin. The packets were then placed in heavy cardboard cartons, and finally in wooden boxes, which were wired shut and stained a neutral color as a camouflage.

Vitamin-filled cookies began the process of packaging K-rations as they moved along the assembly line at the Hiram Walker & Sons Peoria distillery back in April 1944.
(*A Journal Star* **photo, courtesy of Peoria Public Library**)

Hiram Walker's was the only distillery in the country to have a contract for K-ration packaging. The line was worked by women in two shifts, from 6 a.m. to 2:30 p.m. and from 2:30 p.m. to 11 p.m.

K-rations weren't exactly considered gourmet eating by our fighting men at the front, but they were life savers when nothing else was available and they played an important role in our winning World War II.

And yes, it really does

... *seem like only yesterday!*

Griswold was early city leader

One of the north/south streets in Peoria's extreme "south end" is Griswold Street. As a reference point, the "new" Manual High School faces this street, which is named after John Lynch Griswold, a prominent Peoria merchant.

Mr. Griswold was born February 4, 1806, in New York City, the son of Nathaniel and Ann (Sickles) Griswold. Nathaniel was a well known importer in that city, and operated under the name of "N. L. & G. Griswold, East India Merchants." The trade enterprise owned a number of ships which went to all parts of the world.

John went to school in New York City and was trained in the mercantile business when he came to Peoria in 1839. The following year he became a partner with another New Yorker, Alfred G. Curtenius. They formed a mercantile business named Curtenius & Griswold at the "lower end of Quay," which was later listed as 29 South Water Street. They dealt in dry goods, groceries, hardware, "queensware," boots, shoes and leather goods.

On December 9, 1840, John married Elizabeth Smith, the youngest daughter of a widow who owned a farm near Brimfield. Before he brought his bride to Peoria, he built a large brick house at 101 S. Jefferson, where they lived until about 1856.

John sold this home to the Mercantile Library Association and it became a library. It later consolidated with the City Library, the forerunner of today's Peoria Public Library system.

This corner later became the site of the Lehmann Building and is now the location of the new Becker Building.

John and Elizabeth had no children of their own, but when Mrs. Griswold's sister died, they took in her two orphaned boys, Normand and Robert King, to raise. After the boys went to college, the Griswold's adopted a daughter, Myra Howell, who later married one of the foster children, Robert King. Myra, however, died young, a victim of tuberculosis.

In 1845, John Griswold's brother, Matthew, entered into the partnership of Curtenius & Griswold. Then, in March 1857, Alfred Curtenius died and the Griswold brothers carried on the business.

They changed the firm name to Griswold & Co., and the original property on the levee was sold to the Rock Island Railroad, where they built a depot. Today, that building is the River Station restaurant. The Griswold company moved into a new building on South Washington at Liberty Street, where it continued until 1869.

John Griswold was one of the directors of the old Peoria Bridge Association, which was formed to construct the first wagon bridge across the river. It was on the site of today's Franklin Street Bridge.

Griswold was one of the first stockholders of the Peoria Gas and Coke Co., which was organized in 1853, and he later served as its president until his death. John was also instrumental in bringing the Bureau Valley Railroad to Peoria in November 1854.

In 1856, Mr. Griswold decided to build a "country place." He bought a tract of land on "Moss Street," in the West Bluff area. The northern portion stretched along Moss (now Avenue) for more than a block and extended over the hill to Seventh Street (now Dr. Martin Luther King Jr. Drive).

Elizabeth Griswold's cousin, Frederick Law Olmstead, was one of America's first landscape gardeners and held the distinction of laying out New York City's Central Park. Olmstead came to Peoria and designed most of the grounds for the Griswolds' estate,

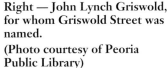

Left — An early sketch of "Woodside," the estate of John Lynch Griswold, built in 1856. (From the Grassel File, Peoria Public Library)

Right — John Lynch Griswold, for whom Griswold Street was named. (Photo courtesy of Peoria Public Library)

"Woodside," which included the arranging of tree groupings and flower gardens.

The property also had a fine vegetable garden which was famed throughout the state. Finally, Olmstead planted a hedge around the estate, which grew very high and gave it a shut-in appearance.

On the hillside below the residence, Griswold had a cave built, with heavy iron doors to protect the entrance. His wholesale grocery firm stored its wine here. Griswold also built Malvern Lane from Moss Avenue down to Seventh Street as a shortcut to town.

The Griswolds joined the First Presbyterian Church in April 1844, where John became an elder and trustee. They later became charter members of the Second Presbyterian Church and John became an elder there in 1853. But the Griswold's returned to the First Presbyterian Church on February 7, 1872.

John Griswold was a member of the Whig political party and later became a Republican, supporting the Union cause in the Civil War. He retired from active business in 1863, and died on January 15, 1883.

After his death, Mrs. Griswold's brother, Eustace Smith, a bachelor, came to live with her. Being somewhat artistic, the first thing Mr. Smith did was take away the hedge, which had grown to huge proportions, and subdivided the property for sale. The estate land, other than for their home, became the residences of Charles S. Jones, Deloss Brown, Frederick Steele, John Neilson and Charles Clark.

In 1890, Mrs. Griswold also donated a tract of ground for the building of the Westminster Presbyterian Church. Workmen, using a mule team and heavy sledge hammers, tore down the wine cave, and some of the stone from the cave was used in the Westminster Church foundation.

Elizabeth Griswold was an active church worker and Sunday School teacher. She died in 1896.

(Sources: A WPA Project story, written in the 1930s and The Peoria Story in the Oakford File, Peoria Public Library.)

You never forget your best buddy

I suppose we can all look back and remember a best friend during our school days. Someone we were always a little closer to than all the others. Someone we could confide in and knew we could trust in any situation. Mine was a great guy named Gil Crotty.

Gil and I first met when my folks moved into a small house at 1512 NE Perry, while I was still attending eighth grade at Irving School. We had moved from the 300 block of NE Madison (which is now an overpass for I-74). But since it was my last grade school year, I was allowed to finish at Irving, rather than transfer to Longfellow, which was just three doors away from our new home.

The Crotty family lived in an apartment above a grocery store on the northeast corner of Monroe at Mary Street, just around the corner from us.

I don't really recall how we met but once we did, we were inseparable. Whenever you saw one of us, you usually saw the other. We went downtown together, to the movies together, and hung out at the corner drug store together. The next year we started our freshman year at Woodruff High School together.

Woodruff was just a block-and-a-half up Perry Street.

Gil was a likeable, happy-go-lucky guy but he also had a temper that could, and did, get us both into trouble more than once. And it was mostly his temper that kept him from finishing high school.

Together, we decided to take the industrial course at Woodruff. The freshman year offered us a chance to try all four workshops the school had to offer: Wood, machine, electric and print shop. Then in our sophomore year, we could choose which shop we wanted to pursue. (It also seemed like a much easier way to get through high school. An academic or business course sounded boring to us).

But what we hadn't reckoned with was mechanical and architectural drawing. These turned out to be much harder than we had planned. I was always interested in drawing, but more of the freehand style rather than the strict adherence to detail and precise measurements. But drawing of any kind just wasn't Gil's cup of tea at all. He really labored at it, and it turned out to be the reason he finally quit school and joined the Navy.

Merle Ririe was our architectural drawing teacher; Melvin Brye, then later, Willis Harms, were our mechanical drawing instructors.

Gil's blood would boil when Mr. Harms corrected our drawings. He had a habit of marking our mistakes with red pencil, which was the next thing to impossible to erase.

One day, one of Gil's drawings came back from Mr. Harms that appeared more red than black. It looked like it had a bad case of the measles. Gil took one look at it, let out a few expletives, tore it to shreds, threw it in the air, and walked out. He not only walked out of class, he walked out of school as well. That's when he decided to join the Navy.

I felt a great loss when Gil decided to go into the service. I knew I wanted a high school diploma and I stayed to get it, but life sure wasn't the same without Gil Crotty.

When Gil and I first met, we were only about 14 years old. We were still two years away from our drivers licenses so, by necessity, our main mode of transportation was the bicycle. Our only other way to get downtown, unless my folks drove us, was to walk or, if we had two dimes between us, the Monroe Street trolley bus.

Monroe Street was the only line that featured trolley buses. They were a regular bus, except they were electric and had double trolleys that operated from two sets of electric lines overhead. They ran on big pneumatic tires instead of on streetcar tracks, which allowed them to pull over to the curb to pick up and drop off passengers.

The time we looked forward to all week long was Friday night at the Rialto Theater. It seemed that all the teen-agers in town hung out in the Rialto balcony on Friday nights. Most would come in doubles or groups of boys... and the same for the girls. It was a great place to just happen to run into someone of the opposite sex, and maybe even sit with them during the show.

The movies were always an action-packed double feature plus a serial and maybe a cartoon. If we were lucky, the main feature would star Roy Rogers or Gene Autry, plus a cops-and-robbers whodunit... or possibly a horror picture, which was great, especially if you were sitting with your arm around a girl. The more scared they were (or appeared to be) the better.

One night around Halloween, Gil and I went to a double-feature horror show at the Rialto, which featured both Frankenstein and Dracula. The show lasted past midnight, which caused us to miss the last bus, so we had to walk home.

It was a blustery, windy night and we were walking up Perry Street. All the big tree limbs were dancing in the wind, cast-

(L to R) Bill Adams with his best buddy, Gil Crotty, after both had returned from the Navy.
(Photo courtesy of Lila Crotty Smith)

ing huge, long shadows in their reflection from the streetlights. To two young teen-agers, these long shadows soon took on the shapes of the Frankenstein Monster and Dracula.

What began as a slow, casual walk home, took on a faster and faster pace. By the the time we hit Spring Street, we were running right up the middle of Perry, as though our very lives depended upon it.

Gil Crotty (right) holding his oldest son, Mike. Gil's brother, Dick (left), was later missing in action in Korea. Gil married Lila Burkholder, a Woodruff classmate.
(Photo courtesy of Lila Crotty Smith)

You never saw two more scared kids when we finally hit our front porch.

But what great days (and nights) those were with my best buddy, Gil Crotty

...and it seems like only yesterday!

Fred Allen brightened radio days

Several years ago I started one of my favorite hobbies, collecting old radio programs. When I play some of these old tapes, which is often, it always takes me on a nostalgic trip back to those pleasant days (and nights) when I would join my parents, listening to one of our favorite programs.

Our Majestic console radio held a prominent spot in the living room between Mom and Dad's favorite easy chairs. I'd usually lay on the floor between them, doing my best imitation of a bear rug, with my head practically in the speaker of that old superheterodyne radio. What great memories of so many wonderful radio programs.

One of my favorites in prime time (we didn't call it that back then) was Fred Allen's program, which had several names over the years. Fred's first program, "The Linit Bath Club Revue," was first heard on October 23, 1932, and his last program, "The Fred Allen Show," made its final bow on June 26, 1949.

In between those dates Allen was heard on "The Salad Bowl Revue" (for Hellman's Mayonnaise) in 1933. Later that same year he began "The Sal Hepatica Revue," which became the "Hour of Smiles." In 1934, Fred formed his famous "Town Hall Tonight" program, which featured "Senator Claghorn" (played by the announcer Kenny Delmar), "Titus Moody" (Parker Fennelly), "Mrs. Nussbaum" (Minerva Pious) and "Ajax Cassidy" (Peter Donald).

It was also on this same "Town Hall" program that Allen started his famous radio feud with Jack Benny, although the two comedians were really close friends away from the microphone.

Fred started the feud on his Wednesday night show by making a crack about Benny's inept violin playing. He remarked that the strings of his violin would have been better off if they had been left in the cat.

Jack Benny picked up on the insult on his following Sunday night show (although the two friends hadn't talked to one another about it off the air). Allen responded to Jack's remarks the next week, and the feud was on.

The verbal fight built big listening audiences for both shows. The whole nation, it seemed, couldn't wait to hear the next barb and it became a natural as a publicity stunt. So the two "friends" slated a "battle of the century," which was aired to a huge national radio audience on March 14, 1937. A radio survey showed that only one of FDR's fireside chats had ever drawn a larger audience. And so many people wanted to see it, live, the program had to be moved from NBC's New York City studios to the ballroom of the Hotel Pierre.

Although this memorable program was intended to be the climax of their on-air fight, the radio "feud" continued until Fred Allen retired from his regular program, 12 years later.

But this wasn't the only feud Fred Allen was involved in. The caustic, nonconforming comedian also carried on some very real ones with network officials and his various sponsors as well. One of his shows was actually cut off the air in the middle of the program. The reason was because of the following scripted dialogue between Fred and his real-life wife, Portland Hoffa, the week after one of his shows had run overtime, which it often did.

Portland: Why were you cut off last Sunday?

Fred: Who knows? The main thing in radio is to come out on time. If people laugh, the program is longer. The thing to do is to get a nice dull half-hour. Nobody will laugh or applaud. Then you'll always be right on time, and all of the little emaciated radio executives can dance around their desks in interoffice abandon.

Portland: Radio sure is funny.

Fred: All except the comedy programs. Our program has been cut off so many times the last page of the script is a Band-Aid.

Portland: What does the network do with all the time it saves cutting off the ends of programs?

Fred: Well, there is a big executive here at the network. He is the vice-president in charge of "Ah! Ah! You're running too long!" He sits in a little glass closet with his mother-of-pearl gong. When your program runs overtime he thumps his gong with a marshmallow he has tied to the end of a xylophone stick. Bang! You're off the air. Then he marks down how much time he's saved.

Portland: What does he do with all this time?

Fred: He adds it all up - 10 seconds here, 20 seconds there - and when he has saved enough seconds, minutes, and hours to make two weeks, the network lets the vice-president use the two weeks of YOUR time for HIS vacation.

Portland: He's living on borrowed time.

Fred: And enjoying every minute of it.

...and it seems like only yesterday!

(The Fred Allen script is from the book, "A Pictorial History of Radio," by Irving Settel.)

Fred Allen and his wife, Portland Hoffa, in a 1932 publicity photo. **(An NBC photo)**

Highs, lows in higher education

According to Ernest E. East's unpublished "History of Peoria," the earliest attempts to establish schools of higher education in this area met with short success. This was, of course, before Lydia Moss Bradley founded her Bradley Polytechnic Institute.

The first among Peoria County's institutions of advanced education was Jubilee College, established in La Grange precinct, which is now Jubilee Township. It was founded by an Episcopal Bishop, the Right Reverend Philander Chase, who had also previously founded Kenyon College at Gambier, Ohio, in 1824.

In 1836, Bishop Chase built a log cabin to house his family in the rugged wilderness of the Kickapoo Creek valley, fifteen miles northwest of Peoria. He said he named it "Robin's Nest" because it was "built of mud and sticks, and filled with little ones". This home later became a post office with Chase as its postmaster.

Reverend Chase laid the cornerstone for the first building, Jubilee Chapel, on April 3, 1839. Soon after, a two-story building was connected to the chapel. A classroom, library and college office occupied the main floor. The upper floor and part of the lower level contained small rooms for male students. Both of these buildings were built from native sandstone.

Bishop Chase purchased more than 2,000 acres of government land adjoining the college grounds. Crops were grown here and a gristmill and a sawmill were constructed. The area provided an abundance of clay for brick, and timber for building purposes. A store was established to handle staple goods, while produce was either grown on the college farm or obtained from nearby farms. Jubilee became a self-contained community.

The first students were admitted to the school in the autumn of 1840, when both preparatory and collegiate courses were offered. Jubilee was principally intended for the training of young men for the ministry but young women were also admitted to the female seminary, although in a separate building.

Jubilee College flourished but only for a decade. Bishop Chase died on September 20, 1852, at the age of 76. His grandnephew, Dr. Samuel Chase, carried on, but the college fell into decline.

The Civil War caused a withdrawal of support from the Southern states. This and other misfortunes, including fire and drought, caused the school to be abandoned in 1862.

Although three more attempts were made to revive the college, none was successful.

Lands held in the name of Bishop Chase were reduced to 96 acres when, under a decree of partition in 1931, the encumbered estate was sold to Dr. George A. Zeller, who presented the ground and dormitory to the Boy Scouts. He reserved the chapel for St. Paul's Church. The Boy Scouts, however, were unable to carry out the terms of the gift so, in December 1933, Zeller gave the property to the state and Jubilee ultimately became a state park.

But Jubilee College fared better than the plans for Peoria University, which was started but never completed.

Peoria U. was planned by the Presbyterian Synod of Illinois, which obtained a charter from the state legislature in February 1855. Its 30 incorporators included 12 Peoria Presbyterians. The Reverend James Smith, pastor of the Springfield Presbyterian Church (of which Mrs. Abraham Lincoln was a member) was authorized to act as its agent. He was also president of the board of trustees.

In April 1856, the Peoria University trustees contracted with William S. Moss for the purchase of a six-acre tract lying north of Moss Avenue and west of the present Orange Street. Construction was begun in June 1857, on a $15,000 two-story brick building. Walls appear to have been completed that autumn, when work was suspended due to a lack of funds to pay the workmen. These walls remained

Bishop and Mrs. Chase as they appeared in 1847.
(Courtesy of Peoria Public Library)

An early view of Jubilee College and Chapel.
(Courtesy of Peoria Public Library)

until May 12, 1858, when a violent wind storm nearly leveled them, and the project was abandoned some months later.

For some reason, the trustees had never acquired title to the real estate, which appears to have been purchased later by the board of school inspectors and re-platted as School Inspectors Addition. Eventually, Washington Grade School was built on, or near, the site of the Peoria University that never was.

Peoria County Normal School, an institution for the training of teachers, was established in September 1868. The city board of school inspectors furnished the building, and the county paid the instructors' salaries.

A two-year course was arranged and 56 students were admitted. Samuel H. White of Chicago was hired as principal. Control passed to the county board of education under a state law that was enacted in 1869.

After 11 years of struggle, Peoria County Normal was closed in June 1879, because the appropriations made by the county board of supervisors were never sufficient to maintain the school.

On May 10, 1879, the *Peoria Journal* announced that Principal White and his first assistant, Louise Ray, had resigned. The newspaper also stated: "Ignorance and bucolic jealousy have at last accomplished their work at the county Normal school."

But then, in 1879, a lady named Lydia Moss Bradley entered the local arena of higher learning, and her Bradley Polytechnic Institute developed into the successful institution we know today as Bradley University!

Diamonds had shining moments

It's sad to hear all the problems surfacing today with our town's Peoria Chiefs baseball team.

As a lifelong Chicago Cubs' sufferer (I mean fan), one of the major blows, to me at least, is the eventual loss of the club's association with the Cubs organization. Well, maybe Pete Vonachen can pull another rabbit out of the hat for us in the near future.

But looking back in the pages of time, Peoria baseball has always had its ups and downs, and old-timers will remember its on-again, off-again association with one of the better minor leagues of the past, the Three I League.

Some older fans might also suggest that old Woodruff Field is still haunted by the ghosts of such former baseball greats as Iron Man Joe McGinnity, Tony Lazzeri, Charley Dressen, Hank Greenberg, Phil Cavarretta, Whitlow Wyatt, Red Ruffing and others.

But if the Three I League had its "peaks and valleys," one of its high point years had to be 1921, when the Peoria Tractors performed not one - but two - triple plays.

The first one occurred on Saturday, June 11, of that year, and thanks to Haven Coleman, then-coach at Manual Training High School, it was caught on camera and preserved for posterity.

The scene was Lake View Park (before it was renamed Woodruff Field, in honor of former Peoria Mayor E. N. Woodruff).

The Peoria team, also known as "the Trax" had such future major league stars as Charley Dressen at third, who went on to become the legendary Brooklyn Dodger manager, and Ossie Bluege at shortstop. The following year Bluege was signed by the Washington Senators, where he played for 18 consecutive years and then managed them from 1943 through 1947. Joey Evers, the younger brother of the Cubs' famous Johnny Evers, was playing second base.

The Peoria Trax manager, "Major" Bill Jackson was playing at first, and Carl Schlee was catching. The Peoria outfield consisted of Mandy Brooks in left, Ted Menze in center and Al Platte in right. The Tractors' pitcher was Tiny Monroe.

The Peoria fans sat in the cool breeze off the river while enjoying the rare treat of the triple play that defeated the visiting Terre Haute team, 1-0.

The photo taken during the play was shot from atop the grandstand, where the press box was located in the old park. Only three players touched the ball and it happened so fast, about a half-minute elapsed before the stunned spectators broke out with cheers and applause.

The play went from center fielder, Ted Menze, to the catcher, Carl Schlee, to second baseman, Joey Evers.

Drew, the Terre Haute second baseman, had opened the inning with a two-base hit, their only extra-base blow in the tightly waged conflict. He then went to third on a passed ball. Winkleman, the visitors' right fielder, walked, setting the scene for the catcher and manager of Terre Haute, Bob Coleman, to come to bat.

Coleman lined a vicious smash to center field. Menze used some nimble footwork to get to the ball, but he caught it on the fly and rifled a throw to the plate.

The picture shows Schlee, the catcher, tagging out Drew, who tried to score from third after the catch. Winkleman also had tagged up at first and is seen in the photo, heading for second, where he was ultimately tagged by second baseman Evers, to complete the sparkling triple play.

The Terre Haute "Tots" were mad as hornets, as they had been during the entire afternoon. They were a hard-hitting team and had pounded the ball all

A picture taken at Lake View Park (later Woodruff Field) on June 11, 1921 while a triple play is in progress by the Peoria Tractors' Three I League baseball team. Photo was taken by Haven Coleman.
(Photo courtesy of Chuck Ginoli)

day, but the Peoria crew were playing inspired ball and caught anything and everything.

Joey Evers figured in a number of other flashy defensive plays, as did Mandy Brooks and Al Platte. Platte also had a three-base hit in the second inning and scored on Mandy Brooks' sacrifice fly, to give manager Jackson's men the 1-0 margin of victory that day.

Peoria pitcher, Tiny Monroe, earned the win with a four-hit performance, and is seen in the picture backing up Menze's throw to the plate.

Carl Schlee was the Tractors' second string catcher to Goldy Goldthwaite that day. When necessary, he filled in for both Goldthwaite behind the plate, and manager Jackson at first.

As mentioned, the Peoria Tractors pulled off a second triple play later in 1921 and, ironically, Carl Schlee figured in that one, too. But this time he was filling in for Jackson at first.

In this one, shortstop Bluege speared a line drive near second base and stepped on the bag to double up a runner. He then pegged the ball to Schlee at first to trap

another runner, which rounded out that triple play.

Incidentally, in the photo, the third base coach for the Terre Haute team is identified as Luke Jackson, a prominent local ball player of an earlier day. A note on the back of the photo also states that the home plate umpire that day was "possibly" Harley W. "Scully" Jones.

From Menze to Schlee to Evers... plus Brooks, Platte, Dressen, Bluege, Jackson and Monroe. What a ball club.

And to some old-timers out there, it might still

... seem like only yesterday!

Book tells TP&W's rail story

On several occasions I've written about Peoria historian Paul Stringham and his infatuation with local rail history. In the past, he's written such books as "76 Years of Peoria Street Cars," and "Illinois Terminal - The Electric Years." In 1979 he also collaborated with two other authors on the "Chicago and Illinois Midland," railroad.

Now, Paul has just come out with another book, and this time it's a thorough documentation of the history of the TP&W Railroad with the appropriate title, "Toledo Peoria & Western - Tried, Proven and Willing."

Railroad buffs should especially enjoy this 158-page edition, which includes 115 photos plus many pages of maps, equipment rosters and corporate history charts. It's just been released this month by Deller Archive, Inc., 1502 W. Barker, in Peoria, and is available at Illinois Antique Center, 100 Walnut; Rex Camera Shop, 222 SW Adams; and Mike's Mainline Hobbies, 1227 W. Glen.

Paul masterfully details the history of this colorful local railroad from its beginning as the Peoria & Oquawka Railroad Co. in 1849, through its many phases and name changes (including the Toledo, Peoria and Warsaw) right up to its recent new beginning as the Toledo, Peoria & Western Railway Corp. This most recent reorganization began in July 1987, under its current president, Gordon Fuller.

Some of this railroad's colorful history includes the famous Chatsworth wreck that occurred on August 10, 1887, just east of Chatsworth, Illinois. This was a devastating wreck of an excursion train that was made up in Peoria and was traveling to Niagara Falls.

More than 600 people were aboard the train when, just before midnight, the engineer noticed what appeared to be a small fire ahead. It turned out to be the wooden railroad trestle that was burning, but it was too late to stop the train. A terrible crash occurred as the trestle collapsed and more than 80 people were killed and many more injured and/or trapped in the wreckage.

The book thoroughly covers the history of the railroad during its various reorganizations and company presidents, including: E. N. Armstrong from 1904 to 1917; George P. McNear Jr. from 1926 until his death in 1947, when he was shot and killed while walking home from a Bradley University basketball game; J. Russel Coulter from 1947 until 1966, when he became chairman of the board; Harold L. Gastler, who was then named president in 1966 for two years; Charles L. Pattison, who took over in 1968 and continued for over nine years; and Robert E. McMillan, who came to the TP&W from the Santa Fe in 1977 and continued as its president until it merged with the Santa Fe in 1984.

But Paul Stringham's book takes you all the way back to the mid-1830s, before the railroads dominated the western frontier. It was a time when river boats provided the most practical means of transportation. Early settlers from the East began settling along the Ohio River, then along the Mississippi. Eventually they settled further upstream along the "Old Muddy" and also up the Illinois River.

There were hundreds of thousands of acres of fertile Illinois land available for cultivation but with no way to get the crops to market.

In 1837, the Illinois state legislature passed the Internal Improvement Act, which was intended to spur the building of railroads, highways and canals. All it accomplished (outside of nearly bankrupting the state), however, was the building of a railroad from Meredosia through Jacksonville to Springfield, plus the Illinois and Michigan Canal, along with a few miles of unoccupied railroad gradings.

One of those grades ran from Warsaw to Hamilton, Illinois, along the

The CB&Q roundhouse in Galesburg, shortly after that line had been acquired by the Peoria & Oquawka Railroad. The second engine on the right was formerly the P&O's "Peoria." Third from the right was formerly the P&O's "Elmwood" engine.
(Photo from the book, courtesy of the CB&Q Railroad)

Locomotive No. 7 appears to be at the former Peoria & Oquawka station between Oak and Elm streets in Peoria, around 1870.
(Photo from the book - the Montague L. Powell Collection)

Mississippi River, then eastward toward Canton and Pekin. But when the railroad was built years later, it was routed to Peoria instead of Pekin.

In 1849, a group of 12 men from central and western Illinois applied for a state charter to build a railroad from Peoria to the Mississippi River at Oquawka. This group included three men representing Peoria County: William S. Moss, Alfred G. Curtenius and Isaac Underhill. Ground was broken at Peoria on October 13, 1851, and about 50 men were put to work grading the line westward.

Oquawka, however, didn't seem interested in having a railroad but Burlington, Iowa did, so the western terminus was changed from Oquawka to East Burlington, Illinois, which was then a ferry landing on the east side of the Mississippi. This location is now known as Gulfport, Illinois.

On July 12, 1853, the Illinois River steamer, "Caleb Cope," arrived at Peoria towing a large barge with two locomotives and their tenders on board. These engines were named the "Peoria," and the "Burlington."

On July 30, the "Peoria" was fired up for the first time and a group of Peorians were given a ride over the completed section of track (which was only about four miles). Peoria's first passenger train had made its first trip, even though the passengers had to ride on construction cars.

Today, the TP&W stretches more than 284 miles, from just west of Fort Madison, Iowa, across north central Illinois to Logansport, Indiana.

Well, that's just a sampling of Paul Stringham's latest book on local railroad history. And, railroad buff or not, I'm sure you'll find it fascinating reading of important times of our local development.

Old bridge got off to a bad start

The opening ceremonies of the new Robert H. Michel Bridge last Thursday reminded me of the long and troubled history of the bridge it finally replaces - the Franklin Street Bridge.

I wish Congressman Bob a long and happy retirement after his 38 years of serving us in Congress. A bridge in his name is certainly a fitting tribute to his many years of service.

But I also wish his new bridge a better start than the one it replaces just a few feet away.

Just 20 days after the Franklin Street Bridge opened, a large chunk of it fell into the river.

When the first pilings were being driven for the bridge in 1906, it wasn't being referred to as the Franklin Street Bridge, and for a very important reason. It's connecting street on the Peoria end wasn't yet named Franklin Street. It was still going by its old name of Bridge Street.

At that time, the bridge was being referred to as the "new wagon bridge," primarily because it was replacing the old wooden wagon and foot bridge, just a few feet south of its new cement arches.

So, what would eventually become the Franklin Street Bridge (which cost $222,088 to build), was first opened to traffic on April 11, 1909.

But 20 days later, at 5:50 a.m. on May 1, a large section of the brand new bridge collapsed into the river, destroying three of its cement arches. Fortunately, because of the early time of the day, no one was on the structure when it toppled over into the river.

In the meantime, the company that built the bridge had also collapsed. The Marsh Bridge Co. of Des Moines, Iowa had gone bankrupt.

Superintendent Jim Finley, the bridge tender, and James Costello, the night watchman for the defunct Marsh Bridge Co., were sitting in the bridge tender's house that morning. They witnessed the tragedy. Here's Finley's description of the event:

"Costello and myself were in the bridge tender's house this morning at 5:30 o'clock when a farmer crossed the bridge driving toward the city. About 20 minutes later we heard a noise like a team driving up on the approach of the bridge. At the same time there was a rumbling noise as if

something had struck the big channel pier where the (bridge tender's) house is located.

"Both of us rushed to the door of the house and when we stepped out, we were just in time to see the first arch on the east side of the big channel pier raise into the air. There was the creaking and cracking sound of splintering steel as ribs of the arch snapped off like matchwood. The arch raised a fearful height into the air and then toppled over into the rushing water below. As soon as it fell, we could see the other arches falling, one after another toward us like cards that had been stood on end and pushed over. We could hardly realize what had happened and stood as if stunned for several seconds after the catastrophe happened. We then ran to the nearest telephone, which was located in the bridge house of the old wagon bridge and spread the alarm."

The news of the disaster spread quickly and hundreds of Peorians rushed to the scene. A number of police were detailed to guard the approaches to keep sightseers from going out on either the old wagon bridge or the Peoria approach of the new bridge, which was still intact but considered unsafe. By 8 o'clock, the river bank and every other vantage point was swarming with people anxious to view the ruins.

The old wooden bridge it was replacing (often called "old tooth picks") was already being dismantled, which left vehicles and pedestrians with no connection

The new wagon bridge (now the Franklin St. Bridge), after its eastern end collapsed on May 1, 1909. The partially dismantled old wagon and foot bridge it replaced is on the left.
(Photo from the Grassel file/Peoria Public Library)

Peoria's first bridge was the old wagon and foot bridge seen on the right. It was built in 1848 and nicknamed "old tooth picks."
(Photo from the Peoria Public Library's Peoria Picture File.)

between Peoria and East Peoria. Work began immediately to rebuild the old bridge for use until the damage to the new bridge could be repaired. But it wasn't until June 13th, nearly a month and a half later, that traffic was again moving on the old bridge.

On September 9, 1910, the last of the remaining arches were cleared out of the river, and on January 26, 1911, a new construction firm, the Milwaukee Bridge Co., was awarded the contract to rebuild the new bridge. It was January 1912 before new steel work could begin.

Finally, on April 6, 1912, three years after its first opening, the new bridge was once again opened to traffic. At 4:55 p.m. that day, 87-year-old Jacob Kock, who saw the construction of Peoria's first bridge, "old tooth picks," in 1848, rode across the new bridge in the first auto, along with Mayor Woodruff and other city officials.

The bridge at that time, however, didn't connect at South Washington Street as it does today. It connected with Bridge Street just about at the doors of the old Gipps Brewery Building. Work on

the viaduct extension, which took it over the railroad tracks and up to Washington Street, got underway in June 1913. A celebration was held at 3 p.m. Christmas Eve, 1913, for the opening of this new viaduct extension.

There is an obvious moral to this story: Don't burn (or dismantle) your bridges behind you. At least for a little while!

(Many of the facts and dates were provided by Peoria historian, Paul Stringham.)

Woe befell 1st bridge over river

Last Monday I wished the new Robert H. Michel Bridge a better start than the one it replaces. That's because what eventually became known as the Franklin Street Bridge collapsed 20 days after it first opened to traffic in 1909.

But the Franklin Street isn't the first bridge to collapse at that location. That honor goes to Peoria's first bridge (and the first to cross the Illinois River), the old "wagon and foot bridge." It wasn't yet completed when the trestlework at the East Peoria end washed out during a flood.

Before this first bridge, a ferry operated there and the street at the Peoria end was named Ferry Street. At various times, this street has also been named Hudson Street, Bridge Street and, later, Franklin Street.

The Peoria Bridge Co. was first chartered to build a bridge here in 1835, but was met with financial problems. It wasn't until October 30, 1846, that Col. William L. May applied for a permit to build a toll bridge on the site of the ferry. On March 24, 1847, an "article of association" was issued for the construction of the bridge and William A. Fessenden handled the sale of stock.

The new toll bridge was opened in 1848 but in the spring of 1849, the east end trestlework was washed out. On October 10, 1849, a local newspaper announced that the rebuilt bridge was (again) nearing completion. In July 1850, work was underway to widen the drawspan an additional 10 feet.

On September 24, 1851, a local paper stated the bridge was again open to the public after "A 324-foot section fell in last spring." This would have been the spring of 1851, and would be the second collapse due to floods.

On January 11, 1853, a new 290-foot drawspan was finished. At this point the river channel had been widened to 132 feet from its previous 85-foot width.

Often referred to as "old tooth picks," this old wooden bridge was later purchased by a Mr. Cole and the bridge became known as the Cole Toll Bridge. Its east end again fell into the river on April 4, 1904.

On November 3, 1886, the City of Peoria purchased the bridge from Mr. Cole for $37,788. Four days later the tolls were removed and a parade and celebration were held. More than 10,000 people crossed the bridge during its first free day. It became known as the Lower Free Bridge after Peoria's second bridge, the Upper Free Bridge, was completed two years later.

It was August 31, 1887, when the citizens of Peoria Township voted to construct a bridge at "the narrows," at Lorentz Avenue, just north of today's McCluggage Bridge. A parade was held from downtown to the site of the newly planned bridge and this was the beginning of what has since become the oldest continuous parade in the United States. We know it today as the Santa Claus Parade.

The following year, on December 4, 1888, merchants along the parade route entered into the celebration with special decorations to celebrate the completion of the new bridge.

Then, in 1889, the Schipper & Block department store (the predecessor to Block & Kuhl's), began sponsoring the parade, which is probably when Santa first entered the festivities. The parade has never missed a year over its 107-year span.

So, with two free bridges now crossing the Illinois River here, this one became known as the Upper Free and the

The old wooden wagon and foot (Cole) bridge after one of its collapses into the river, probably on April 4, 1904.
(Photo courtesy of Peoria Public Library)

The Upper Free Bridge at "the narrows" of the river, just above where the McCluggage Bridge is today.
(Photo courtesy of Peoria Public Library)

old wagon bridge downtown became the Lower Free Bridge.

And when the old downtown bridge was finally and permanently replaced in 1912 with what is now the Franklin Street Bridge, it, too, carried the Lower Free name. It was built with a 30-degree curve in the middle so that it could be built around the old wagon bridge (which had to be used while it was under construction). This also afforded the building of a sound footing in the middle of the river.

As old-timers as well as newcomers will recall, the Franklin Street Bridge has had a long and storied history of closures for repair. It became a way of life, especially for those who depended on it as the only downtown connection between Peoria and East Peoria, until the Murray Baker Bridge was opened in 1958. Over the years, mechanical problems caused the bridge to be locked in an up position anywhere from a few hours to a few weeks, primarily because new parts had to be custom made.

Even with all its problems and faults, the old Franklin Street Bridge will be missed by many of us. But probably not by the barge operators who risked banging into its pilings as they carefully maneuvered their boats and cargo barges through its narrow area, or actually crashed into it during rough weather and once when the span didn't rise in time.

But in a few years, this too

... will seem like only yesterday!

(Many of the facts and dates were provided by Peoria historian, Paul Stringham.)

Adventure on the way to Alaska

It was July 4, 1975, and if I didn't take a vacation soon, I, too, would explode like a firecracker.

The reason for my stated mental condition was because of my responsibility for installing a computer system in WEEK-TV's sales and traffic departments.

I can see my friend, Stu Sheehan, rolling on the floor laughing as he reads this. He and I, alone (until now), have any idea how little I know about computers, although he has since coerced me into writing the column via this mysterious system.

So, I packed Flossie and our three children who still lived at home - Lesa, Rob and Brad -into a rented 27-foot Champion motor home and headed for Alaska. The kids had a ball with their own bunk beds, a big king-size bed in the rear, plus access to the refrigerator all day.

Since childhood, I had dreamed of going to Alaska. Although I only had a three-week vacation, we didn't immediately head for that far-away state. First, I wanted my family to enjoy some sites out West that I'd enjoyed as a youngster. So, our first stop was Mt. Rushmore in the Black Hills of South Dakota, followed by the site of Custer's Last Stand in Montana, and then on to Yellowstone National Park.

We also squeezed in a visit to Virginia City, Montana, an old silver mining town where Flossie's grandfather, Thomas Castle, had settled as a printer during the frontier days. He eventually became the owner and publisher of "The Madisonian," the oldest newspaper in the Montana Territory.

Here we found his grave in the cemetery on a mountain overlooking his old newspaper building which, by the way, is still in operation. We also visited with an old blind saloonkeeper, who had been a personal friend of Grandpa Castle back in those wild and wooly frontier days.

After all the side trips, we finally headed north to Alaska.

We drove through the Canadian province of Alberta via Calgary, home of the famous Calgary Stampeed rodeo, on through Red Deer, Edmonton and Grand Prairie, to Dawson Creek in British Columbia.

From there, we began the most adventuresome part of our trip, the 2,000-mile trek on the Alaska Highway, across the northeast corner of British Columbia, through Fort Nelson and into the Yukon Territory at Watson Lake. Then it was on to the Yukon town of Whitehorse and, finally, Fairbanks, Alaska.

More than 900 miles of this historic Alaska Highway was gravel road.

As if that wasn't rough enough, the area had just suffered its worst flood in memory. Most of the bridges had either been washed out or had their underpinnings removed by the rushing water filled with uprooted trees.

The Alaska oil pipeline was also under construction at the time and the highway was packed with semi-trailer trucks, loaded with pipeline materials, racing to meet their deadlines.

Traffic became so bad that, when I would see a truck coming either toward us or from behind, I'd pull off the road and let it pass. Even so, by the time we returned home, I counted 11 windshield holes made by flying rocks thrown at us from those speeding trucks.

By the time we reached Dawson Creek, tourists in motor homes and trailers were bumper-to-bumper coming back down the highway. They had turned around because of the bridge washouts and highway damage caused by the floods and they strongly advised us to go no further.

We had a family meeting of sorts about continuing. Lesa, Rob and Brad were somewhat game to go on but I knew Flossie wasn't. But I told them I'd waited for this trip most of my life and I didn't

Flossie poses in front of her grandfather's newspaper building in Virginia City, Montana.

The driver visits with (L to R) Brad, Rob and Lesa during a rare coffee break on the road to Alaska.

Waiting my turn to drive our motor home across a partially washed out bridge on the Alaska Highway in 1975.

want to quit after being so close. We continued, but I promised them I'd turn around if I thought we were getting into any life-threatening situations.

The bridges were so bad, we were only allowed to move across them one vehicle at a time, and at no more than five miles an hour, as they precariously suspended us above the rushing water.

At last we made it!

It's hard to believe the 90-plus degree temperatures in the Yukon Territory that July. The mosquitos seemed big enough to saddle; they swarmed so thick at night that we had to stay inside the rig. Brad ventured out once and came back with welts all over his body.

After visiting Fairbanks, we traveled the inner circle road down past Alaska's highest mountain, Mount McKinley (20,320 feet), the peak of which we never saw through the thick clouds. From there, we traveled to Anchorage.

Having been penned up in the motor home for days, we took the luxury of renting two rooms in an Anchorage hotel for a couple days before heading home.

We retraced our trail back down the Alaska Highway as far as Watson Lake, where we entered British Columbia, then on to Prince George. From there it was a fairly straight shot down the Cariboo Highway on the west side of the Rocky Mountains.

I took this western route for a selfish reason. It would bring us back into the United States through Washington and Oregon. After being in Alaska, these were the only two remaining states to which I hadn't traveled.

Now I'm glad we chose the route for another reason. The view from the Cariboo Highway in the high mountain ranges, down into the sweeping valleys below, was one of the most beautiful panoramas we've ever witnessed... anywhere in the world.

We made our final camp just a few miles inside the Oregon border, and the next morning I made a beeline for home.

We got back to Peoria on July 25, 1975, just 21 days after our trip began. We had traveled 9,400 miles in just three weeks... and, even in those days of 75-cents per gallon gas, our gasoline bill was $1,006. No wonder I could see the needle moving on that gas guzzler's fuel gage.

It was a great family adventure that happened more than 18 years ago

...but it seems like only yesterday!

Tom Mix married a circus star

A few years ago, I told the story of Gene Autry and his Peoria connection, early in his career.

While he was still playing the vaudeville circuit and appearing on the "WLS Barndance" in Chicago, Autry made a "pilot" film in Peoria. He used this film to promote himself with Hollywood producers, which ultimately led to his motion picture star status.

But my very first cowboy hero was a movie star, even before Gene Autry.

His name was Tom Mix.

So, you can imagine my surprise when I recently discovered that this bigger-than-life hero of mine also had a Peoria connection, and an important one at that. He was married to a former Peorian named Mabel Hubbell.

Although this rugged he-man (off the screen as well as on) was publicized as being born in Texas and Indian-blooded, Thomas Hezikiah Mix was actually born at a place called Mix Run, Pa. (named for an ancestor) on January 6, 1880.

When he was ten years old, Tom was enamored with the glamour of Buffalo Bill and his Wild West Show at the Clearfield County Fairgrounds there.

From that moment on, the youngster was obsessed with horses, guns and anything to do with the West.

But even before his Hollywood stardom, young Tom Mix lived an exciting life, as well as portraying one. He was a soldier in the Spanish-American War, the Boer War and in China's Boxer Rebellion. After he returned to the states, he became a sheriff in Kansas and Oklahoma and also a Texas Ranger.

In 1905, four years before making his first movie, he was hired by Col. Joe Miller as a full-time cowboy with his Miller Brothers' 101 Ranch and Circus. His pay was $15 a month plus board. In 1906, he was hired by the old Selig movie company in Hollywood to supply them with horses, extras, and atmosphere, while the studio shot silent films on location.

By 1909, his masculine good looks had earned him a spot before the cameras - his first big break was in a Western documentary, "Ranch Life in the Great Southwest." It wasn't long until he became a star as the nation's number one boyhood hero.

During his entertainment career, Tom Mix also became a director, producer and screen writer as well as a vaudeville, circus and rodeo performer. But in front of the cameras, he fought the bad guys and rescued damsels in distress to the joy of his millions of fans who idolized him and his famous horse, Tony.

Tom Mix never smoked in his movies nor frequented saloons (except to shoot villians). And he usually wound up marrying the rancher's daughter or the local schoolteacher.

In 1932, his horse, Tony the Wonder Horse, rolled over on and badly injured Mix. That was the same year he married former Peorian, Mabel Hubbell, who had become a famous circus aerialist in her own right. The two had become acquainted while they were appearing with the Sells-Floto Circus.

Mabel Hubbell was the daughter of Isaac Hubbell of 1101 E. Melbourne Avenue. Her father and two younger sisters were still living at that address at the time of her marriage. She was born in Middle Grove, Illinois, but had moved to Peoria with her parents as a young girl. She attended Columbia School in Peoria.

Mabel left Peoria around 1917 with her Uncle Jacob Hubbell, to join a circus. A few years later, she and her two sisters, Irma and Jessie, joined the famous aerial act from Bloomington, Illinois called "The Flying Wards" and she took the stage name of Mabel Ward.

The year before her marriage, Mabel performed an unequalled feat under the big top when she accomplished 300 one-

Tom Mix resented doubles and preferred to do his own stunts. A scene from "The Big Diamond Robbery" (1929).
(From the book, "The War, the West, and the Wilderness.")

arm revolutions on the high bar without the protection of a net. She had played Peoria with circuses several times before, but in the summer of 1931, she and Tom both appeared here with the Sells-Floto Circus.

Tom and Mabel were married in Mexicali, Mexico, on February 15, 1932. His cowboy actor and friend, Monte Blue and his wife, were their attendants, along with Mix's daughter by a previous marriage, Thomasina. Tom was 52 and Mabel was 28. The marriage was the third for Mix (not counting one annulment) and the first for Miss Hubbell.

Tom Mix was 60 years old when he met his tragic death in an accident not unlike the one when his horse rolled over on him.

Tom was an advance agent for a circus, and driving his car on a highway south of Florence, Arizona, on October 12, 1940, when the crash occurred. When the rescuers dragged him from the wreck, they found him impeccably dressed, unmarked by wounds, and with thousands of dollars in cash and checks. But apparently a metal suitcase had struck him on the back of the neck, killing him instantly.

His car had pitched at a highway detour... and rolled over on him

... and it seems like only yesterday!

Birger: A killer in the midst

First of two parts

Back in the 1920s, long before Carl, "Big" Earl and Bernie Shelton made Peoria their gambling headquarters, they and their gang played a major role in the bloody Williamson County gangland war in southern Illinois.

Their big antagonist in that war was a former partner of theirs, Charlie Birger, who also had a gang of his own.

Shachna Itzik Birger, later known as Charles, was (according to him) born in Guanbainy, Russia, on January 1, 1880. Some members of his family gave different dates and locations but, in any event, the Birgers, a Jewish family, emigrated to New York City in 1887 and then on to St. Louis.

Charlie remembered living there in the 2200 block of Biddle Street as a youth and delivering newspapers for the *St. Louis Post-Dispatch*. His father drove horses and wagons for a living and his mother died when Charlie was a youth. He had two older brothers, Oscar and Sam, and an older sister, Rachel.

The Birger family later moved to Glen Carbon, Illinois, a coal mining town in Madison County where Charlie gave his occupation as a bricklayer.

He joined the 13th U.S. Cavalry on July 5, 1901, and learned to use a revolver and carbine rifle while serving on the Western frontier at Fort Meade, South Dakota; Fort Assinniboine and Fort Keogh, Montana.

After three years, Charlie returned to Glen Carbon. In 1905, he headed back out west, where he joined a round-up crew operating out of Deadwood, S. D. He had become a good horseman and broke outlaw horses at $1.50 a head.

Birger later came back east to live in Edgemont and Staunton, Illinois. A city directory stated he had a wife, Sarah, but there's some question as to an actual marriage. Charlie also claimed he ran a lunchroom, but that was probably just a front for bootlegging.

"Yes, I've killed men," he admitted near the end of his almost 50 years of life, "but never a good one."

Birger's first victim was William "Chubby" Oughten, in 1908. Their feud began as a simple argument over some cigars and a beer, but when Chubby came at him with a razor, Birger fired a warning revolver shot in the air, then shot Chubby three times in the chest. The jury acquitted Birger on grounds of self-defense.

Charlie became a bartender and spent a short time in Springfield and Christopher, Illinois, in 1912. Then he moved to Saline County, which became his home the rest of his life.

It was at Ledford, southwest of Harrisburg, where he first became prominent in southern Illinois. Here he lived with his wife, Edna, a statuesque blonde from East St. Louis, whom he married in Clayton, Missouri, on March 22, 1913. (He and Edna had a daughter but would later divorce. Charlie remarried a couple more times and also had a second daughter).

In the summer of 1913, he bought a lot in Ledford near the spur of a streetcar line and soon he was in the business he knew best: selling whiskey and beer to miners, most of whom were Lithuanians, Hungarians and Poles. Charlie provided extra touches to the miners' hard, drab lives, with every drink imaginable for the thirsty (including champagne) and women for the lonely.

He had barrels of beer shipped to Eldorado via the Big Four railroad, where they were switched off onto the Ledford spur. The railroad conductor was John Small, who would one day become sheriff of Saline County and complicate Birger's life.

In June 1923, that same John Small, then sheriff, made a raid on Birger's operation in Saline County, so Charlie moved his operation to neighboring Williamson County, although he continued to live in Saline County.

He moved to a "resort" between Marion and Johnston City known as "Halfway." This was actually a big house on the west side of the road, with a road-house on the east side, which he ran with three other partners. One of the bartenders there was Cecil Knighton.

Birger and Knighton became close friends but Cecil had a quick temper and was almost never without a pistol. After an argument between the two at the road-house on November 15, 1923, Charlie walked across the road to the big house. Knighton followed him and took a shot at Charlie, who grabbed a shotgun and blasted Knighton twice, killing him instantly.

The next afternoon the coroner's jury exonerated Birger on the grounds of self-defense. Various newspapers depicted the killing as bearing an uncanny resemblance to that of Chubby Oughten, 15 years earlier.

Cecil Knighton's killing was the real beginning of Charlie Birger's notoriety in southern Illinois.

But three days later, Birger was credited with killing another man. This time it was a St. Louis gangster named William F. "Whitey" Doering. In this battle, how-

Charlie Birger, the man who headed the gang that fought the Sheltons in the bloody Williamson County war.
(From the book, "A Knight of Another Sort," by Gary DeNeal)

ever, Birger was also seriously wounded but he eventually recovered.

By now the local folks were beginning to realize that a dangerous man with a winning smile was operating in Williamson County.

NEXT WEEK: The Birger gang and its war with the Ku Klux Klan, followed by the bloody Williamson County war with the Shelton's.

(Some of the highlights and dates in this article are from the book, "A Knight of Another Sort," by Gary DeNeal.)

Birger had a date with a hangman

Second of two parts

As mentioned last Monday, Charlie Birger's notoriety in southern Illinois began with the killing of his bartender and friend, Cecil Knighton, on November 15, 1923.

Three days later he also killed a St. Louis gangster, "Whitey" Doering in a shootout at his "Halfway" roadhouse. Birger was also wounded in that battle, but he recovered.

Charlie Birger and Carl, "Big" Earl and Bernie Shelton became friends back when the Sheltons were transporting booze for his operations, as well as their own, in the early days of Prohibition. By the end of 1925, the two factions had formed a partnership and shared the profits in their slot machine operations.

The Ku Klux Klan, opposed to the lawlessness and open violations of Prohibition, moved into the southern Illinois area in May 1923. The Klan initiated 200 local members, blocked roads and burned a cross to show their opposition. This represented a frontier vigilante society which automatically made it a mortal enemy of both Birger and the Sheltons.

In 1923, S. Glenn Young, the leader of the Klan, began cleaning up Herrin, Illinois. About 35 were arrested and open warfare began. In a short time, the coroner filed 153 cases of death from "unknown causes" or "by person or persons unknown," and the sheriff called for troops.

On February 8, 1924, the Klansmen and bootleggers clashed in the center of Herrin, killing Constable Caesar Cagle. Carl and Earl Shelton were indicted for Cagle's murder. Then on January 24, 1925, Glenn Young, the Klan leader, was killed in Herrin. Charlie Birger was jailed at Harrisburg for the murder, but then released. None of these indictments were ever prosecuted.

In April 1926, a battle on the Masonic Temple lawn in Herrin took six more lives and destroyed the KKK in Williamson County.

It was in the summer of 1925 that Birger built his Shady Rest roadhouse, that figured so prominently in an upcoming war with the Sheltons. The following summer several killings again occurred around Herrin, even though the Klan was gone. It was an indication that a gang war was in the making.

A feud developed between Birger and the Sheltons, apparently over a territory dispute. Birger split with them and Art Newman also deserted to become Charlie's partner. On August 22, 1926, former Klansman Harry Walker and Everett Smith were killed in a fight in a roadhouse north of Marion.

Then, on September 12, Max Pulliam, his wife and a friend, "Wild Bill" Holland, were machinegunned, killing Holland and wounding the Pulliams. On October 4, 1926, Art Newman's car was fired on while traveling on Route 13, west of Harrisburg, and Mrs. Newman was wounded. Ten days later the Shelton's roadhouse was fired on.

The County Line Roadhouse was fired into on October 28, and the Sheltons were believed to be responsible. On November 10, a homemade bomb was tossed from a passing car at the barbeque stand in front of Birger's Shady Rest.

This was followed by the Shelton's big 280-pound friend, Joe Adams' house being fired on. Birger thought the Sheltons hid their armored truck in Adams' garage.

Birger and the Sheltons began tipping off the authorities on one another. The Sheltons were indicted for a Collinsville mail robbery, and a few hours later the Sheltons retaliated by dropping bombs from an airplane on Shady Rest. Then, on December 12, 1926, their friend Joe Adams was murdered, supposedly by two of Birger's boys: his partner Art Newman and Ray Hyland. Birger, though, was charged with the Adams killing.

Finally, Shady Rest was destroyed at midnight on January 8, 1927.

The Birger gang in front of Shady Rest. Birger is in the center, seated on top of the car, in shirt sleeves and with machine gun.
(From the book, "A Knight of Another Sort," by Gary DeNeal)

Charlie Birger on the scaffold shortly before his hanging for the murder of Joe Adams.
(From the book, "A Knight of Another Sort," by Gary DeNeal)

The Sheltons were sentenced to 25 years in Leavenworth for the mail robbery but were freed in 1931, due to a confession by Harvey Dungey. They were then convicted for robbing the Kincaid Bank but, again, were freed.

But Birger, Newman and Hyland weren't as lucky. All three were found guilty in the Adams murder, but only Birger received the death penalty. Birger did receive one stay of execution on October 7, 1927, but after a sanity hearing the following April, he was found sane. Charlie Birger was hanged for the murder of Joe Adams at 9:48 a.m. on April 19, 1928.

A highway patrolman, Lory Price, and his wife, Ethel, turned up missing. And after a confession by Art Newman, Ethel Price's body was found in an abandoned mine. On January 7, 1929, the remainder of the Birger gang were charged with the murder of Mrs. Price. They all pleaded guilty and each was sentenced to a total of 157 years.

On October 18, 1929, another member of Birger's gang, Connie Ritter, was arrested in Gulfport, Mississippi, after a long search. He also pleaded guilty to the murder of Joe Adams and was sentenced to life in prison. Ritter died at Menard prison in 1948.

The Sheltons managed to survive six years of murders and robberies plus the Klan and bootleg wars of Williamson County. They moved their operation to East St. Louis and became the biggest wholesale bootleggers in Illinois outside of Chicago.

In the early 1930s, the Sheltons were run out of East St. Louis and Prohibition was about to be abolished. But Carl realized the gambling potential of downstate Illinois and began putting together a racket empire.

He had the charm and reputation to move in on local gamblers and become their "partner." Soon, the Shelton gang controlled gambling through the center of Illinois from Peoria to Cairo... and their new gambling headquarters? Peoria, Illinois!

...and it seems like only yesterday!
(Some of the highlights and dates are from the book, "A Knight of Another Sort," by Gary DeNeal.)

Train had a date with disaster

First of two parts

In the recent column about Paul Stringham's new book on the TP&W Railroad, I mentioned an incident he covered regarding the Chatsworth train wreck.

That horrible accident occurred before the turn of the century and was closely associated with our town because the train had just begun an excursion trip out of Peoria, headed for Niagara Falls.

At the time, it was considered the third worst train disaster in the nation.

In 1970, Mrs. Helen Louise Plaster Stoutemyer, a Chatsworth resident and former school teacher, published a book on the catastrophe titled "The Train That Never Arrived." Her book details the accident and also describes Chatsworth's early days. It also includes the news coverage of the train wreck by area newspapers, including the *Chatsworth Plaindealer*.

Louise was interviewed for a teaching position after graduating from the University of Illinois in 1928, and eventually accepted one at Chatsworth. Upon her arrival there, she met a Mr. L. J. Haberkorn, who ran a local music store.

He had taken part in the rescue work at the wreck sight that fateful night and, being a good storyteller, would often reminisce about it.

Mrs. Stoutemyer became interested in the wreck's history and began collecting clippings, pictures and souvenirs. Around 1950, she accepted a part-time job with the local newspaper and each year, on the anniversary of the wreck, she would collect more and more material, including interviews of people who still recalled the event. She compiled all this material into one volume, including many historic photos, and here's just a sample of her story:

In 1832, Franklin Oliver drove his family in a fancy horse-drawn carriage through a rich timber land, then held by the Kickapoo Indians, called Kickapoo Grove. He was on his way from New Jersey to Missouri, but decided to stay here instead. He built a log cabin for his family and the area became known as Oliver's Grove.

The railroad, originally named the Peoria & Oquawka Railroad, began in Peoria in 1849, first building westward to the Mississippi River. By 1857, the railroad was being built eastward through the Oliver Grove area, some 65 miles due east of Peoria.

Some of the local citizens didn't like the double name of Oliver's Grove, so when a new town was plotted on the railroad's right-of-way, the name was changed to Chatsworth. It's believed the name came from the famous estate of Chatsworth in England, which was the home of the Duke of Devonshire.

The railroad went by different names over the years - including the Toledo, Peoria and Warsaw - but in 1879, it became the Toledo, Peoria & Western Railroad.

In those early railroad days, the various companies searched for ways to encourage more people to ride the train, much the way airlines and travel agents do today. To make a trip especially attractive, excursion rates were advertised for round trips to popular areas. One of the most popular destinations was Niagara Falls.

In the summer of 1887, the TP&W began advertising an excursion trip from Peoria to Niagara Falls and return, for the special rate of $7.50. For weeks the trip was promoted in towns all along the TP&W line. Even though it was a special rate, $7.50 was a lot of money for someone working for wages of two and three dollars a week.

People didn't take annual vacations then, and two-week vacations were

Helen Louise Plaster Stoutemyer, the author of "The Train That Never Arrived." (Photo courtesy of Mrs. Stoutemyer)

A portion of nine cars which were piled in a space 40x60 feet, in the Chatsworth train wreck. (Photo courtesy of the Peoria Public Library)

unheard of. A trip like this for the average person was a once-in-a-lifetime thing.

Although the trip was advertised as leaving from Peoria, it actually originated in La Harpe, Illinois, near the western end of the line. The bulk of passengers, however, boarded the train in the Peoria vicinity. The date was Wednesday, August 10, 1887.

More people and cars were added along the way and it was later quoted that the train was 15 cars long by the time it reached Chatsworth - so long it required two engines to pull it.

On board the fatal train were newly-weds, families with children, women with babies, elderly couples, single people, a youth group known as "Parker's Juvenile Brass Band," and a vocal quartet from Peoria, all bent on having a good time.

The train was due in Chatsworth at 10:33 p.m., but it arrived close to mid-night because of the many stops to pick up crowds of people all along the line.

Some of those boarding the train at Chatsworth noticed a fire of some sort up the line. As it turned out, that fire was what would cause a horrifying crash in the next few minutes - killing 85 and wounding around 370, many of them mangled and helplessly trapped in the splintered and burning wreckage.

NEXT WEEK: A description of the actual Chatsworth wreck.

Bridge fire caused a calamity

Second of two parts

Last Monday I explored the book by Helen Louise Plaster Stoutemyer titled "The Train That Never Arrived." It's the fascinating story of the horrible Chatsworth train wreck.

A Toledo, Peoria & Western excursion train that left Peoria for Niagara Falls on Wednesday, August 10, 1887. The crash occurred just before midnight, shortly after it left the station at Chatsworth, Illinois, about 65 miles due east of Peoria.

That summer, the TP&W had announced plans for an excursion to Niagara Falls for a special round trip fare of $7.50. Tickets for sleeping and special chair car accommodations could also be purchased by contacting TP&W ticket agent A. F. Haskins at Peoria's Union depot.

The train, later estimated to be about 15 cars long, arrived at Chatsworth shortly before midnight. Some who boarded at the Chatsworth Station noticed a fire further up the line.

The long string of wooden cars (this was before all-steel cars were developed) required two steam engines to pull it. The first engine, No. 21, was a large freight engine, piloted by engineer David Sutherland. The second engine, No. 13, was a small passenger engine with E. B. McClintock at the throttle. Next came the baggage car, then the private car of the TP&W superintendent, Mr. Armstrong, followed by chair cars and coaches. The six Pullman sleeping cars were placed as usual, at the rear of the train.

August 1887 had been unusually hot and dry. No rain had fallen for weeks and fires had been reported at various spots along the tracks. Section men had also been burning weeds the day of the wreck, along the right-of-way just east of a wooden bridge, spanning a small stream, which was just two and one-half miles east of Chatsworth. It was that same bridge that caught fire and burned - unnoticed - that fateful night.

Apparently, it had apparently been slowly burning for quite some time because the entire structure was now resting on charred embers.

The train, reported to be traveling anywhere from 20 to 40 miles per hour, hadn't had much time to gain momentum out of Chatsworth, due to a small rise in the level of track just east of the station. Engineer Sutherland had just topped the rise and was starting down grade when he first caught sight of the burning bridge. With the heavy load pushing from behind, he knew it meant disaster.

If you're superstitious, you might note that the heavier lead engine, No. 21, made it safely across but the smaller second engine, No. 13, crashed through the burning bridge, plowed along the ditch and tipped over, killing Engineer McClintock. The fireman, Alex Applegreen, thrown up and out of the cab, managed to escape.

The cars following Engine 13 dropped their trucks, one by one, into the chasm, each sliding into the next car, telescoping the splintering wooden seats and crushing the passengers. Some of the wooden coaches, oil soaked from broken kerosene lamps, caught fire.

As the Pullman cars approached the brink, the rear of the train slowed down. The first Pullman, named "Tunis," teetered dizzily with its front end hanging over the edge of the gaping hole.

L. J. Haberkorn, who later ran a music store in Chatsworth, was one of the rescuers who ran to the scene immediately following the crash. He said a brakeman from the derailed train ran back down the track to Chatsworth to sound the alarm. Engine 21 had proceeded on to Piper City, the next stop, to do the same.

Engine No. 13 lies on its side in the wreckage of the Chatsworth train disaster.
(Photo courtesy of Peoria Public Library)

The sleeper, "Tunis," (left) lies behind three telescoped cars where the heaviest loss of life occurred. In the background is Superintendent Armstrong's car.
(Photo courtesy of Peoria Public Library)

As rescuers ran from Chatsworth toward the wreck, they met Mr. & Mrs. T. Y. Brown, an elderly couple, toddling back to town. They had boarded at Chatsworth and hadn't yet found their seats when the crash occurred. They had just stepped into the first Pullman car as the train approached the bridge, which undoubtedly saved their lives.

Mr. Haberkorn told of a badly injured man begging for someone to shoot him. His family had all been killed and he, too, wanted to die. He eventually did get hold of a gun and took his own life. Another man was found out in a field, crawling around and pulling up grass in his agony and delirium.

The local newspaper, "The Chatsworth Plaindealer," later described the scene this way:

"Would-be rescuers were chilled by the scene of mutilated bodies and the screams and groans of the dying. The cars were heaped 12 to 15 feet in the air. To rescue the injured it was necessary to build a system of ladders and planks to carry the injured out and slide the dead bodies to the ground...

"To add to the misery, a thunderstorm rolled in about 3 o'clock (a.m.), soaking everything and turning the dust into a sea of mud. Yet it was a blessing as it removed further danger from the fire."

Early reports stated 81 killed and 372 injured, but it was said that several more died soon after, bringing the death toll to 85. It placed the Chatsworth wreck as third in the list of train wreck fatalities in the nation.

(Mrs. Stoutemyer has also written a 319-page hardbound book, "The Sands of Time - 150 Years Around Chatsworth, Illinois," and a booklet, "The Heritage of the One Room Country School." She is currently working on a new book tentatively titled, "Niagara Nightmare.")

100 years later, club celebrates

When I was a youngster, I vividly recall going out of my way to walk up the incline of Liberty Street, between Adams and Jefferson, just to see all the portly old gentlemen sitting behind the big arched windows of the Creve Coeur Club. No matter what the time of day, they'd be sitting in those big comfortable chairs, reading their newspapers.

I'd never heard of the *Wall Street Journal* back then. All I knew was that those gents must have been awfully rich to belong to such an exclusive club, and I'd catch myself daydreaming about what it must be like to be a member of such a wonderful place.

Little did I know I'd one day be fortunate enough to belong to it but, unfortunately, it would be some time after that grand old building was torn down. The new modern one that replaced it (at least to me) never held the charm of the one I remembered as a kid.

Well, here it is 1994, and the Creve Coeur Club is celebrating its 100th Anniversary. That milestone will be commemorated next Monday evening at the club's 96th Annual Washington Day Banquet, just across the street at the Peoria Civic Center.

This annual banquet has traditionally highlighted the club's promotion of business, civic leadership and community service over the years, by bringing many celebrated speakers to Peoria.

This year, banquet chairman Henry Holling and his committee have deviated from the usual format so that the club can celebrate its 100th birthday and, at the same time, pay tribute to one of its own, U.S. House Minority Leader Robert H. Michel, a local boy who made good in Washington the past 38 years and is retiring at the end of his current term.

In the congressman's honor, the Creve Coeur Club has created the first annual Robert H. Michel Lifetime Achievement Award, to go to an individual the club feels has served the community "far above and beyond the expectations of normal, responsible citizenship." A gift of (at least) $25,000 will also be awarded to a local charity in Michel's name.

Among the dignitaries who plan to honor Michel at this black-tie event are Illinois Governor Jim Edgar; Speaker of the U.S. House Thomas Foley; and U.S. Senate Minority Leader Robert Dole.

The beginnings of the Creve Coeur Club were considerably less auspicious.

It was on March 13, 1894, that 13 young area business and professional men first met in the old YMCA building at 111 N. Jefferson, to form a young men's club to "promote the business interest of Peoria: and the social enjoyments of its members." Theodore Kuhl was elected chairman and Joseph Callender, secretary.

A week later the name "Creve Coeur Club" was adopted. The club was named for Fort Creve Coeur, the first European settlement in the Peoria area, established in 1680 by French explorer, Robert Cavelier Sieur de LaSalle.

On October 13, 1894, the club agreed to lease the Kruger residence (known as "The Alhambra") at 213 S. Jefferson, as its first club house. Its formal opening took place in 1895.

In December 1897, plans were first discussed for an annual club banquet. A year later it was decided the banquet would be held February 22, 1899, in honor of President George Washington's birthday. This first banquet included five speakers: Hon. Peter S. Grossup, the Rev. Simon J. McPherson, Commander Thomas W. Ryan, the Hon. Marcu Kavanaugh Jr., and Bishop John Lancaster Spalding. It was held at the old National Hotel at the corner of North Jefferson and Hamilton; 325 paid $5.00 to attend.

The grand old building I remember as a youth was built in 1903-04 at Liberty and South Jefferson. It was a three-story brick structure that included bowling alleys, billiard rooms, lounging rooms,

Left — An early view of the Creve Coeur Club building that was built in 1903-04 at the corner of Liberty and S. Jefferson streets. (A Bert Powers photo, courtesy of Peoria Public Library)

U.S. Congressman, Robert H. Michel (A *Journal Star* photo)

and a large dining room and banquet hall. By then, the membership had grown to 733.

Some of the club's early banquets were very long affairs featuring a multitude of speakers. The 1906 banquet, for instance, featured four major and six minor speakers plus five songs. When it finally came time for the keynote address by Thomas W. Larson, he refused to speak, indicating that his remarks would take at least two hours, and his train was due to leave in one.

Many of the club's early banquets were held in the old Peoria Coliseum at 515-31 N. Adams Street. This 4,000-seat arena was built in 1901 and was destroyed by fire in 1920. In 1927, the banquet moved into the brand new Hotel Pere Marquette.

In 1967, a new $1 million dollar building was proposed to replace the old club house. It was a cooperative effort with the Commercial National Bank (now First of America) and would double the club's space.

While the old building was being razed and the new one built, the club was temporarily housed across the street in the Hotel Jefferson. The new facility opened in February 1971, and was dedicated in May.

The club began to decline after its 1978 peak of 1,600 members and, after various renovations, membership drives, and ongoing financial ills, the club closed in 1991. It reopened in July of that year at Carnegies Restaurant in the Hotel Pere Marquette and currently serves its members there exclusively, during the lunch hour.

...but it seems like only yesterday I was admiring those portly old gents, reading their newspapers in the windows of that grand old Creve Coeur Club!

Club sees a century of service

Last Monday I wrote about the 100th anniversary of the Creve Coeur Club, which was formed by 13 young businessmen on March 13, 1894.

But just three weeks before that, on February 20, 1894, a small group of Catholic women met "to sew and see what could be done for those who needed help in the community."

A short time later, they named their group the Catholic Women's League in Peoria, and elected Mary H. Spalding as its first president. She was a most appropriate selection since she was the sister-in-law of Bishop John Lancaster Spalding, the Peoria diocese's first bishop.

The club's current president, MaryEllen Strode, and her board began the anniversary year last fall with a Mass celebrated on September 18 by Bishop John J. Myers at St. Mary's Cathedral, followed by a luncheon and musical revue at the Madison Theater.

Several events have since occurred, including an annual style show, but the high point of the year will be Saturday evening, April 30, when the ladies will bring back a part of the past: a revival of the Catholic Women's League Charity Grand Ball. It will be held in the ballroom of the Holiday Inn City Centre. A prime rib dinner will be followed by dancing to the music of Bill Hardesty and his big band.

For many years the league's Grand Ball was "the glamorous social event of the winter" in Peoria and this one should be no exception. I have this on good authority, since my wife is chairperson of the ball.

A hundred years ago, the women who formed the Catholic Women's League decided that their first venture, to raise funds for their charity work, would be a supper and dance. The first one was held in Rouse's Hall on Main Street, near N. Jefferson. It immediately became an annual event and grew until the "huge crowds" forced it to move into the larger Peoria Coliseum, in the 500 block of North Adams.

The Hotel Pere Marquette was built in 1927, and in later years the Grand Ball was traditionally held there.

Back in 1905, the CWL was one of the various women's clubs that united to form the Peoria Women's Civic Federation. There had been a growing truancy rate in the schools and local women were concerned for the children. When the care for children of working mothers became evident, they opened a day nursery at Neighborhood House in 1906. League members helped care for the children there for many years.

In 1930, the CWL formed a St. Josephine Sewing Club that met at least two days a month in the large ballroom of Mrs. Edward (Josephine) Cashin's home at 131 Columbia Terrace. They operated 22 Singer sewing machines to make children's garments. A group at one end of the ballroom made layettes of 26 pieces each, all handmade and edged with crochet. Quilting frames were set up at the other end of the room to make quilts and comforters.

Sewing continued to be an important club function for many years. A 1941 report stated that in ten sewing days 162 women made: 105 dresses, 30 comforters, 15 layettes, 243 diapers, 42 baby comforters, 52 baby nightgowns, 26 gertrudes (a slip-like garment for infants), five rompers, 36 boys' polo shirts, two baby dresses, 30 baby shirts and 31 pairs of baby hose.

Wartime has always found the CWL in evidence. During the Spanish-American War, they sent great quantities of bandages and fruits and jellies to the front lines. World War I found them selling defense stamps and Liberty Bonds and sewing harder than ever. And during World War II, league members helped staff the local USO.

Over the years, the CWL has given much time and financial support to the Catholic Social Service. They formed a group of "Marillacs" who gave untold

Mrs. John (Katherine L.) Gallagher, president of the Catholic Women's League in 1912, died in 1972 at age 93.

The Peoria Coliseum in the 500 block of N. Adams Street. Because of the huge crowds, the Catholic Women's League Charity Ball was moved there from Rouse's Hall. (Picture courtesy of Peoria Public Library)

hours transporting babies and children for CSS.

During the days of Peoria State Hospital in Bartonville, the league formed ward parties for its patients. A group of CWL members would go monthly to the women's ward and entertain them. Most of the patients had been institutionalized for many years and these parties were one of their few contacts with the outside world.

The league now gives monthly birthday parties to residents at St. Joseph's Home, as well as annual get-togethers for residents at St. Augustine Manor.

Supporting Catholic education has long been a CWL tradition. Dating back to at least 1937, they were giving a scholarship to girls attending the Academy of Our Lady. And in May of 1993, eight scholarships covering half the cost of tuition were awarded for students to attend Peoria Notre Dame High School.

The annual charity balls were the major source for CWL funds over the years, although changing times led to their demise by the late 1980s.

The club's 100th anniversary, though, will be celebrated in its past traditional style, with one more "Grand Ball" on April 30.

The committee, which has been planning the event since fall 1992, has gotten donations from businesses and private citizens to defray the cost of putting on the ball. That means all of this year's proceeds can be used for scholarships to Peoria Notre Dame High School.

The committee consists of: Mary K. Barkley, Pat Ciccerelli, Juanita Deeb, Joann Landon, Dorothy McNamee, Rose Seghetti, MaryEllen Strode, Oneita Volz, Ann Wombacher, Jean Zellmer and Flossie Adams.

Happy 100th Anniversary to the Catholic Women's League... which continues to prove that its initials truly stand for Charity, Worship and Love.

Ingersoll had a way with words

First of two parts

For 20 years, back in the mid-to-late - 1800s, Robert Green Ingersoll, was an outstanding Peoria lawyer. He also became a famous orator, and was nationally known as the great infidel, the great agnostic and, to many, the devil incarnate. (Agnosticism is the theory that God is unknown or unknowable.)

He was born in Dresden, N.Y. on August 11, 1833, the youngest son of the Rev. John Ingersoll. Being a Congregational minister, Rev. Ingersoll was a revivalist by temperament and three years was as long as he ever spent in one place. He moved the family from one pastorate to another in New York, Ohio, Wisconsin and then Illinois.

Young Robert's mother died when he was two years old and his father remarried several times. He was always close to his brother, Ebon Clark Ingersoll, and was an avid reader and a good student.

In 1852, the family lived in Mount Vernon, Illinois, where his father was a preacher and his stepmother ran an all-girls' school. Bob got a teacher's certificate and rounded up 40 or 50 students on a subscription basis and began teaching. But after about six months, he moved to Marion, Illinois.

In Marion, the brothers took up the study of law. They passed the bar in 1854 and moved to Shawneetown to begin practicing law. His brother, Eben Clark, moved to Peoria in the autumn of 1857. Robert followed him here in 1858 and they opened offices at No. 4 N. Adams Street.

The Peoria city directory of 1859 lists him as living in the Peoria House, an early Peoria hotel. In 1860-61, he was listed as residing at 141 Monson Street.

In 1860, young Ingersoll ran for Congress but was defeated by Judge William Kellogg. During the first six months of the Civil War, he spoke at rallies, inciting his listeners to action. At first his political views were Democratic but the Civil War became a turning point for Ingersoll. He completely reversed his political stand and became a staunch Republican.

In 1861, just a few days before leaving for the Civil War battlefront, he married Eva Parker, the daughter of a Groveland justice-of-the-peace, whom he had met while working on a case in that town.

Mrs. Ingersoll was as independent as he was, and they shared a lasting affection for one another. They had two daughters, Maude Robert and Eva Robert. His wife, Eva, was a rationalist with some unorthodox beliefs and, at about this same time, Ingersoll began questioning his own religious training.

In September 1861, he organized and commanded the 11th Illinois volunteer cavalry and served four years, until the end of the war. He saw action at the battles of Shiloh and Jackson, Mississippi. He was also captured but later released.

After the Civil War, from 1865 until 1876, his residence is listed as being at 105 N. Jefferson. During this time, he was also a partner in a law firm with his brother and Sabin D. Puterbaugh.

In 1867, then Governor Oglesby named Ingersoll the first attorney general of Illinois. At the Republican convention of 1876, he nominated James G. Blaine for president in a speech that attracted worldwide interest, and it became known as "the plumed knight speech."

As an orator and writer he had few peers. Although many opposed him for his agnostic religious views, he garnered much publicity for Peoria and gained prominence as an able attorney, an eloquent orator, and a controversial free thinker.

It is said that Clarence Darrow tried to copy his style but gave up, and Henry Ward Beecher said he was "the most brilliant speaker of the English tongue of all the men on the globe." His peers were such people as Patrick Henry and Daniel Webster.

Left — A portrait of Robert G. Ingersoll, painted in 1881 by Henry Ulke.
(Photo courtesy of Peoria Public Library)

Right — Robert G. Ingersoll's home in the 200 block of N. Jefferson.
(Photo courtesy of Peoria Public Library)

In 1877, Ingersoll had moved his residence and office into a building at 201 N. Jefferson, which is the northeast corner of N. Jefferson and Hamilton. This massive three-story structure was later moved to the adjoining lot at 217 N. Jefferson, to make room for the National Hotel, which was built on this corner in 1883.

At its second location, the building housed the Frank P. Lewis Cigar Co., and the general offices of the Distillers and Cattle Feeders Trust, which became known as the "whiskey trust." This trust controlled the national regulation of the output and value of whiskey in the entire United States.

The National Hotel was destroyed by fire in 1911, and in later years, the Ingersoll home next door became the New National Hotel.

While living in Peoria, Robert Ingersoll became famous as the "great agnostic," although he may not have been a true agnostic. It seems more likely that, being the son of a strict preacher (whom he truly loved), he just couldn't take the "hell-fire and damnation" religion of those days. Besides, it paid well to make the preachers mad and it also got him a lot of publicity, which built attendance at his lectures.

Ingersoll once said: "When I was a boy, Sunday was considered altogether too holy to be happy. Sunday used to commence when the sun went down on Saturday night... A darkness fell upon the house 10,000 times deeper than that of night. Nobody said a pleasant word; nobody laughed; nobody smiled... In those days no matter how cold the weather was, there was no fire in the church. It was thought to be a kind of sin to be comfortable while you were thanking God... The minister asked us if we knew we all deserved to go to hell, and we answered 'yes.' Then we were asked if we would be willing to go to hell if it was God's will, and every little liar shouted 'yes'... When we got home, if we had been good boys... sometimes they would take us out to the graveyard to cheer us up."

NEXT WEEK: The religious debate between Ingersoll and Peoria Catholic Bishop John Lancaster Spalding.

"Agnostic" launched a big debate

Second of two parts

As described in last Monday's column, Robert G. Ingersoll came to Peoria in 1858, shortly after his brother, Ebon Clark Ingersoll, settled here. The two opened a law office and for several years were in practice with another Peoria lawyer, Sabin D. Puterbaugh.

While living in Peoria, Robert Ingersoll became a famous orator and gained a national reputation as "the great agnostic."

In 1877, he gave up his law practice and began a series of lectures. He received much criticism for his religious views, a position that cost him the governorship. But Ingersoll was a very generous individual who made and spent money freely.

Robert moved to Washington D.C. in 1879 and he later lived at Dobbs' Ferry, N.Y. He continued to build his reputation as a great orator and writer, and was considered to be on a par with such people as Patrick Henry and Daniel Webster.

As an agnostic, he drew great criticism from many quarters, including the Catholic Church, and one of his severest critics was another famous Peorian, the Right Reverend John Lancaster Spalding, the first bishop of the Peoria Catholic Diocese.

The two debated in a Boston-based magazine, *The Arena*. In its January 1890 issue, the nationally circulated publication printed an article by Ingersoll titled "God in the Constitution." Three months later, in its April issue, it printed Bishop Spalding's rebuttal. To give you an idea of what the debate was all about, here, in part, is Ingersoll's opening position in the January issue:

"In this country it is admitted that the power to govern resides in the people themselves; that they are the only rightful source of authority. For many centuries before the formation of our Government, before the promulgation of the Declaration of Independence, the people had but little voice in the affairs of nations... The king sat on his throne by the will of God, and for that reason was not accountable to the people for the exercise of his power. He commanded, and the people obeyed. He was lord of their bodies, and his partner, the priest, was lord of their souls...

"The Feudal system was supposed to be in accordance with the devine plan...

"In 1776, our fathers endeavored to retire the gods from politics. They declared that 'all governments derive their just powers from the consent of the governed.' This was a contradiction of the then political ideas of the world; it was, as many believed, an act of pure blasphemy - a renunciation of the Deity. It was in fact, a declaration of the independence of the Earth. It was a notice to all churches and priests that thereafter mankind would govern and protect themselves. Politically it tore down every altar and denied the authority of every 'sacred book' and appealed from the Providence of God to the Providence of Man."

Ingersoll's scathing comments drew blood in the religious communities of our country. So much so that Bishop John Lancaster Spalding was asked to answer his former Peoria antagonist. And he did so in the same Boston magazine, *The Arena*, just three months later, in its April 1890 issue.

Here, again in part, is his response:

"The founders of the colonies from which the United States has sprung were deeply religious. Their faith was the chief motive which impelled them toward the New World, as religious zeal had led Columbus to his discovery. When the War of Independence broke forth, the descendants of the original settlers were still believers in God and Christ, as their fathers had been. To represent them as skeptical and irreligious is a perversion of the truth of history. And this is what Colonel Ingersoll has done in the article to which I have been asked to write a reply. In declaring that 'all governments derive their powers from the consent of the governed,' they certainly did not

Left — Peoria Catholic Bishop John Lancaster Spalding, who debated with Robert G. Ingersoll in 1890.
(Photo courtesy of Peoria Public Library)

Right — The Robert Ingersoll family pose around his statue at its dedication. Mrs. Ingersoll seated. Behind her are her two grandchildren and George W. Curtiss. On the left are the Ingersoll's two daughters and Walston Brown of New York City.
(Photo courtesy of Peoria Public Library)

believe they were 'guilty of an act of pure blasphemy - a renunciation of the Deity.' They were not declaimers and had no thought of making 'a declaration of independence of the earth,' which would have been false and foolish both from a scientific and a rhetorical point of view. In making this simple declaration, our fathers did not dream that they thereby 'politically tore down every altar, and denied the authority of every sacred book, and appealed from the providence of God to the providence of man.' They were not critics, but creators; not destroyers, but builders; and for them the providence of man was but a phase of the providence of God..."

This exchange in a national magazine was not the end of the great debate between the two. Ingersoll answered Spalding in an "unfinished" reply, which was later reprinted in "The Works of Robert G. Ingersoll" (Volume 11 of 12 volumes) published in 1900, the year after his death.

And Bishop Spalding, in his book "Religion, Agnosticism, and Education," published in 1902, reprinted this statement:

"Colonel Ingersoll forgets that religion is not, in any proper sense at all, a subject for verbal fence, a question to be settled by a debating club... As it takes a hero to understand a hero, a poet to understand a poet, so only a reverent and religious mind can rightly deal with questions of religion. We are offended less by what Ingersoll says than by the spirit in which it is said."

Colonel Robert G. Ingersoll died at Dobbs' Ferry, N.Y., about 20 miles north of New York City, on July 21, 1899.

In 1911, Peoria honored the man, who became a legend in his own time, with a life-size statue, unveiled at the lower entrance to Glen Oak Park. The figure, in an oratory pose, was sculpted by another famous Peorian, Frederick "Fritz" Triebel. It still stands at the foot of the Glen Oak Park hill, although it was thrown from its pedestal by vandals and damaged in 1943.

Parents bring fond memories

Being an only child, I was always very close to my mother and father. Wherever my folks went, I tagged along, until I began working steadily at the age of 16. During those times I heard many stories about Peoria and the people who were a part of those stories.

Looking back now, I know my deep feelings for my home town are something I acquired from Mom and Dad. Over the years, those memories became a part of me, but most of them layed dormant in my mind until I began writing this column. You've possibly read many of them before, but here are a few that deal directly with my family.

My dad, William Virgil Adams, was born in Peoria on June 4, 1903, the second of five children of William Samuel and Beulah Baxendale Adams. Mom was Anna Fern Zimmerman. She was born here September 16, 1904, the youngest of the seven children of Joseph B. and Arletta Cooper Zimmerman.

My parents were married July 27, 1924, and I came along the following year, on June 16, 1925.

One of Dad's earliest jobs was with the Electrical Testing Co. at 300 Knoxville, but by the time I was born, he was driving a delivery truck for Bourke's "Big White" Laundry at the corner of Main and Globe streets. He was still driving for the laundry when the market crashed in 1929.

He was making $25.00 a week during the Depression, when others were either out of work or making little or nothing. I'm sure it's because of his good job in those days that I don't recall any great hardships of the Depression.

In 1932, his older brother, Gene Adams, was elected Peoria County recorder on the Democratic ticket. He and most of the other Democratic candidates took office on the coattails of Franklin Delano Roosevelt's presidential landslide. Until then, most of the local political offices were controlled by Republicans. Then, for the next eight years, Dad was Uncle Gene's chief deputy recorder in the old court house.

Dr. Diller was the Peoria County coroner in those days and Dad became good friends with his chief deputy, Glen Gumm. It was because of Glen that I was on the scene of the spectacular Pascal Hotel fire at the corner of Hamilton and North Adams streets.

Glen stopped at our house in the middle of the night, on the way to the fire, to pick up Dad to go along with him and, of course, I tagged along. I wasn't about to miss a big fire if I could help it and Glen made my day (or night) by turning on his siren all the way downtown, just for my benefit. It was at this same fire that Dad's youngest brother, Gerald "Red" Adams, a fireman, was credited with rescuing two people via the hook-and-ladder.

And, by the way, I'm not the only one of my family to have been associated with the *Journal Star*. Back in the 1950s, Dad worked there for a man named Carl Heppe. He drove a truck and also worked on the crew that unloaded the huge rolls of newsprint from railroad cars and transported them to the *Journal Star* presses, which were then located downtown.

My mother also worked most of her life. Before she was married, she was a seamstress (as were some of her sisters) at the Chic Manufacturing Co. on South Adams Street, making housedresses and aprons. Next, she was a seamstress at the Galesburg Overall Co. in Peoria.

But I first recall her working at Peoria Tent and Awning Co. on Franklin Street, where my uncle, Ed Williams, was shop foreman. She sewed canvas awnings there and later painted the lettering on awnings made for store fronts and other commercial companies.

She last worked for the K. L. Burgett Co., a local firm that made golf gloves. The company was at 220 Persimmon

My mom and dad (Virg and Ann Adams) posing next to Dad's brand new Model T Ford.

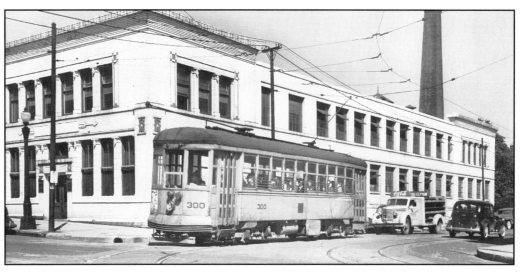

Bourke's Big White Laundry, behind the streetcar, at the corner of Main and Globe streets.

(Photo courtesy of Paul H. Stringham)

Street when she started, but it later took over the building at 918 S.W. Jefferson, which was the former Trinity Lutheran School. She was a leather cutter there and later ran the shipping department.

My parents both loved to dance and during their dating days they frequented all the old dance halls - such places as the Inglaterra, the National Roof Garden and Fernwood Gardens. They often ran into another Peoria couple at many of those dances, Jim and Marian Jordan, who later became famous as radio's "Fibber McGee and Molly."

But of all the family stories, the one I enjoyed the most was when Dad first worked at Bourke's Laundry. Although trucks were in commercial use by then, the laundry was still using horses and wagons.

Dad's delivery route was in the center bluff of town and he said his wise old horse knew the route almost as well as he did. Without being tied, the horse would wait patiently while Dad delivered an order at a residence. Then, as soon as he got back in the wagon, the horse would move on to the next stop.

This worked out fine until a new customer was added or an old one was dropped. Then it would take the horse a few days to learn the new routine. But the worst moment of the day always came after the last stop of the day, at a house at the top of Knoxville hill.

The horse would stop, as usual, and patiently wait for the delivery to be made, but he knew the next stop was the barn. So, as soon as Dad's foot hit the wagon's running board, that horse would take off down Knoxville hill as fast as he could go, and no pulling on the reins could keep him under control. To Dad, that last ride to the horse barn each day, with driver and wagon careening wildly behind, was as exciting as a roller-coaster ride at Al Fresco Park, and a heck of a lot more dangerous.

Some wonderful old family stories

... that seem like only yesterday!

Alas, these time travels must come to an end

YESTER DAYS

— Bill Adams

It seems like only yesterday

...but it's actually been nearly six years since this column began in the *Journal Star*. It first appeared on May 9, 1988, and has been running every Monday since, in the Vintage Point section.

Now, with deep emotions, the time has come to tell you that this will be my last Yester Days column.

In more than 300 columns, I've had the opportunity to share many nostalgic and historic adventures. To me, the column has been like a wonderful time machine that you and I could jump into each Monday and, at the flip of a switch (or, in this case, a turn of the page) go back in time and visit, or revisit, many exciting events in Peoria's past.

All the columns were trips into the past except one. On February 19, 1990, our time machine moved forward to 1995, to see what a train between Peoria and Chicago might be like once again. I'm pleased to say that train is right on track and, with a little luck, will become a reality... and on time!

The looks back at our town's past all those other Mondays have allowed us to revisit many old downtown Peoria landmarks: the Madison, Palace, Rialto, Apollo, Princess and Columbia theaters; the older folks might even remember the Grand Opera House, Hippodrome, Orpheum and Majestic theaters... and maybe even Rouse's Hall.

Peoria's great entertainers were there, too: opera star Emma Abbott; radio's Charles Correll, Jim and Marian Jordan and Ken Carpenter; songwriter Richard Whiting; movie writer Frank Wead and Hollywood actor Marshall Thompson.

Then there were all the great big band days of Glen Gray & his Casa Loma Orchestra, the Tiny Hill band, the local groups of Charlie Cartwright, Jack Wedell, Billy Hill, Joe Kilton, Verle Bogue, Freddy Stevens, Henry Mastronardi, Cary Robards (Senior & Junior), Bill Hardesty and Bill Hogan's Hotel Pere Marquette Orchestra.

Old radio was revisited beyond Fibber McGee & Molly and Amos & Andy, too.

We stopped off to remember the Jack Benny Program, the Fred Allen Show, Edgar Bergan & Charlie McCarthy, Orson Welles, Bob Hope, Burns & Allen, Sam Spade, Lum & Abner, Ma Perkins, Vic & Sade, Jack Armstrong, Little Orphan Annie and many more.

Our journeys gave us looks at Peoria landmarks: Block & Kuhl's Big White Store, the Inglaterra and National Roof Garden, Al Fresco Park, Kramer's Drive-In, the Empire, the Alcazar and Lekas' Sugar Bowl.

And there were the moving landmarks of Peoria's old streetcars, plus the tragedies of the sinking of the Columbia riverboat, the Chatsworth train wreck, and the spectacular fires of Hiram Walker's (The World's Largest Distillery) and the Seneca and Pascal hotels.

Our Monday trips allowed us to remember some early local radio and TV personalities; Jack Brickhouse, Gomer Bath, Milton Budd, Betsy Ross, Jimmie & Eleanor Bickel, Ozzie Osborne, Dick Coffeen, Bob Burton, Bob Arthur, Tom Connor, Hank Fisher, Bill Houlihan. And who could forget Captain Jinks & Salty Sam, portrayed by Stan Lonergan and George Baseleon.

Other Peorians who are gone now but still remembered were two of my old bosses, Great States Theaters city manager Len Worley and WEEK-TV's Fred Mueller. Other Peorians included Bradley coach and athletic director Robbie Robertson, Peoria artist Elmer King, and photographer Lee Roten, plus the unforgettable Chief Coy.

The most popular features of the column became the stories of Peoria's wide-open days of the Shelton Gang, the kidnapping of Bill Urban, the attempted kidnapping of Clyde Garrison and murder of his wife, Handsome Jack Klutas and others.

But one of the big opportunities our time machine provided was the covering of some major historic events: The building of the Duryea and Glide automobiles, the history of Peoria aviation, and the history of Peoria's newspapers, plus many prominent Peorians of another day such as Joseph Greenhut, Fritz Triebel and Robert Ingersoll.

The biggest challenge came during Peoria's Tricentennial Year (1991-92), with one column each month for 12 months dedicated to Peoria's 300-year history, from 1691 up to the 20th century.

Those are just a few of the subjects covered the past six years. The column has been a great experience and I've enjoyed every minute of it.

But the time has come to see if there is life after the column.

If one thing has come through, I hope it is the deep feeling I have for my home town. Peoria has been very good to me over the years. I feel very privileged to have been able to document some of its rich history.

I want to publicly thank *Journal Star* managing editor Jack Brimeyer and the then managing editor Marge Fanning, for offering me a shot at being the newspaper's 63-year-old rookie columnist back in 1988.

And finally, a special thanks to you, the readers. It's really your support that gave Yester Days a chance to "Play in Peoria" the past six years. Thanks for sharing the memories... it's been a grand trip!

Letter from the editor

Through all his years as a Peoria broadcaster, Bill Adams could move about town with relative anonymity.

But plaster his face on a weekly newspaper column and a couple of books, and he can go nowhere without being recognized and buttonholed.

Such is the price of fame. And such is the loss for readers of the *Journal Star* as our friend Bill Adams closes the book on Yester Days.

We didn't want Bill to hang up his pen. Nor, he tells us, did he really want to. But he and his wife, Flossie, their kids and grandkids deserve the uncluttered retirement he'd tried once before.

How does one replace Bill Adams? You don't. It'd be nigh impossible to find someone with Bill's mix of energy, verbal skills, savvy and sense of community. So we'll retire Yester Days along with its writer.

But we'll nurture the seeds Bill Adams planted by asking you readers to write a column in his place. This new column, called "Times Past," will run in Vintage Point, weekly if possible.

You could write of your memories of some local event, building, person, whatever. Or you could research some such topic in newspapers or interviews with elders. We'd love to see young people offer material.

We'll run this with a minimum of rules: One, it must be historically accurate; two, stay under 700 words; three, have it typed, double-spaced; four, try to find pictures to go with your story. Send your column to Times Past in care of Dennis Dimond, Journal Star, 1 News Plaza, Peoria, Ill. 61548.

We'll review your article for freshness, accuracy, style, reader interest, and such. If we use your piece, we'll send you $50. If we use a photo you provide with it, we'll send $75.

Don't disappoint us. Bill got a good thing started that we'd hate to see become just a memory.

One last note: We can't let Bill move on without a final tribute. So the *Journal Star* is planning a public reception for Bill and Flossie at the Madison Theater - the place they met - on Monday, April 11. An ad in today's paper provides details.

Jack B.
Jack Brimeyer
Managing Editor